TERRORISM IN EUROPE

Terrorism in Europe

Edited by Yonah Alexander and Kenneth A. Myers

ST. MARTIN'S PRESS   NEW YORK

St. Martin's Press, Inc., 175 Fifth Avenue, New York, NY 10010
Printed in Great Britain
First published in the United States of America in 1982

Library of Congress Cataloging in Publication Data
Main entry under title:

Terrorism in Europe.

   1. Terrorism – Europe – Addresses, essays, lectures.
2. Terrorism – Europe – Prevention – Addresses, essays,
lectures. I. Alexander, Yonah. II. Myers,
Kenneth A.
HV6433.E85T47 1982   363.3'2   81-21306
ISBN 0-312-79250-6   AACR2

CONTENTS

INTRODUCTION

Yonah Alexander and Kenneth Myers

In May 1981, in one of the spectacular incidents in the history of contemporary ideological and political violence, a Turkish terrorist
attempted to assassinate Pope John Paul II in front of St Peter's Cathe-
dral in the Vatican. The Pontiff, who was seriously wounded in the
attack, has since fully recovered. The assailant, Ali Agca, a member of
the Gray Wolves, a right-wing Turkish extremist group, was appre-
hended, convicted and sentenced to life in an Italian prison.

Several months later, in September 1981, a German terrorist squad,
apparently affiliated with the Red Army faction (RAF), used Soviet-
made RPG-7 grenade launchers, as well as Heckler and Koch 33 assault
rifles, to attack the car of US army General Frederick Kroesen near
Heidelberg. Although the vehicle was hit in the trunk area, it managed
to speed away. The General and his wife were slightly wounded while
his aide and driver were uninjured. And according to news reports in
October 1981, a Libyan hit team was sent to assassinate Maxwell M.
Rabb, US Ambassador to Italy, in retaliation for the US downing of
two Libyan jets over the Gulf of Sidra several months earlier. Partly as
a precautionary measure, the Ambassador had left Rome temporarily
while Italian police conducted an investigation.

These latest assassination attempts, as well as some 400 additional
incidents of ideological and political violence in Europe recorded in
1981 alone, clearly illustrate that we are living in an 'Age of Modern
Terrorism' with all its frightening ramifications. Indeed, during the past
two decades, pragmatic and symbolic terrorist acts in Europe — including arson, bombing, hostage-taking, kidnapping and murder — undertaken by extremist groups for the purpose of producing pressures on
governments and peoples to concede to the demands of the perpetrators, have victimised, killed and maimed thousands of innocent
civilians. These casualties include government officials, politicians,
judges, diplomats, military personnel, police officers, business executives, labour leaders, university professors, college students, school
children, travellers, pilgrims and Olympic athletes.

Terrorist acts have also inflicted considerable damage on nonhuman
targets. Terrorists have already attacked government offices and police

1

stations, pubs, restaurants, hotels, banks, supermarkets, department stores, oil pipelines, storage tanks, refineries, railway stations, air terminals, jetliners, broadcast stations, computer and data centres and electric power facilities.

In sum, from 1970 to 1981, some 3,851 domestic and international terrorist operations have occurred in Europe, with a toll of some 1,464 individuals killed, 2,834 wounded and with property damage of approximately $500 million.[1] It is safe to assume that ideological and political violence is now an established mode of conflict. Terrorism will continue and probably intensify because many of the roots of contemporary violence will remain unsolved and new causes will arise in the coming months and years of this decade.

To be sure, the threatened and actual resort to ideological and political violence for the purpose of achieving limited and broad realistic or imaginary goals by both established regimes and opposition forces is not new in the history of Europe. Ancient civilisations such as Greece and Rome have, in the struggle for power with other nations, utilised 'extra-legal' psychological and physical force. For example, they, as well as other European maritime states between the sixteenth and late eighteenth centuries, have found it expedient to employ pirates, or privateers, to terrorise the seas for the purpose of advancing some national policy objectives. Similarly, terrorism was practised by the party in power in France during the Revolution of 1789-94, and the government established the 'reign of terror' in 1793-94.

Moreover, terrorism from 'below', utilised by sub-state groups against their own governments as well as against other social organisations, became popular in the nineteenth and the early years of the twentieth centuries. Cases in point are the activities of the Narodnaya Volya movement targeting Imperial Russia; the use of violence by nationalist groups such as the Irish, Macedonians, Serbs and Armenians, all struggling for sovereign existence; and the resort to 'propaganda by the deed', as a strategy of political action by radicals and anarchists determined to overthrow the established order.

While these groups have failed in achieving their strategic aims, none the less they attained some tactical success. They assassinated, for example, Tsar Alexander II in 1881, French President Carnot in 1894, Spain's Prime Minister in 1897, Austria's Empress Elizabeth (Zita) in 1898 and Italy's King Umberto in 1900. Regicide and other terrorist acts continued in several European countries, including Russia and Spain, until 1914, but abated in central and western Europe. In the inter-war period ideological and political violence was on the rise once again. Nourished by right-wing and nationalists' ideologies rather than by anarchic theories, various extremist groups operated in France, Germany, Hungary, Italy and Rumania. Among the successful assassinations are those of King Alexander of Yugoslavia and Barthou in Marseilles in April 1914.

During World War II ideological and political violence was undertaken by various European resistance movements and directed against the Nazi occupiers. But it was not until the late 1960s and the following decade that Europe, primarily Western Europe, led all other regions in the world in the incidence of terrorist activities. Unique political circumstances led to this development: the defeat of the Arab states in the June 1967 war and the subsequent rise in Palestinian terrorism abroad; the Vietnam war and the widespread demonstrations against it; and the Paris students' revolt of 1968. These circumstances, coupled with developments in modern technology, particularly inexpensive and convenient travel and communication facilities, have contributed to the rise of European imitators of ideologically motivated extremist movements in the Third World, and to the strengthening of indigenous European ethnic and separatist groups.

Indeed, over 200 terrorist groups have been active in Europe since 1970. Among the most publicised are the Irish Republican Army (IRA), a militant Catholic movement, which is campaigning for the unification of the predominately Protestant province of Northern Ireland — Ulster — now under British rule, with the Irish Republic; the Red Army Faction (RAF, Baader-Meinhof gang), an extremist urban group in West Germany, wishing to overthrow capitalism and the present parliamentary system in the country; the Red Brigades (Brigate Rosse), a radical Marxist movement in Italy, determined to destroy the 'capitalistic domination' of the government and to create a Communist state; and Basque Nation and Freedom (Euzkadi ta Azkatasuma, ETA), a clandestine militant movement seeking a separate homeland in Spain.

To be sure, many of the various terrorist groups in Europe are able to survive simply because they enjoy the support of thousands of sympathisers within their own country and abroad, as well as assistance from foreign states. As Brian Jenkins explained this phenomenon: 'Relatively few terrorist movements are entirely homegrown and self-sufficient, although it is equally true to say that unless a group has roots in its home territory, it is unlikely to flourish, regardless of foreign support. The point, however, is that foreign support does enable such groups in many cases to increase their effectiveness and pursue their efforts until final victory.'[2]

Another factor contributing to the proliferation of terrorism is the toleration, encouragement and even the support of ideological and political violence by some states. It is becoming increasingly clear that ideological and political violence is, to paraphrase Clausewitz, a continuation of war by other means for the purpose of compelling an adversary to submit to specific or general demands. Indeed, terrorism is escalating into a form of surrogate warfare, whereby small groups are able, with direct and indirect state support, to conduct political warfare at the national level, and ultimately may even succeed in altering the balance of power on the international scale.

This trend has been explained succinctly by John Collins:

Terrorism is cheap to activate and costly to counter. State leaders who lack compassion can carry the fight to foes without fear of reprisal, if surrogates conceal true responsibility. Risks of escalation can be reduced to acceptable levels. Ninth-rate nations consequently could put great pressure on a superpower, such as the United States, using terrorist tactics.[3]

Elaborating on this same development, Ray S. Cline writes:

The deliberate use of terrorism as a technique of disrupting the fabric of civilized order in open societies is one of the most menacing facts of international life today. As a form of 'low-intensity' attack below the threshold of what is clearly perceived as regular, organized military aggression, terrorism is seldom recognized as a form of warfare and is rarely met with effective countermeasures in democratic nations. It is a destabilizing element that benefits militants and extremists while putting tolerance, moderation, and political pluralism in peril.[4]

It is not surprising, therefore, that the strategic thinking of Communist states, as exemplified by the Soviet Union's policies and actions, calls for the manipulation of terrorism as a suitable substitute for traditional warfare, which has become too expensive and too hazardous to be waged on the battlefield. By overtly and covertly resorting to non-military techniques, and by exploiting low-intensity operations around the world, the Soviet Union is able to continue its revolutionary process against the democratic pluralism of the Free World, as well as against a wider target area.

For instance, the American Secretary of State, Alexander Haig, has charged that 'Moscow continues to support terrorism and war by proxy', and 'with a conscious policy, programs if you will, which foster, support and expand international terrorism'.[5] That is, terrorism, whether backed directly or indirectly by the Soviet Union or independently initiated, is an indispensable tactical tool in the Communist struggle for power and influence within and among nations. In relying on this supplementary instrument, Moscow aims at achieving strategic ends when the use of armed might is deemed either inappropriate or ineffective.

Some of the broad goals which the Soviet Union hopes to achieve through terrorism in Europe would include the following:

(1) Drawing non-Communist European states into the Soviet system or at least into the Soviet sphere of influence. For example, Moscow's activities in Portugal — ranging from subsidising the Communist Party to infiltrating the administrative machinery of the country — culminated in chaos and almost enabled the 'revolutionaries' to seize power in the 1970s.

(2) Weakening the political, economic and military infrastructure of anti-Soviet alliances such as NATO. A case in point is the Soviet support of the IRA. Moscow hopes that if the violence in Ulster continues, Britain, a member of NATO, may be somewhat neutralised as a potential adversary.

(3) Frustrating efforts of non-NATO countries from joining the alliance. For instance, the Spanish government has accused Moscow of fomenting Basque terrorism, apparently for the purpose of forcing a military coup in the country as a reaction to this form of political violence. The assumption may be that Spain, under a dictatorial government, would not be accepted as a full-fledged member of the European community.[6]

(4) Destabilising relatively prosperous Europe because stabilisation of the West is an attraction to East Europeans, and, hence, a threat to the consolidation of the Soviet alliance system. The recent events in Poland illustrate the tangible dangers which the Soviet Union is facing in Eastern Europe, and, thus, destabilisation in West Europe could neutralise some of the temptation of the inhabitants in the Soviet sphere to look to the West.[7]

Obviously, there is another school of thought which tends to discount the role of the Soviet Union in European terrorism. This school asserts that stability in Western Europe is also in the interest of the

East. After all, it is argued, the state system which up to now has so well reflected the true balance of power in Europe that has emerged from the crises of this century possesses a strong lease on the future.

Regardless of how the controversy over the Soviet role in destabilising Western Europe is resolved, the fact remains that terrorism in that region is steadily growing. Clearly, the advances of science and technology are slowly turning the modern European societies into potential victims of terrorism, with no immunity to the noncombatant segment of the world population, or to those nations and peoples who have no direct connection to particular conflicts or to specific grievances that motivate acts of violence. Justice Arthur Goldberg, in assessing this development, has noted that modern terrorism, with sophisticated technological means at its disposal and the future possibility of access to biological, chemical and nuclear weapons, presents a clear and present danger to the very existence of civilisation itself.

It is out of this realisation that this violence grew. The purpose of this book is threefold: first, to present an historical perspective on some aspects of European terrorism; secondly, to analyse some of the common regional problems of contemporary ideological and political violence; and thirdly, to present selected case studies of contemporary terrorism in several European countries.

The editors wish to thank the authors for their contributions and to express their appreciation to the Center for Strategic and International Studies of Georgetown University for its continuing support.

Notes

1. These statistics are derived from the information provided by Risk International, a private consulting firm. The various terrorist incidents are based on the following categories: (1) kidnapping, (2) hijacking, (3) assassination, (4) maiming, (5) attacks against facilities and (6) bombing. Information contained in this data is derived from foreign and US government reports, police reports and the foreign/English language press. Data relating to damages, persons killed and wounded and hostages taken are dependent upon the accuracy of such reporting. In many nations governmental policies preclude the publication of such data. Accordingly, the figures cited for these categories can give only a relative approximation of actual human and material losses.

2. See Brian Jenkins, 'High Technology Terrorism and Surrogate War: The Impact of New Technology on Low-Level Violence' (The Rand Corp., Santa Monica, Ca, November 1975), p. 2.

3. John Collins, 'Definitional Aspects' in Y. Alexander and C. Ebinger, *Political Terrorism and Energy: The Threat and Response* (Praeger Publishers, New York, 1981), p. 6.

4. 'Foreword' in Y. Alexander and John Gleason, *Behavioral and Quantitative Perspectives on Terrorism*, (Pergamon Press, Elmsford, NY, 1981).

5. *The Washington Post*, 15 April 1981.
6. Ernest Halperin, 'Patron States and State-Sponsored Terrorism' (unpublished paper, May 1981).
7. Ibid.

1 PROPAGANDA BY THE DEED: TERRORISM AND ANARCHIST THEORY IN LATE NINETEENTH-CENTURY EUROPE*

Marie Fleming

There have been instances of terrorist activity throughout the course of history, but terrorism as an integral part of a revolutionary strategy to overthrow the established order dates from late nineteenth-century Europe. Since this period the terms anarchism and terrorism have sometimes been closely linked and frequently used interchangeably. Yet strangely, however, there has also emerged a fierce denial of any necessary relationship between anarchism and terrorism. In 1894 the social scientist and anarchist sympathiser Hamon insisted that the 'true' anarchists were men such as Peter Kropotkin, Elisée Reclus and Jean Grave, lovers of liberty, altruistic, sensitive and intelligent, while the terrorists of that time who claimed to be acting in their name were a small minority with imperfectly formed brains.[1] George Woodcock, whose study of anarchism is one of the most authoritative to appear in the post-World War II period, maintains that: 'The association of anarchism with political terrorism is still well established in the popular mind, but it is not a necessary association, nor can it be historically justified except in a limited degree.'[2] In his recent book on the Spanish anarchists, Murray Bookchin has asserted that violence and terrorism are not 'intrinsic features' of anarchism.[3] So, to put it mildly, there is a mixed opinion on terrorism and anarchist theory (and practice) as these developed in late nineteenth-century Europe.

Certainly, many modern anarchists, as well as scholars and publicists who sympathise with certain of the anarchist points of view, deeply resent a direct and simple identification of the terms anarchist and terrorist. Violent acts, and the terror which is their psychological counterpart, it would be maintained, are not peculiar to anarchism; almost all political groups, from the far left to the far right, the legal and the extra-legal, have, at one time or another, sanctioned the use of such practices. None the less, in their justifiable exasperation at the notion that anarchism and terrorism are equivalents, writers such as Woodcock and Bookchin have surely been overly hasty in dismissing the role of violence within anarchism. They do not make it clear how one is to judge what would constitute a 'necessary association' or what would represent an 'intrinsic feature'. Their approach merely denies the importance of violence and terror within anarchism, without leading to a resolution of what is obviously an important issue for an understanding of anarchism and/or the lineage to anarchism claimed by some terrorists.

This paper is an attempt to establish the links between terrorism and anarchist theory in late nineteenth-century Europe, since, I shall submit, the issues at stake in the controversy were adumbrated then and there. Thus, I shall examine anarchist Communism or socialist (non-Marxist) anarchism, wherein we find the ideological foundations of the anarchist movement. The focus will be upon the thought of Peter Kropotkin and the well-known geographer Elisée Reclus, and the emphasis will be placed upon French events, though an attempt will also be made to assess developments elsewhere. I am convinced that, if we are to uncover the links between European anarchist theory and practice in this period, it is important to begin where they are most evident. This is not to deny that contributions were made by figures such as Michael Bakunin, Errico Malatesta, Johann Most, Emma Goldman and Alexander Berkman, nor that events outside France, especially in Spain and the United States, had a significant impact in shaping the thought of Kropotkin and Reclus. However, in the other cases the relationship between theory and practice was more indirect.

For example, Bakunin had given a powerful thrust to the direction which the theory of anarchism was to take, but he did not live to participate in the debate on theory and practice which led to the adoption of political terrorism by self-professed anarchists. Malatesta's assumptions, as I shall indicate, steered him in a somewhat different direction from that taken by Kropotkin and Reclus. From 1880 Most's *Freiheit* and his incitement to violence had a significant impact upon anarchist activities in Germany and Austria, but he left Europe for the United States as early as 1882. And after the unfortunate Haymarket affair in 1887 he, as well as Goldman and Berkman, increasingly lost touch with aspirations among the native American working class and were reduced to an American following composed largely of immigrant families. In contrast, Reclus and Kropotkin developed their theories in response to events happening around them. They were especially influenced by developments in France. Reclus was of French origin; Kropotkin who had adopted France as his native land was probably even more attached to it than Reclus. Both men, with more than a touch of traditional French chauvinism, expected that France, which had always played a leading role in revolutionary theory and practice, would provide the clues to future revolutionary successes.

For these reasons, then, I shall examine the theory of anarchist Communism, give particular attention to the thought of Reclus and Kropotkin and explore the significance, for their theories, of acts of violence, especially those in France. I shall show why, from the late 1870s, propaganda by the deed was central to the elaboration of their theory of anarchism and how a philosophical justification of violence and terrorism developed logically out of it. This becomes especially apparent in the thought of Reclus whose writings, until recently largely neglected, reveal important dimensions of European anarchism and help to clarify how propaganda by the deed fits into the larger framework of anarchist theory.[4] Those anarchists who were frequently ambivalent and even contradictory when confronted with the reality of acts of violence, notably Kropotkin, but also Most and even Goldman, misunderstood the nature of their own conception of such 'propaganda' techniques.

Development of an Anarchist Framework for Action

The notion of propaganda by the deed can be traced to some Italian anarchists in the 1870s. It began to gain recognition in anarchist circles in other parts of Europe after the famous Benevento affair of April 1877 when Carlo Cafiero and Errico Malatesta provoked an uprising among the peasants of southern Italy in which tax records were burned and the deposition of Victor Emmanuel declared. The strategy was outlined by one of Malatesta's comrades who described how a small group of armed men could 'move about in the countryside as long as possible, preaching war, inciting to social brigandage, occupying the small communes and then leaving them after having performed there those revolutionary acts that were possible and advancing to those localities where our presence would be manifested most usefully.'[5] For some anarchists, propaganda by the deed came to be accepted as a suitable means of 'educating' the masses (especially when many were not able or had no time or desire to read), to stimulate them to action and to draw them into the movement.

In August 1877 an article entitled 'Propaganda by the Deed' appeared in the Swiss-based revolutionary journal, *Bulletin de la Fédération Jurassienne*. The article was written by Paul Brousse, with the support of Kropotkin, and it heralded the new age of propaganda.

Traditional forms of propaganda, discussion and personal contact, it was explained, were inherently limited in their ability to reach the masses; these, it was argued, must henceforth be supplemented by deeds. The Paris Commune was offered as a powerful example of what ordinary men might achieve, by way of spreading the anarchist message, but even more modest performances, such as the demonstrations which were being held around that time at Berne, were thought immensely worthy of emulation.[6] Anarchist ideas had to be spread not only by speech and by the pen, Kropotkin insisted in 1879, but also and especially by action.[7]

What precisely was meant by propaganda by the deed was not clear. But it is not difficult to understand the dilemma of those wanting to *do* something about what they perceived as wrong, and being virtually impotent to do anything. It would have been well within anarchist principles to have provided a forum for the discussion of the moral and political implications of specific kinds of deeds which might be used as propaganda, and the failure to do so must be seen partly as a reflection of the existing state of anarchist revolutionary practice. Even giving consideration to the notion of propaganda by the *deed*, however, might seem to imply that there had already been either too much, or only, discussion. In general, it should be said, anarchists continued to think in terms of the rising at Benevento; they did not foresee that propaganda by the deed might be used by self-appointed individuals as a theoretical justification for acts of political terrorism, as was to happen in the years to come. This uncritical acceptance of the conception of propaganda by the deed becomes more understandable when we consider the peculiar historical, intellectual and psychological position in which the anarchists found themselves in the late 1870s.

Up until the mid 1870s European anarchism had represented one wing of the wider socialist movement. More specifically, it had been part of the 'anti-Authoritarian' International which had been established in Switzerland in 1872, in essence a protest against Marx's call for tighter control of the General Council of the International Working Men's Association (or First International) over the Association's sections.[8] However, as ideological positions within the anti-Authoritarian International became more sharply defined, the anarchists became ever more isolated until they emerged as a separate group among the anti-Authoritarians, with a fairly coherent 'non-authoritarian socialist' philosophy, but lacking a plan of action.

The effectiveness of modern means of repression at the disposal of governments, as demonstrated during the Paris Commune, had placed severe limitations on the value of the tradition of the barricades. Anarchists rejected the Marxist approach to politics after 1871 as an attempt to introduce the element of authority into the struggle for a socialist society.[9] Those such as Kropotkin and Reclus who were emotionally and intellectually repulsed by the savage repression and violence of the Paris Commune, also dismissed any other possibility for political agitation within the existing political system, as condemned, by definition, to failure.[10] (Reclus rejected violence to the point of being, from his youth, a deeply committed vegetarian.) The anarchists in Switzerland were soon faced, therefore, with bleak prospects. On the one hand, police harassment and the failure to establish a popular base encouraged many of their number to find an outlet in some form of municipal or parliamentary socialism, while on the other, the more deeply committed painted themselves into a corner where they had to accept the *status quo* and/or any way of showing their total rejection of it.

In the late 1870s, with no hope of a successful wide-ranging revolution, the core which persisted in its anarchism, none the less, generally restricted its activities to spreading the word, mainly through the press, and via addresses to the already initiated. For those whose aim was to foment universal social revolution, such scope for action was exceedingly narrow; in fact, the anarchists looked as though they might be reduced to a small band of impotent and eccentric ideologues totally out of touch with the demands of modern society and politics. The inherent appeal of propaganda by the deed becomes apparent once we understand that it appeared to point the direction of resolving the paradox of a non-authoritarian revolution. In the early 1870s, Frederick Engels had argued that a revolution without organisation and authority was an impossibility, but the socialists grouped around Bakunin (who was to live until 1876) had remained adamant that there would be no revolution at all if it were to be carried out in an 'authoritarian' fashion, as this would automatically create a new force for oppression. As positions within the socialist movement hardened, this difference of view became ever more pronounced. In the late 1870s Kropotkin and Reclus were singularly insistent that it was not sufficient that the masses *support* the revolution; they must also *make* it. Propaganda by the deed appeared in some way to provide a framework for action which promised to expose the vulnerability of the bourgeois order without compromising anarchist principles of opposition to organisation and authority. It could also be seen as a logical extension of a deep-seated belief in the importance of rebellion, and adhered to the idea that man was by 'nature' free, though everywhere in chains.

The intellectual and emotional roots of late nineteenth-century anar-chism are complex, but the immediate inspiration had come from Bakunin, according to whom: ' . . . the power to think and the desire to rebel . . . represent the essential factor, the negative power in the posi-tive development of human animality, and create consequently all that constitutes humanity in man.'[11] In the late 1860s Bakunin was intro-duced to the religious commitment to violence of the notorious Nechayev. 'The revolutionary is a doomed man', states Nechayev's *Catechism of the Revolutionary*. 'He has no personal interests, no affairs, no sentiments, attachments, property, not even a name of his own. Everything in him is absorbed by one exclusive interest, one thought, one passion — the revolution . . . To him whatever aids the triumph of the revolution is ethical; all that hinders it is unethical and not criminal.'[12] Bakunin in time rejected Nechayev, but he did not lose his fascination for violence and direct action. And sentiments which he expressed in this period were to reappear with profound consequences in the theory and practice of the later anarchist movement. His pro-gramme, as he wrote to Nechayev, was: 'Total destruction of the world of the legal state and of all the bourgeois so-called civilization, by means of a popular revolution, directed not by an official dictatorship, but by a collective, imperceptible and anonymous dictatorship of the partisans of the complete liberation of the people from all oppression, firmly united in a secret society and acting everywhere and always with the same goal and according to the same programme.'[13]

The Marxist/anarchist debate is usually traced to the Marx/Bakunin quarrel, but it is clear that there did not emerge a distinctive anarchist position until the late 1870s. With the elaboration of this anarchist position, the notion of rebellion bequeathed by Bakunin to his spiritual heirs began to take on added significance. The key to all social and political change became ever more clearly perceived as the spirit of revolt which, it was believed, had existed in all men from the beginning of time. In an 1880 article Kropotkin summed up the anarchist position on revolt by outlining how the natural desire of men to rebel gives rise to action by courageous individuals and groups even before the masses are fully prepared for revolution

Men of courage, not satisfied with words, but ever searching for means to transform them into action, — men of integrity for whom the act is one with the idea, for whom prison, exile, and death are preferable to a life contrary to their principles, — intrepid souls who know that it is necessary to *dare* in order to succeed, – these are the lonely sentinels who enter the battle long before the masses are sufficiently aroused to raise openly the banner of insurrection and to march, arms in hand, to the conquest of their rights.

In the midst of discontent, talk, theoretical discussions, an individual or collective act of revolt supervenes, symbolizing the dominant aspirations.[14]

An examinatin of Kropotkin's remarks in the late 1870s demonstrates how firmly he believed that there ought to be no interference with the natural spontaneity of such acts of revolt. There was no need to be concerned about whether or not the social and political conditions were appropriate for rebellion, he assured his comrades; the masses were well aware of such things and they would be ready.

Late nineteenth-century European anarchist intellectuals deliberately fostered an identification of themselves as *'le parti des révoltés'* – the party of the rebels. Their organ *Le Révolté* first appeared in Switzerland in 1879 and it symbolised the mood of the anarchists as they worked out more fully the implications of the notion of revolt. The rebellious mood of the French anarchist groups also extended to the German anarchists who were exposed to the even more openly radical paper *Der Rebell*, beginning in 1881. By contrast, previous anarchist journals (1877-8) had been entitled *Le Travailleur* and *L'Avant-Garde*. A strict interpretation of anarchist theory, as worked out by Kropotkin and Reclus, placed the course of revolution so completely with the people that theoreticians forfeited all right to make any contribution beyond that of spreading the word and stirring up the (natural) spirit of revolt. Scrupulous in the extreme, they found comfort in the belief that they alone among the socialists had not violated the true spirit of the Working Men's Association, that 'the emancipation of the Workers will be made by the Workers themselves'. The irony of the situation is that while theoreticians of modern anarchism were moving in the direction of accepting propaganda by the deed, in order, thereby, to increase the possibilities for 'anarchist' action by the masses, they were reducing the importance and scope of their own activities.

Propaganda by the Deed and the Evolution of Anarchist Thought

The inclination of the leading anarchist theoreticians to sympathise with the idea of propaganda by the deed, as it developed up to about 1880, was to have an important impact upon the subsequent evolution of anarchist thought. First of all, anarchist theoreticians began to relinquish the role of political actors, much less leaders, for propaganda by the deed would demand that anarchists be prepared to submit to the revolutionary course mapped out by the people as they struggled to create a socialist society. Secondly, such a submission created a situation in which the work of the theoreticians — if they were not to become completely obsolete — must intellectualise and/or justify the acts of the masses. They could do this only by taking it as their task to discover the revolutionary significance of all acts of revolt.

The implications of the anarchist position on propaganda by the deed were becoming clear as early as 1878, the year in which there was a number of sensational attacks on European authorities and heads of state. In February Vera Zasúlitch shot at the chief of the St Petersburg police, Trepov, in protest over his treatment of the 'go to the people' movement. Two attempts were made to kill the German emperor, in May and June respectively. There was an assassination attempt against Alfonso XII of Spain in October, and in November King Umberto of Italy was attacked. These events were generally linked with the anarchists and, sometimes for political reasons, to other socialists. The Swiss authorities suppressed the anarchist paper *L'Avant-Garde* for what were claimed to be its extreme views, and arrested the editor Brousse and brought him to trial.[15] The anarchist response to the events of 1878, however, was more ambivalent. *L'Avant-Garde* had made some effort to distinguish the individual acts of the assassin from the collective deeds of 'conscious' anarchists such as those at Benevento in 1877. The suggestion was also made that assassination was of limited propaganda value, although the feeling persisted that under certain conditions it could lead to revolution. Such an equivocal reply indicates that either the anarchists were not fully aware of the implications of their framework for action or were extremely reluctant to admit them.[16]

Anarchists were more decisive, however, in their interpretation of the terrorism of the Russian Narodnaya Volya (People's Will) which was struggling against the impossible odds of Tsarist autocracy. In July 1879 Reclus wrote that the nihilists 'were the salt of the earth. Their devotion to duty, their contempt of death, their spirit of solidarity, their tranquility of soul amaze me, and I turn red in comparing myself to them.'[17] Sophie Perovskaya, one of the five who were executed for their part in the assassination of Tsar Alexander II in March 1881, became a true inspiration. Kropotkin wrote: 'By the attitude of the crowd she understood that she had dealt a mortal blow to the autocracy. And she read in the sad looks which were directed sympathetically towards her that by her death she was dealing an even more terrible blow from which the autocracy will never recover.'[18]

It is hardly surprising that such unqualified approval could be given to Russian revolutionaries. Throughout Western Europe there was an awareness of the extent of Tsarist oppression, so that even liberals might in all conscience extend their sympathies. But for the ever-anxious anarchists (and most other socialists) in the dark post-Paris Commune days, there was at last a revolutionary spark, and it seemed all the stronger because it glowed in Russia, the darkest corner of the civilised world. Marx, too, who in this period is supposed to have supported the strategy of taking the parliamentary route to socialism, was cheered at the prospects for revolution. For anarchists in particular, in so far as Russia provided specific lessons, it is clear that these largely consisted in a reaffirmation of the importance of spontaneous acts of revolt within the context of propaganda by the deed. In spite of the enthusiasm with which anarchists might be expected to greet revolutionary events in Russia, however, their lack of anxiety over what constituted acts of revolt there may be taken to indicate that the ambivalence of 1878 was gradually abating. Many anarchists must have been thinking of events in Russia in July 1881, four months after the assassination of Tsar Alexander II, when they met in the famous London International Congress and officially recognised propaganda by the deed. The Congress pointed the direction to later events by advocating a study of the new technical and chemical sciences from the point of view of their revolutionary value.[19]

Few leading anarchists understood so fully and accepted so readily the implications of propaganda by the deed, as did the German Johann Most. From late 1880 the pages of his *Freiheit* (published outside Germany) throbbed with articles inciting workers to rebel against injustice through violence and terrorism. Information and instructions were provided on the effective use of lead, knives, poisons, fire and explosives. The journal urged the destruction of homes and churches, offices, shops and factories. All methods of achieving the social revolution were justifiable; it was time to demand an 'eye for an eye'. 'Comrades of *Freiheit*,' screamed the pages of the journal, 'we say murder the murderers. Rescue mankind through blood, iron, poison, and dynamite.'[20] *Freiheit* was intended for clandestine distribution in Germany and Austria, and in the early 1880s it had considerable influence among the anarchist groups there. Almost prophetic in terms of its response to propaganda by the deed, it no doubt also had an important influence in preparing the way for the fuller acceptance of the role of violence and terror within later anarchist theory. This was true even though Most's enthusiasm for violence had begun to wane markedly by the early 1890s when the full force of the European anarchist movement was making itself felt. By this period Most had become so disillusioned with the role of violence that he publicly condemned Goldman and Berkman, provoking Goldman to the point where she physically attacked him.

By 1882 propaganda by the deed was becoming identified by anarchist theoreticians, such as Reclus, with any act of revolt, even when the act was not performed consciously to elicit support for the anarchist cause.[21] On 24 March 1882 the young unemployed Fournier shot at an employer whom he considered responsible for the crisis in the weaving industry at Roanne in France. From August of the same year there was extensive terrorist activity by the *Bande Noire* (Black Band) directed against the mine owners of Montceau-les-Mines in the Lyons area. Fournier had not acted under the banner of anarchism, but none the less *Le Révolté*, the paper launched by Kropotkin in 1879, referred to his act as 'propaganda by the deed, the most fecund, the most popular'.[22] The terrorism of the *Bande Noire* was likewise considered an event of 'immense significance, and hence the consequences from the socialist-revolutionary point of view, are inestimable'.[23] There is little question that underlying such deeds was the unrest caused by a French economy which had been experiencing stagnation from 1873. But whether the cause was socio-economic or simply personal, the anarchists chose to regard these acts as encouraging and as indications that revolution was not entirely out of the question in Europe. For those who doubted the power of popular protest there were the terrorist activities of the Spanish *Mano Negra* (Black Hand) in 1883. In Spain, as well as in France, police authorities responded with intense efforts to round up anarchists, regardless of whether or not they were involved in the outbursts of terrorism.

Despite the uneasiness which may well have been experienced by some anarchists, the very nature of anarchist theory as the intellectual expression of the acts of the masses demanded the accommodation of incidents of broadly defined revolt. The Lyons trial of 1883 provides an important example of how anarchists played this role to the extent of becoming identified as instigators of terrorism. It is not difficult to imagine how the Lyons authorities could conclude that the 'moral solidarity' provided by the anarchists was instrumental to, if not the root cause of social revolt in their area. In any event, in an effort to bring terrorism under control, they arrested and brought to trial 65 anarchists, including such prominent figures as Kropotkin and Emile Gautier, on the charge of alleged membership in an international organisation whose goal was the destruction of the bourgeois state.[24] Kropotkin did little to distinguish his position from that of the bombers when he declared: 'I have said that when a party is put in the position of having to use dynamite, it ought to use it, as, for example, in Russia where the people [as a force] would have disappeared, if they had not used the means put at their disposal by science.'[25]

Shortly after the Lyons trial a placard was posted up around Paris. It was signed by the *groupe parisien de propagande anarchiste* and printed by the *Le Révolté* press, at that time under the supervision of Reclus who had assumed responsibility for the paper when Kropotkin had been sent to prison. 'Yes,' the placard read, 'we are guilty of proceeding with the practice of our theories by all means, by the word, by the pen, BY THE DEED – that is to say by revolutionary acts whatever they may be.' With an anticipation of things to come, the text continued: 'Yes, we acknowledge them loudly. We claim them as ours. We glory in them.'[26] This placard represents a noticeable psychological adjustment to the implications of propaganda by the deed. In other words, some anarchists had turned from somewhat opportunistic approval to open advocacy of rebellious acts. The rebel Kropotkin languished in prison, but the trial had brought him and his comrades a good deal of notoriety. In keeping with the mood Reclus decided upon *Paroles d'un Révolté* as the title of a collection of Kropotkin's essays which he published in 1885.

It might be argued that anarchist theory and political terrorism not only were not opposed, but that in fact they were coming to complement and sustain each other. At the very least it must be admitted that the theoreticians came to provide a sense of legitimacy for acts of social revolt. Increasingly there occurred incidents which were the work of individuals who had absorbed sufficient anarchist theorising to be able to translate specific grievances into an ideological hatred of the whole bourgeois order. An example of this had taken place as early as 1881 when Emile Florian went to Reims with the intention of killing Gambetta, and in 1883 when the youth Paul-Marie Curien went to Paris hoping to kill Jules Ferry. A more consciously anarchist act was that of Louis Chaves who in 1884 killed his former employer, the Mother Superior of a convent near Marseilles. In 1886 there was the case of

Charles Gallo who attempted to accomplish an act of 'propaganda by the deed of the anarchist doctrines' by throwing a bottle of prussic acid from an upper gallery of the Paris stock exchange and shooting at the panic-stricken brokers.

Such incidents and the accompanying coverage in the popular press no doubt reinforced the self-image of the anarchists, and by.1885 some observers were recognising the 'anarchist party' as a 'manifestation expressive of the state of spirits in the working class milieu'.[27] It is quite understandable how, by the period of the *attentats* of the 1890s, the French establishment had come to believe that just about every anarchist, from the theoretician to the bomber, was guilty of crimes against the French state. In the 1895 analysis of criminal lawyer Garraud, an interested observer, the anarchists represented a division of labour in which each person contributed to the destruction of society according to his temperament and abilities. Some anarchists were *'practiciens'*, those who propagated the doctrine by means of the deed, that is by theft, burning and assassination. At their side were the frequently gifted intellectuals who diffused the anarchist idea through newspapers, brochures, songs and pictures. Then there were the anarchist 'door-to-door salesmen' who could be found selling newspapers in the working-class districts and in general inciting rebellion in every corner of the land.[28] Garraud's analysis was simplistic, but it had sensed important elements of the underlying logic of anarchist theory. His analysis also evokes the reasoning of Johann Most who came to believe, after 1890, that anarchists divided, naturally, into thinkers and doers.

The Period of the *Attentats*

Propaganda by the deed, as developed from the late 1870s, was built upon a number of convictions: that all revolt against oppression was in itself progressive, that the transformation from blind and spontaneous responses to injustice into 'conscious' and calculated revolt represented significant advances, that decisions to commit specific acts of revolt had to rest with the people. In sum, anarchism was able to provide an intellectual justification for asserting that acts perceived by the existing order as 'terrorist', or simply criminal, were revolutionary deeds heralding the coming of socialism. While most socialists in this period expected that there would be *collective* violence in the revolution, anarchists were compelled, through their insistence upon a strict interpre-

tation of the principle of individual autonomy, to admit the legitimacy
of *individual* acts of violence as well. Arguing on behalf of the right of
individuals to act as they saw fit, many anarchists looked sympathetically upon the violence which reached crisis proportions in the 1890s.
The Paris explosions of March 1892 initiated a period of terror which
continued for over two years.

A man known as Ravachol was arrested and tried for the explosions
of March, as well as for a number of earlier crimes, including murder.
The French establishment was somewhat startled when Ravachol
refused to regard himself as a mere criminal, and insisted on presenting
himself as an anarchist redresser of wrongs, claiming that he had killed
and robbed, first to satisfy personal needs and then to come to the aid
of the anarchist cause. The verdict of death he greeted with 'Long live
anarchy!' and he marched to the guillotine on 11 July 1892, singing an
anti-clerical song. From this point onwards there seemed no shortage
of aspiring candidates for anarchist martyrdom, and some people were
able to achieve a glorious end to an otherwise miserable life.

The young shoemaker, Léon-Jules Léauthier is remembered among
anarchists for his words, 'I shall not strike an innocent if I strike the
first bourgeois I meet', and he earned himself a place in history by
seriously injuring the Serbian Minister Georgewitch on 12 November
1893 with his (shoemaker's) paring knife. On 9 December Auguste
Vaillant threw a bomb from the gallery of the Chamber of Deputies,
injuring several Deputies, some of them seriously, as well as a number
of spectators, an usher and himself. Although no one was killed, Vaillant
was condemned to death. He became a martyr of anarchism, having
neither stolen nor killed, but only having attacked a 'corrupt' Chamber
severely discredited in the public eye by the recent Panama scandal. On
12 February 1894, one week after the execution of Vaillant, Emile
Henry blew up the Café Terminus (of the Saint-Lazare Station),
injuring twenty people, one of whom later died from his injuries.
Henry, sometimes known as the Saint-Just of Anarchy, expressed his
regret at the failure of the explosion to claim more victims; he said that
his aim had been to kill, not to injure. The *attentats* reached a climax
with the killing of President Sadi Carnot, highest symbol of the
bourgeois Republic, by the young Italian Santo Caserio at Lyons on 24
June 1894.

The *attentats* were by no means restricted to France. The early
1890s brought widespread bombings, insurrections and assassinations
in Spain, especially in the Andalusian area. In 1893 an anarchist called
Pallas was executed for an (unsuccessful) attempt to blow up the

Captain-General of Barcelona. His friend Salvador avenged his death by bombing the Liceo Theatre and killing twenty people. The killings increased as police intensified efforts to root out anarchists, causing an international outcry by its savage treatment of suspects at the Mont-juich prison. In Germany and Austria, however, the anarchist move-ment of the early 1880s had collapsed. In Italy there was also no parallel to events in Spain and France. The Italian movement had weak-ened considerably. Many leading Italian anarchists had emigrated. Others were lost through defection to parliamentary socialism; Cafiero became insane. Italians were active within Spain and were, moreover, noteworthy for spectacular acts of terrorism within the international anarchist movement. Caserio killed the president of the French Republic in 1894; Angiolillo shot the Prime Minister of Spain in 1897; Luccheni killed the Empress of Austria in 1898; Bresci executed King Umberto of Italy in 1900.

The period of the *attentats*, however, was more than the story of a handful of individuals who were driven by their own wretched exist-ence and inspired by anarchist theory to express their anger through acts of violence against the political order. In France there was a con-siderable number of political dynamiters whose explosions were not serious enough to warrant lasting attention. In addition, there were numerous instances of threatening letters sent anonymously to property-owners, warning them to expect an explosion and sometimes informing them that they should vacate the property by such and such an hour, in order to escape personal injury. In the Paris Police Archives there are several boxes of documents dealing with explosions in the 1880s and 1890s; the vast majority of these documents concern the period 1892 to 1894. There are also three boxes which contain 'threatening letters' passed on by their recipients to the police in the year 1892. (One suspects that many more were discarded upon receipt.)[29] The more sensational *attentats* were committed amid general excitement, panic in bourgeois circles, approval (or at least no dis-approval) in the anarchist press, even extreme enthusiasm in some papers. Pictures of Ravachol were produced and distributed, as if they were images of a saint, and his deeds were celebrated in song. For one anarchist he was seen as 'a sort of violent Christ'.[30]

Although approval had been given to certain acts of violence in the 1880s, the enormous scale of the terror of the 1890s seems to have caught some theoreticians unprepared. It was not until after Ravachol's appearance in court that the anarchist paper *La Révolte* (successor to *Le Révolté*) gave a hesitatingly favourable appraisal, suggesting that a distinction should be made between his earlier crimes and the Paris explosions.[31] And only after the death sentence had been passed did it come out in open support of Ravachol.[32] Kropotkin seems to have been genuinely troubled lest innocent people should become victims, and he wrote a letter intended for publication in *La Révolte* denouncing an explosion which had killed and maimed a large number of people in Spain. These initial waverings were overcome with the help of the arguments of Jean Grave who has reported how he explained to Kropotkin that there was no basis on which to condemn the wretched, as they struggled to overcome their miserable existence.[33] There is reason to suspect that, none the less, Kropotkin underwent a fair amount of soul-searching in choosing to refrain from a condemnation of terrorism, and we catch a glimpse of his agonising in his comments to a friend concerning his regrets over the assassination of the Austrian Empress Elizabeth in 1898.[34]

It had been less difficult for Kropotkin to support the efforts of angry, unemployed persons seeking redress for immediate grievances in the 1880s than to sanction the acts of bombers who were now professing to be carrying out in practice what a number of anarchist intellectuals were advocating at a theoretical level. At one point he even attempted to deny that he had had any part in the 1870s formulation of propaganda by the deed.[35] But Kropotkin's position comes as less of a surprise, once we recall that his earlier statements supportive of violence at a theoretical level showed a reluctance to envisage the use of violence as a calculated political weapon outside Russia. It is also well to remember that, though his writing in the 1870s had been bold, he had been thinking in terms of the rising at Benevento and had not anticipated individual acts of violence on the level of the *attentats* of the 1890s. It was his acceptance of the principle of individual autonomy which left him with no option but to submit to the imperatives for terrorist action which developed logically out of his theorising. Kropotkin's Italian friend Malatesta, who had been instrumental in propagating the notion of propaganda by the deed in the 1870s, had avoided the theoretical trap by his refusal to yield before individual autonomy and by his insistence upon some elementary form of organisation of the revolutionary forces.[36] Thus Malatesta and other leading Italian anarchists could advocate organised violence against the established order, but at the same time reject individual acts of violence.

Kropotkin recoiled at the sight of blood, but remained steadfast in his resolve to stand by the wretched as they carried out, on their own terms, the fight against the system. This acceptance of the fact of terrorism, however, did not rest upon a willingness to abide by the logic of the framework of propaganda by the deed. Instead, his analysis took a new and rather unexpected turn. The explanation of terrorism offered by Kropotkin depicted the bombers as mental and emotional cripples, victims of a vicious society, and echoed significant elements of the sentiments of middle-class intellectuals. 'In fact,' Kropotkin declared, 'we have not suffered from the persecutions as they the workers, suffered; we who, in our houses, seclude ourselves from the cry and sight of human sufferings, *we are no judges* of those who live in the midst of all this suffering . . . Personally I hate these explosions, but I cannot stand as a judge to condemn those who are driven to despair . . .'[37] Such a response was hardly consistent with his above-mentioned eulogy of the 'lonely sentinel' whose courage and integrity were crucial to the success of the revolutionary struggle. 'So long as contempt for human life shall be taught to men,' wrote Kropotkin in 1898, 'and so long as they will be told that it is good to kill for what one believes to be beneficial for mankind − new and newer victims will be added, even though the rulers should guillotine all those who take sides with the poor.'[38]

The hesitancy of Kropotkin (humaneness or weakness depending on one's view) was compensated by the determination of Reclus (courage or fanaticism) to admit the implications of a theoretical position and to approve action carried to its logical conclusion. Reclus refused to condemn acts which were the result of 'horrible forces, the consequences of inevitable passions, the explosion of a rudimentary justice',[39] and he insisted that anger had its 'raison d'être . . . its day and its hour'.[40] Within this analysis Ravachol had risen above the status of a mere victim; he had become a primitive lover of justice, striving for what was right, an inevitable phenomenon in the progress towards justice. 'I admire . . . his courage,' wrote Reclus, 'his kindness, his grandeur of soul, the generosity with which he pardons his enemies, in truth his denunciators. I know few men who surpass him in nobleness.'[41]

Reclus' response is wholly consistent with the position which he had developed in the 1880s, namely that the struggle for legitimate rights ought not to be equated with violence, but rather viewed as 'defence armed with a right'.

> If it is true, as I believe it is, that the product of a common work ought to be common property, it is not a call to violence to demand one's share. If it is true, as I believe it is, that no one has the right to deprive another man of his freedom, he who rebels is completely

within his rights.[42]

In another place Reclus had maintained that the word 'violent', if pursued to its primitive meaning, really only meant 'strong'. It was a question, he emphasised, of putting force at the service of justice and goodness, that is a question of being strong.[43] In 1892 he could declare: 'It goes without saying that I regard every revolt against oppression as a just and good act.'[44] In modern language he would say that acts are branded as 'terrorist' from the outside, by society at large, but that this was itself a value judgement disguising their revolutionary character.

In contrast to Kropotkin and Grave, Reclus unhesitatingly defended the position that 'the end justifies the means'. The means, he said, were only the instruments. Just as hands could indifferently serve good or ill, the means could contribute to progress or regression. It is startling — as well as insightful into modern justifications of violence — to read his words on this point. The comrade who lied to save a friend did well to lie; the revolutionary who stole to serve the needs of his friends might 'calmly and without regret allow himself to qualify as a thief'; the man who killed to defend the weak was 'a murderer with honourable intentions'. To be sure, those persons who merely called themselves anarchists in order to justify lies, theft and murder were motivated by purely selfish concerns. The principle which guided their actions was 'the pretext justifies the means'. The principle itself should be subjected to moral scrutiny, not the means which were an essentially neutral thing.[45] Few anarchists in the *La Révolte* group were daring enough to follow the logic of their views to this extent.

Reclus' position closely represented the underlying logic of the anarchism of the terrorists, who insisted on being self-proclaimed anarchists as well. But he was not alone in his insistence upon the essential neutrality of means. Goldman and Berkman, for example, fully embraced this view, which led them, in 1892, to attempt to assassinate Henry Clay Frick for his part in the bloodshed arising out of the Homestead steel strike. Goldman and Berkman, who were to live well into the twentieth century, came to modify their views upon the neutrality of means and the efficacy of violence, moving from the position adopted by Reclus to one which approximated that of Kropotkin. This was an uncomfortable theoretical position to which Goldman never became reconciled. She could not resist the judgement that violence was an inevitable accompaniment of social change, even as she insisted upon the view that violence did nothing to hasten the coming of the revolution. It was doubtlessly a feeling of helplessness in the face of this dilemma which led her, in her later years, to devote much effort to exposing the violence of the existing order rather than advocating the use of violence against it. Perhaps she hoped that an understanding of the nature of violence would contribute to its ultimate eclipse in every form.[46]

Propaganda by the deed was a significant strategy for political action which was formulated in the 1870s by a few socialist revolutionaries who felt that the avenues of the existing political order could offer no prospect for significant social and political reform. In the context of severe socio-economic hardship, the bureaucratisation of political life and the decreasing likelihood of a mere overthrow of the existing order, as well as the 'organisation' of politics, a number of anarchist theoreticians insisted on holding to the view that the impossible — major social revolution — was literally around the corner. It has not been my aim to explore the socio-economic conditions which led to the adoption of the anarchist strategy for action by the few committed groups and individuals. My interest has been rather to examine the elaboration of anarchist theory by radical intellectuals such as Reclus and Kropotkin in response to certain acts of violence in Western Europe and in conjunction with their subjective sense of impotence.

As we are led to believe by Karl Mannheim, the predilections of the politically committed operate as a function of their own versions of the 'perfect world'. It is also well known, if not as widely accepted, that advocates of change (or persistence) are motivated by drastically different conceptions of the 'perfect world'. The theoreticians of anarchist Communism, as these made their views known in the late nineteenth-century literature and in the countless discussions, had their views as well and distinguished themselves by the *means* which they were prepared to adopt. They were torn between the self-imposed sterility of a rejection of organised activity — with the 'authoritarianism' that implied — and the notion of the one against the many. Grasping at the ever-present metaphorical straw, these theoreticians quite naturally were drawn to those who, regardless of how 'correct' their reasons, were prepared to suffer, and even to die, for the cause. Anarchist theory came to represent a highly conscious effort to intellectualise, even to rationalise, certain social occurrences, but this very intellectualising became, in turn, an impediment to the political activism of the theoreticians. In fact, propaganda by the deed bound theoreticians and terrorists in a working alliance against the existing system to the point where theory was at the mercy of practice and compelled by its own internal logic to respond favourably to the violence committed in its name.

Notes

An earlier version of this chapter was published in *Terrorism: An International Jaimal*, vol. 4, nos 1-4 (1980). Permission to reprint this article is acknowledged.

*I should like to thank Robert Gellately for his many helpful suggestions.

1. A. Hamon, *Psychologie de l'Anarchiste-Socialiste* (Paris, 1895); see also Félix Dubois, *Le Péril Anarchiste* (Paris, 1894); Cesare, Lombroso, *Les Anarchistes* (Paris, 1896; Italian edn, 1894); Jehan-Préval, *Anarchie et Nihilisme* (Paris, 1892).

2. George Woodcock, *Anarchism* (Pelican, 1963), p. 12.

3. Murray Bookchin, *The Spanish Anarchists* (New York, 1977), p. 17.

4. For a detailed description of Reclus' position, see Marie Fleming, *The Anarchist Way to Socialism, Elisée Reclus and Nineteenth-Century European Anarchism* (London, 1979), esp. chaps. 8, 10.

5. Quoted in James Joll, *The Anarchists* (London, 1964), p. 121.

6. 'La propagande par le fait' in *Bulletin de la Fedération Jurassienne*, 5 August 1877.

7. *Le Révolté*, 1 November 1879.

8. See Fleming, *The Anarchist Way to Socialism*, chap. 6. See also David Stafford, *From Anarchism to Reformism: a Study of the Political Activities of Paul Brousse 1870-90* (London, 1971), p. 12ff.

9. See the proceedings of the St Imier Congress held from 15-16 September 1872 in protest at the decisions reached by the Hague Congress of the International Working Men's Association; Jacques Freymond (ed.), *La Première Internationale*, vol. III (Geneva, 1971), pp. 3ff.

10. The 'myth' of the Commune seems to have been an important impetus in the development of anarchist theory; see especially the Genevá-based *Le Travailleur* (1877-8) which contributed to this 'myth', as well as to the development of anarchist theory. See also Fleming, *The Anarchist Way to Socialism*, chaps. 5, 6.

11. Michael Bakunin, *God and the State* (Dover, 1970), pp. 9-10.

12. Quoted in Paul Avrich, *Bakunin and Nechaev* (London, 1974), p. 12.

13. Quoted in James Joll, 'Anarchism – A Living Tradition' in David E. Apter and James Joll, *Anarchism Today* (New York, 1972), p. 250.

14. Peter Kropotkin, 'The Spirit of Revolt' in Roger N. Baldwin (ed.), *Kropotkin's Revolutionary Pamphlets* (Dover, 1970), p. 39.

15. For an account of Brousse's arrest and trial, see Stafford, *From Anarchism to Reformism*, pp. 126ff.

16. For the position of Brousse, see ibid., pp. 122ff.

17. Reclus to his brother Elie, 20 July 1878, *Correspondance*, 3 vols. (Paris, 1911-25), vol. II, p. 214.

18. Quoted in George Woodcock and Ivan Avakumović, *The Anarchist Prince, Peter Kropotkin* (Schocken, 1971), p. 343; cf. Kropotkin's comments on Perovskaya's personality in his *Memoirs of A Revolutionist* (Dover, 1971), pp. 317ff.

19. There were 31 delegates representing 56 federations and 46 sections or groups without ties to federations. According to *La Révolution Sociale*, 24 July 1881, delegates came from Germany, America, England, Belgium, Egypt, Spain,

France, Holland, Italy, Russia, Serbia, Switzerland and Turkey. For the proceedings of the congress, see *Le Révolté*, 23 July 1881.

20. Quoted in Andrew R. Carlson, *Anarchism in Germany*, vol. 1 (Metuchen, NJ 1972), p. 254.

21. In Reclus' view, even enemies of the anarchists were engaged in making incessant propaganda on their behalf. See his 'An Anarchist on Anarchy' in the *Contemporary Review*, May 1884 (as pamphlet published in Boston, 1884).

22. *Le Révolté*, 1 April 1882.

23. *Le Révolté*, 2 September 1882.

24. See *Le Procès des Anarchistes devant la Police Correctionnelle et la Cour d'Appel de Lyon* (Lyons, 1883).

25. Ibid., p. 29.

26. Police reports of 28 January and 17 February 1883, B a/1502, *Préfecture de Police*, Paris, contain copies of the placard. On 28 October 1882, *Le Révolté* had published the placard of the *Justiciers du Peuple* which advocated burning the furniture of property-owners whose harshness singled them out.

27. J. Garin, *L'Anarchie et les Anarchistes* (Paris, 1885), p. 1.

28. R. Garraud, *L'Anarchie et la Répression* (Paris, 1885), pp. 17-18, cf. P. Fabreguettes, *De la complicité intellectuelle et des délits d'opinion. De la provocation et de l'opologie criminelles. De la propagande anarchiste* (Paris, 1894-5).

29. For the documents collected under the heading *Explosions*, see B a/66, B a/67, B a/136, B a/139, B a/140, B a/141, B a/142, B a/143; see also B a/508, B a/509, B a/510 entitled *Lettres de manaces*, 1892. In addition the Paris Police Archives contain many files on general anarchist activities, as well as on the more prominent individuals within the movement.

30. Victor Barrucand in *L'En Dehors*, 24 July 1892; quoted in Jean Maitron, *Le Mouvement Anarchiste en France*, 2 vols. (Paris, 1975), vol. I, p. 224.

31. *La Révolte*, 23-30 April 1892.

32. See *La Révolte*, 7-14 May 1892 for an article by Octave Mirbeau and 1-7 July 1892 for 'Declarations de Ravachol'.

33. Jean Grave, *Quarante Ans de Propagande Anarchiste* (Paris, 1973), pp. 296-7.

34. Kropotkin to Brandes, *Freedom*, October 1898; Martin A. Miller, *Kropotkin* (Chicago, 1976), p. 174.

35. Miller, *Kropotkin*, p. 150.

36. See Vernon Richards (ed.), *Errico Malatesta, His Life and Ideas* (London, 1965), esp. pp. 53ff.

37. Quoted in Woodcock and Avakumović, *The Anarchist Prince, Peter Kropotkin*, p. 248.

38. Kropotkin to Brandes, *Freedom*.

39. Reclus to Richard Heath, nd, *Correspondance*, vol. II, p. 425.

40. Reclus to Lilly Zibelin-Wilmerding, 7 June 1892, *Correspondance*, vol. III, p. 118.

41. Reclus to Sempre Avanti, 28 June 1892, ibid., p. 120.

42. Reclus to Heath, 18 February 1883, ibid., p. 279.

43. Reclus to Heath, 10 January 1885, *Fonds Elisée Reclus*, 14 AS 232, *Institut Français d'Historie Sociale*.

44. Reclus to Zibelin-Wilmerding, *Correspondance*, vol. III, p. 118.

45. Reclus to Grave, 21 May 1893, *Correspondance*, vol. III, *op cit.*, pp. 139-40. It is sometimes suggested that Reclus' dislike of violence led him to write a letter condemning the explosions and, specifically, Emile Henry's *attentat* at the Café Terminus on 12 February 1894. Such a letter appeared in *Le Travail* on the day after the Terminus bomb and was reprinted in other papers. However,

Reclus publicly denied responsibility for the letter and claimed that it was a forgery (see letter from Reclus to *l'Eclair*, 2 May 1894, *Correspondance*, vol. III, p. 163).

46. See Alix Kates Shulman (ed.), *Red Emma Speaks* (New York, 1972), esp. pp. 205ff. Cf. Alexander Berkman, *What is Anarchist Communism?* (New York, 1972), esp. pp. 173ff.

2 SOME ASPECTS OF INDIVIDUAL TERRORISM: A CASE STUDY OF THE SCHWARTZBARD AFFAIR

Yosef Nedava

The literature dealing with individual terrorism throughout the age is voluminous.[1] Assassinations have occurred since the dawn of civilisation, and tyrannicide has been the subject of philosophical discussion and analysis since the formative stages of human society. At first the act of killing a tyrant was not frowned upon, and it carried no suggestion of moral obloquy. On the contrary, it was considered a legitimate means of meting out justice where no other remedy was available to the afflicted, thus reflecting commendable, and not only justifiable, vengeance. With the growth of some semblance of an organised, democratic society, assassinations came to be regarded as a threat to recognised authority. Such a resort to extra-legal means seemed liable to lead to anarchy, thus endangering the very basis of existence of society. Assassinations soon came under the heading of criminal acts and were dealt with accordingly.

Nowadays both democratic and authoritarian regimes alike look askance at acts of individual terrorism. To be sure, Soviet rule, more particularly during the 'black years' of Stalinism, has applied both *mass* and *individual* terror to ensure obedience, but they were used as a means to an end. Marxism does not condemn terrorism from an ideological point of view; it simply does not believe in its practicability in bringing about a substantial change in society.

Individual terrorism is still prevalent in our days. In practically every country of the globe there are to be found 'lone wolves' who aspire to change the state of affairs of men through the removal of latter day tyrants — kings, presidents and dictators. We shall limit our study to one particular class of assassins, namely, those motivated by an urge to avenge acts of *genocide*.

Shalom Schwartzbard set out to avenge the slaughter of Jews in his native Ukraine; Salomon Teilirian was driven to avenge his martyred Armenian people; Maurice Conradi killed V.V. Vorosky with a view to protesting, even though vicariously, against the murderous excesses of Bolshevism; and David Frankfurter killed Wilhelm Gustloff, the Swiss Nazi leader, as a warning against the imminent perpetration of the crime

29

of genocide in Hitlerite Germany.

We shall concentrate almost entirely on the Schwartzbard affair, not only on account of its universal repercussions at the time, but also because it can aptly serve as a fit pattern for a case study of individual terrorism. But first a few facts about the case:

On 25 May 1926, Shalom Schwartzbard, a Jewish watchmaker, assassinated Simon Petliura, the chief Ataman of the Ukranian Republican Army. During Petliura's reign, prior to his defeat by the Red Army in 1920, the Jews in the Ukraine were subjected to pogroms and slaughter on a scale unknown since the massacres of 1648-9 under Bogdan Chmielnicki.[2] Petliura was killed in rue Racine, in the Latin Quarter of Paris; Schwartzbard surrendered to the police, and following a dramatic trial was acquitted on 27 October 1927. The verdict was almost universally acclaimed. Following his release, he expressed his wish to settle in the Land of Israel (Palestine at the time), but the British Mandatory authorities viewed his deed with disfavour and, fearing further trouble from a 'temperamental' type in a 'troubled' area, refused him permission to land. He died in March 1938, in South Africa, and his remains were transferred to Israel in 1967.

Schwartzbard's trial turned on one pivotal issue: could Petliura be held responsible for the pogroms in the Ukraine, and, consequently, be accountable for their grim results, as claimed by the defence; or was he innocent of the crimes imputed to him. For, the prosecution maintained, he had tried his best to stop the massacres by publishing exhortatory proclamations to his soldiers. As was to be expected, Schwartzbard turned from accused to accuser; yet in spite of this change of roles, the onus of proof still rested on him. The prosecution and its witnesses persisted in their argument that Petliura had been a friend of the Jews; his proclamations to the army had denounced the pogroms unreservedly. The prosecution further claimed that he had contributed from the funds of the Directory, which he had headed, towards relieving the sufferings of the victims' families, and that he had manifested in diverse ways his resentment of the activities of the 'irregulars' who had joined his forces in the struggle against the Bolsheviks and for the independence of the Ukraine. The defence rejected these claims *in toto*, yet found it difficult to produce in court any *written* incriminating evidence. It lacked clear-cut documentary proof definitely to condemn the 'Chief Hangman', as Schwartzbard's attorney, Henry Torrès, called Petliura.

It seems that from time immemorial, perpetrators of genocide have tended to hide behind the backs of their assistants and henchmen in order to be able to wash their hands of any responsibility when called to account. The Wansee Conference (January 1942), which was held in the presence of some of the highest officials of the Nazi hierarchy, refrained from putting down in writing any of its deliberations. It was ostensibly a 'social' gathering, although the lines were laid down for co-ordinating efforts to carry out the 'Final Solution' of the Jewish problem. Among those present was Adolf Eichmann, who to the very end never admitted being anything but a minor functionary in any decision making. It was his consistent practice to avoid putting his signature to incriminating documents. He, too, like Petliura, pretended to have been a friend of the Jews bent 'on finding a piece of land that they could call their own'. But he was naturally unable to safeguard himself entirely against all 'foolhardy' actions on the part of his minor subordinates. Following a telephone conversation with Franz Rademacher, an expert on Jewish affairs at the German Foreign Office inquiring what should be done to some Yugoslav Jews, Rademacher noted: 'Eichmann says no possibility of reception (of Jews) in Russian and General Government . . . Eichmann proposes shooting.'[3]

In Schwartzbard's case, too, the defence had to a great extent to rely on circumstantial evidence. This problem was dealt with by the well-known historian of the Ukrainian pogroms, Elias Tcherikower, in his comprehensive work.[4] Tcherikower was invited to Paris by the Zionist leader, Leo Motzkin, in order to preside over the preparation of the background material for the defence. From the numerous testimonies and documents collected, Petliura's culpability clearly stood out, but it was established somewhat indirectly, for the defence could lay its hand on no single document bearing the Ataman's signature incriminating him in the massacres.

A special chapter in Tcherikower's book deals with 'Petliura and the Proskurov Pogrom (February 1919)'.[5] The shadow of this pogrom in particular hovered over the entire proceedings of Schwartzbard's trial because of its savagery and ferociousness. For three and a half hours on 15 February ('The Proskurov Sabbath'), over 1,500 Jews were slaughtered and more than 1,000 wounded. Hetman Semesenko's soldiers, who belonged to Petliura's Haidamacks, showed no mercy towards the old, women or children. On the eve of the pogrom they swore to deviate from their customary rule of conduct — to refrain from robbing their victims and content themselves with their killing. As usual, the massacre was carried out under the slogan: 'Kill the Jews and save the Ukraine', and the pretext was that the Jews were Bolsheviks and ought to be eradicated mercilessly. The army marched in procession along the main street of the town to the strains of a military band. In order to save ammunition the pogromists were ordered to kill their victims with lances and bayonets only.

To what extent was the pogrom organised at the behest of Petliura, and what written material was available to incriminate him?

(a) Among the witnesses for the defence summoned to Paris, but not called to stand,[6] was a Jew, Z. Zecker, who had been a member of a commission appointed to investigate the Proskurov pogrom. He had access to the official archives when the town was temporarily under Bolshevik rule. Among the documents which he discovered there was a cable in code, dated 13 February (that is, two days before the pogrom), signed by the Chief Ataman (namely, Petliura): 'Top Secret. Any attempt on the part of the Jewish population to bring about a Bolshevik rebellion should be ruthlessly suppressed by the armed forces, so that no treacherous Jewish hand would dare to be raised against independent Ukraine.' But this cable was no longer to be had. In June 1919, Petliura's forces recaptured Proskurov from the Bolsheviks. Zecker had entrusted a packet of cables to a friend who, however, fearing a search in his house, burned all the documents in it, including 'the only direct proof that Petliura was to blame for the Proskurov pogrom'.[7]

(b) Another relevant document was the testimony of Henryk Pszanowski, a Pole in the service of the Danish Red Cross in Proskurov. He was the only non-resident to witness the horrors. In his deposition to the Examining Magistrate at the Schwartzbard trial in Paris, Pszanowski wrote that a few days after the pogrom he had met with Petliura in his official capacity when suddenly their conversation was interrupted by Semesenko, who burst into the room, impatiently to report his activities to his chief: 'By order of the Chief Ataman I started the pogrom at 12 o'clock at noon; 4,000 [sic] Jews were killed . . . ' Semesenko was so eager to impart his news that he failed to notice the presence of a stranger. Petliura was greatly embarrassed, but was unable to stop his henchman's flow of words without raising the suspicions of his guest. Pszanowski's testimony was absolutely trustworthy;[8] yet, again, it was merely hearsay.

We are therefore forced to draw the conclusion that in cases of genocide, where perpetrators of horrendous crimes are all too careful to work in the dark, some relaxation of the rules of evidence must be admitted. Circumstantial evidence counts comparatively little in ordinary criminal procedure, but is often of decisive importance in *political* trials. In this respect, all cases involving acts of genocide are political by nature, even though there is always the danger that the admission of second-rate evidence may lead to a travesty of justice.

Another relevant factor in practically all cases involving crimes of genocide is the state of mind of the avenger. Psychiatrists are called in to observe the mental behaviour of the accused with a view to determining the extent of his responsibility. The *a priori* assumption is that the act of assassination is a result of a morbid state of mind and is due to an obsession. An irresistible instinct to avenge the dead of one's family and nation is bound to drive a man to commit some act over which he has no control. Can such an avenger be regarded as normal, more particularly where his victim was chosen by him virtually at random? Conradi is a case in point, for he planned at first to kill the Soviet Commissar of Foreign Affairs, Chicherin. However, on finding that statesman beyond his reach (he had left the Lausanne Conference before its conclusion), Conradi killed Vorovsky instead, and in fact, his mind was set on killing *any* Bolshevik leader.[9]

The state of mind of the Armenian student Teilirian might well have been the decisive factor leading to his acquittal. He was examined by several psychiatrists, who diagnosed him as a psychopath. On the witness stand Teilirian declared that his mother had appeared to him in his dreams, urging him to avenge the Turkish crime against his people.[10]

In Schwartzbard's case it was the prosecution which made an attempt to represent the accused as insane, in order to obviate the need of going into the full details of the Ukrainian pogroms.[11] But the three psychiatrists, who were officially entrusted with the task of delving into Schwartzbard's state of mind, concluded that he was in full control of his faculties. One of them, Dr Claude, stated that 'as far as our understanding of the workings of the human mind goes, he (Schwartzbard) makes the impression of an honest man, an idealist, pursuing wholeheartedly the course of justice'.[12]

As has already been stated above, Schwartzbard's case was primarily a *political* rather than a *criminal* one, and it therefore naturally tended to assume a dramatic turn and aroused considerable interest all over the world. By a stroke of providential luck Schwartzbard's act of vengeance was committed in Paris and not in London. Under Anglo-American jurisprudence such a trial could not have taken place 'with all of its hearsay, its theoretical opinions, its wild conclusions, its disorder and perfervid elocution'.[13] Neither British nor American law recognises a *political* murder as such, and equal treatment is meted out both to a person committing a deed politically motivated and to one committing a deed of a purely criminal character. In the entire history of British jurisprudence, no single case can be cited where a man was acquitted of murder merely because the jury had sympathised with the motives of his deed. British jurisprudence would not permit an individual to take the law into his own hands, nor would it subscribe to the French conception of *crime passionel*. A person killing his or her mate because of faithlessness, will not necessarily be absolved of criminal guilt. Allowance is sometimes made under British law only in cases of *provocation* — where an act is committed as a result of an irresistible impulse, in 'hot blood', testifying to a situation where the doer is unable to control his feelings and is therefore not fully responsible for his acts. But this rule is of very limited application and is construed with great reserve. In order to apply it, ample and incontrovertible proof must be adduced to the effect that the act in question was done spontaneously, on the spur of the moment, with no trace of malice aforethought.

Consequently, British legal criteria could never have been applied to Schwartzbard's case, for the killing of Petliura was committed as an act of vengeance for genocide perpetrated seven years earlier. Moreover, it was by no means committed 'on the spur of the moment', for it took Schwartzbard many days to trace Petliura's whereabouts in Paris and to decide to kill him, buy a gun and lie in wait for him and seize the opportune moment for the act. Even by a considerable stretch of the imagination one cannot place such a case within the orbit of the strict British definition of provocation, unless one admits some kind of permanent state of 'hot blood'. Such an artificial extension of a legal term would be quite consistent with the 'legal' histrionics inherent in a typical French criminal lawyer like Torrès.[14]

The Anglo-American and French systems differ not only in their basic conception of criminal jurisprudence, but also in the very nature of criminal trial and procedure. The French system admits to much informality. The investigation or 'instruction' of criminal cases lies exclusively in the hands of the public officer known as *Juge d'Instruction* ('Examining Magistrate'), whose discretionary powers are wide, for he is supposed to do everything 'pour decourvir la verité' (Art. 268, Code Instr. Crim.). He is not limited by any strict rules of procedure. He asks any questions he feels may throw some light on the occurrence, and on the responsibility, reason and motive for the act. When a trial is connected, however remotely, with politics, speeches are in great abundance. The substance of the depositions is more often than not connected only remotely with the legal aspect of the case. Nobody seems to stop any redundancies, hearsay or rhetoric. For instance, on the second day of the trial of the Schwartzbard case, Torrès spent a great deal of time dramatically demonstrating how the shots were fired, even using a revolver in the portrayal. A common feature is what may be called 'confrontation'. In the midst of the witness's evidence, the judge may interrupt him by addressing the accused: 'Is that true?' The court's record swells boundlessly with seemingly hopeless irrelevancies, opinions of prominent persons, 'expert' testimony and philosophical-moral expositions.[15]

In sum one might say that the elasticity of the French legal criminal system is conducive to adjudicating in political cases by responding to the Latin temperament, preferring the humanistic rather than the dogmatic approach to 'extra-judicial' situations. The less insistence there is made on observing strict technicalities, the easier it becomes to overcome obstacles inherent in the lack of sufficiently *direct*, as opposed to circumstantial, evidence necessary to assure convictions in cases involving acts of genocide.

There is still another aspect which points to the advantageousness of the Continental legal system. It provides a remedy in cases which do not fall strictly within the scope of the ordinary criminal law. The avenger of acts of genocide can find a hearing for his motives. Where could Teilirian, Schwartzbard, Conradi and Frankfurter have turned for redress in an objective adjudication of their deeds? To the League of Nations? To the International Court of Justice at the Hague? Could they have appealed to what was bound to be a deaf public opinion, or could they have made any effective representations to a non-existent universal body representing World Diplomacy and the entire enlightened world? Was there anyone else at hand to avenge the sorrowful fate of their peoples? There seemed to have been no alternative but to take the law into their own hands.

In his speech for the defence in the Schwartzbard case, Torrès referred to 'individual justice, which is a substitute for the failing collective justice'.[16] The implications of the fateful lacuna in international law to provide for the punishment of perpetrators of atrocities was brought up in the testimony of the renowned French natural philosopher, Professor Langevin: 'Schwartzbard expected that justice would be meted out against the perpetrators of atrocities. Only when he despaired of obtaining such justice did he regard himself as a would-be judge.'[17]

Lanvevin further expounded his view by stating: 'When organized justice exists, there is no room for acts of violence, nor are such acts excusable. But . . . in the absence of organized justice individual acts of violence interpose. It is only because there is no international justice that we have wars . . . individual justice as in the case before us, seems to belong to the same category.'[18]

In his deposition, Maxim Gorki gave yet another reason for the justification of acts of vengeance: 'I am not a partisan of terror, but I cannot refuse a man the right of self-defence. It seems to me that murder can be committed out of fear that the past may recur, and through a natural desire to forestall the possibility of greater horrors than one's own moral death.'[19]

To what extent has this lacuna in international justice been filled in modern practice?

Incidents of genocide have been haunting civilisation for all time, yet not until World War II was an attempt made to provide a legal framework by means of which cases of mass extermination of peoples could be dealt with.[20] On 9 December 1948, the General Assembly of the United Nations unanimously and without abstentions approved the Convention of the Prevention and Punishment of the Crime of Genocide.

Genocide was defined as 'a crime under international law which the civilized world condemns, and for the commission of which principles and accomplices are punishable'. Since the Convention came into effect (1951) it has been ratified by a substantial number of states. Its enforcement can be effected either by the incorporation of genocide into domestic law, or by the trial of violators ('constitutionally responsible rulers, public officers, or private individuals', Art. IV) by an international criminal court to be established, whose jurisdiction is accepted by the contradicting parties.

The Genocide Convention was hailed as an 'epoch-making event in the development of international law',[21] yet it is very doubtful whether it can acquire practical value, as punishment of acts of genocide is entrusted primarily to the municipal courts. 'There is nothing revolutionary in the Convention', writes Professor Kunz. 'The new crimes are merely an addition to the *delicta juris gentium*, such as piracy, slave trade, counterfeiting, and so on. The crimes under Article II and III are "crimes under international law", but not crimes against international law'.[22] The drafters of the Convention were not prepared to accept international provisions, although it was evident from the very beginning that domestic jurisdiction would not be sufficient.

Following the approval of the Genocide Convention various suggestions were made in respect of an international court. The International Court of Justice at the Hague was not the appropriate body, since its jurisdiction was limited to states only; other proposals too were unsatisfactory. Finally, a draft resolution of the General Assembly was approved to the effect that an International Law Commission be requested to study the desirability and possibility of establishing an independent international criminal court for the trial of persons charged with genocide. The General Assembly put this problem on its agenda at several sessions, but has not so far acted upon it. Great difficulties were encountered. The Soviet Union, for instance, would not adopt any kind of international criminal law.[23] Then, as political crimes are generally not subject to extradition, it would seem that the state refusing extradition would itself have to prosecute the accused.

The attempts to establish an International Criminal Court have a long history. Two international judicial bodies were established after World War II: the International Military Tribunal for the trial of the major war criminals at Nuremberg, and the International Military Tribunal for the Far East. On the initiative of the General Assembly of the United Nations several draft statutes for an International Criminal Court were submitted, but so far this has not materialised. The discussion of the drafts was formally postponed until aggression was properly defined. The matter was further dealt with at the 1971 Belgrade World Conference on World Peace Through Law, and one of its working sessions was devoted to the subject 'Towards a Feasible International Criminal Court'.[24] At the 1971 and 1972 Wingspread-Bellagio Conferences, a Draft Convention on International Crimes and a Draft Statute for an International Criminal Court were drawn up. A long list of crimes, including crimes against humanity and genocide, fall within the scope of the international body to be established.

However, no progress has been made in this direction since then, and the decision to set up a truly competent international criminal court is in abeyance. Collective justice has not so far found a substitute for individual justice in the most sensitive and threatening field of human experience — genocide. The development of international justice has so far not reached such as stage as to obviate the possibility of the appearance of new would-be avengers as Schwartzbard, Teilirian and their like. It seems that individual terrorism will go on engaging the minds of men and public opinion for many years to come.

Notes

1. For a partial citation of authorities see, e.g. Luis Kutner's 'A Philosophical Perspective on Rebellion' in M. Cherif Bassiouni (ed.), *International Terrorism and Political Crimes*, (Springfield, Illinois, 1975,) pp. 51-64.

2. The exact toll of Jewish victims in the pogroms in the Ukraine during 1919-21 has never been ascertained. The number of pogroms was estimated at about 2,000 in 700 towns. In the YIVO (New York) Archives some 20,000 names of victims are listed, yet clearly these are partial lists, for many victims were buried in mass graves and never identified. According to other sources the toll is believed to be between 50,000 and 170,000.

3. Gideon Hausner, *Justice in Jerusalem* (New York, 1968), p. 125. In the case of the Armenian atrocities the number of incriminating documents was somewhat greater. See *Der Prozess Talaat Pascha* (Berlin, 1921), pp. 129ff. See also James Nazer, *The First Genocide of the 20th Century* 1968) and for authentic and corroborating oral evidence, see Henry Morgenthau, *Ambassador Morgenthau's Story* (New York, 1918), pp. 301ff

4. Elias Tcherikower, *Di Ukrainir pogromen in yor 1919* (Yiddish) (YIVO, New York, 1965).

5. Ibid., pp. 145-63.

6. On the seventh day of the trial Henry Torrès surprised the court by announcing that he would refrain from calling some eighty defence witnesses. This was a calculated, dramatic as well as a thought out move, which paid off, for it greatly contributed to the acquittal of the accused; lengthy testimonies of atrocities would have certainly wearied the court and blunted their effectiveness on account of their repetitiveness.

7. Tcherikower, *Di Ukrainir pogromen*, p. 146.

8. He too was summoned to Paris, but, like most witnesses for the defence, was not called. His report is included in H.B. Shekhtman, *Les Pogromes en Ukraine sous les Gouvernments Ukrainiens 1917-1921* (Paris, 1927). See also *L'Europe Nouvelle – Russia 1917-1927* (Paris, 1927), p. 1524.

9. Veridicus, *Suisse et Soviets (Histoire d'une Conflit)* (Paris, 1926), p. 157.

10. *Der Prozess Talaat Pascha*, pp. 8, 17, 70ff. See also Emil Ludwig, *The Davos Murder* (London, 1937).

11. Shalom Schwartzbard, *Inem loif fun yoren* (Yiddish) (Chicago, 1934), pp. 263-9.The Ukrainian representatives in Paris, too, urged the Schwartzbard Defence Committee to agree to declare Schwartzbard insane. They maintained that, by leaving Petliura's black record untouched, Jewish-Ukrainian friendship would be preserved. See Zosa Szajkowski, 'A Reappraisal of Symon Petliura and Ukrainian-Jewish Relations, 1917-1921: A Rebuttal' in *Jewish Social Studies* (New York, 1969), vol. 31, pp. 203-4. Paradoxically, some leaders of the American Jewish community were of the same opinion. 'If this had occurred in the United States,' wrote Louis Marshall to the Russian-Jewish communal leader Henry Sliosberg on 18 August 1927, 'the defense interposed would have been that Schwartzbard killed Petliura while emotionally insane, that he had become obsessed with the idea that Petliura had murdered his relatives, and that acting under an uncontrollable impulse he fired the shot. It was for that reason that I suggested that the defense should be sought in the field of mental irresponsibility . . . Sometimes they are referred to as brainstorms, at other times as acts of temporary aberration . . . Consequently the effort of a number of irresponsible and self-constituted Jewish leaders like Motzkin to attempt to justify Schwartzbard's act is in my judgment a crime tenfold as great as that committed by Schwartzbard of Petliura, because it jeopardizes the Jews who are now living in the Ukraine and will tend to re-open wounds which have closed and to occasion

new pogroms.' Louis Marshall Collection, box no. 1599, American Jewish Archives, Hebrew Union College, Jewish Institute of Religion, Cincinnati, USA.

12. *Official Record of the Schwartzbard Trial Proceedings* (YIVO, New York, Micr. n.d.).

13. Louis Marshall Collection, box no. 1599, letter to Mr Wiernik, 29 October 1927.

14. Henry Torrès, *Le Procès des Pogromes* (Paris, 1928), p. 31.

15. Derick Goodman, *Crime of Passion* (London, 1958).

16. Torrès, *Le Procès des Pogromes*, p. 11.

17. *Official Record of the Schwartzbard Trial Proceedings* and Torrès, *Le Procès des Pogromes*, pp. 185-6.

18. Torrès, *Le Procès des Pogromes*, pp. 185-6.

19. *Official Record of the Schwartzbard Trial Proceedings* and Torrès, *Le Procès des Pogromes*, p. 131.

20. An attempt to deal with a somewhat cognate phenomenon, namely war crimes, preceded the problem of genocide. Following the defeat of Germany in World War I the Allied Powers demanded that some 900 Germans accused of war crimes be handed over for trial. By way of compromise, the Germans were allowed to try their own 'war criminals'. The Kaiser was out of reach; Holland, to which he fled in November 1918, refused to extradite him. In respect of other war criminals in 1921 and 1922, trials were conducted by the Supreme Court of Germany, sitting in Leipzig; but the matter turned into a fiasco; nearly all were acquitted or allowed to escape their very short prison sentences.

21. Nehemiah Robinson, *The Genocide Convention (A Commentary)* (New York, 1960), p. 43.

22. Josef L. Kunz, 'The United Nations Convention on Genocide', Editorial Comments, *American Journal of International Law*, vol. 43, p. 738.

23. Robinson, *The Genocide Convention*, p. 86.

24. L. Kos-Rabcewicz Zubkowski, 'The Creation of an International Criminal Court' in Bassiouni (ed.), *International Terrorism and Political Crimes*, pp. 519-36.

25. Ibid., pp. 522ff.

3 POLITICAL TERRORISM IN WESTERN EUROPE: SOME THEMES AND VARIATIONS*

Dennis Pluchinsky

Western Europe has the most active terrorist environment in the world. By one estimate, 33 per cent of all 'international terrorist attacks' from 1968 to 1980 took place in Western Europe.[1] Latin America ranked second with 21 per cent. According to another estimate, which used different criteria, 47 per cent of all 'significant terrorist actions' from 1970 to 1978 occurred in Western Europe.[2] In this estimate, Latin America again ranked second with 24 per cent. Regardless of the criteria used to measure terrorist activity, Western Europe has been and continues to be the foremost battlefield for political terrorist activity. Essentially, this results from Western Europe's encounter with four different but interrelated levels of terrorist activity. It is the combination of and interaction between these four levels or types of terrorist activity that has presented Western Europe with the destabilising problem of multi-tiered terrorist activity. The four levels of terrorist activity which are found in Western Europe are *indigenous, supra-indigenous, international* and *state-directed*.[3] While one or more of these levels can be found in other regions of the world, only Western Europe is faced with all four to a significant degree.

Indigenous Terrorist Activity

At the lowest level, Western Europe is faced with significant and, at times, serious indigenous terrorist activity. To a lesser degree and more limited scope, such activity is also found in Latin America (Guatamala, Colombia, Peru and Chile), the Middle East (Syria and Israel) and the Far East (Thailand and the Philippines).[4] In Western Europe this activity is an actual or potential problem for most countries in the region. It is an actual problem for Spain, Turkey, Italy and Northern Ireland, where special anti-terrorist legislation has been enacted, the capability and responsibilities of the security forces have been increased and enhanced and the political fibre of the country has been occasionally shaken. Indigenous terrorist activity in these countries has also caused signifi-

40

cant casualties, and, at one time or another, has provoked the government to either employ or be challenged by the respective military forces in these countries.

In Spain, the indigenous terrorist threat comes primarily from the military wing of the separatist 'Basque Fatherland and Liberty' group (ETA-M). To a lesser extent, the political-military wing of ETA (ETA-PM), the rightist, anti-Basque 'Spanish Basque Battalion' (BVE) and the leftist, anarchist, 'Groups of Anti-Fascist Resistance, First of October' (GRAPO) have augmented the ETA-M attacks. All of these groups have contributed to the escalating political violence in Spain which in 1977 claimed only 29 deaths, but 88 in 1978, 127 in 1979 and 126 in 1980.

It was this proliferation of terrorism, primarily in the northern Basque region, which was the determining factor in provoking an attempted military coup by several rightist Spanish Civil Guard officers in February 1981. Although there were certainly other contributing factors which prompted this attempt, escalating indigenous terrorism was the determining factor, the 'last straw'. In a communiqué issued immediately after the seizure of the Spanish Cortes or Parliament by rightist elements on 23 February, the rebel Civil Guardsmen stated: 'We do not accept separatist autonomies and want a decentralised but not fractured Spain . . . do not accept impunity for terrorist murders . . . do not accept insecurity . . . ' and want 'the unity of Spain, peace, order, and security'. Although the attempted coup failed to generate the support necessary to succeed, the Spanish government did have to make some concessions to the military. On 23 March 1981, exactly one month after the attempted coup, the government announced new measures to combat separatist violence in the Basque area, including supplementing the security forces in the region with military units. More stringent anti-terrorist legislation has also been passed since the coup. While placating hard line elements within the Spanish military, the government's 23 March decree also recognised the destabilising effects of indigenous terrorist activity in the Basque region.

Increasing political violence has also been a serious problem for Turkey. Since 1977, over 5,000 people have died there as a result of indigenous terrorist activity emanating from both the right and the left. In 1977, the death toll was 231. In 1978, it rose to 1,170 and then approached 2,000 in 1979.[5] During the first eight months of 1980, over 1,600 died and about 10,000 people had been injured as a result of political violence. Unlike Spain, where the terrorist threat was separatist in nature and geographically restricted to the northern Basque region, the threat in Turkey was generally anarchist and country-wide. Combined with a degenerating economy and ineffective political leadership, this escalating political violence was leading the country towards possible civil war. On 12 September 1980, the Turkish military, for the third time in the last 20 years, seized power from the civilian leadership. In the first communiqué issued after the take-over, the military stated that they had assumed control of the government in order to ensure national unity, 'prevent civil war' and 'restore the authority and existence of the state'.[6] During the following months, the military conducted a search and destroy campaign against extremist elements throughout Turkey.[7] Compared to the 1,600 people killed in Turkey prior to the September take-over, only 140 were killed between September and December 1980. According to the Turkish government, 'the number of people killed in terrorist incidents has been reduced from a daily average of 22 before the coup to less than one a day now'.[8]

On 14 August 1968, Major James Chichester Clark, Prime Minister of Northern Ireland's Parliament, made the following dramatic announcement: 'I have called in the British Army, it is an emergency operation which will last no more than two weeks.'[9] Twelve years later, the British army remains in Northern Ireland. While initially called in to contain sectarian riots, the army has remained there because of the indigenous terrorist activity of the Provisional Irish Republican Army (PIRA). Like Spain, the indigenous terrorist threat for the United Kingdom is separatist in nature and geographically limited to Northern Ireland. Like Spain, indigenous terrorism for the United Kingdom is a single-issue problem fuelled primarily by the activities of a single terrorist group. Since 1969, this indigenous terrorist problem has caused more than 2,060 deaths (334 army, 245 members of the security forces, 1,286 civilians and about 195 IRA members), over 20,000 injuries, and caused the British government to pay nearly $146 million in compensation for death and injury and $884 million in compensation for the destruction or damage of property in Northern Ireland. Security in Northern Ireland has cost the British taxpayer about $200 million a year.[10]

Unlike Spain, Italy and Turkey, where the indigenous terrorist threat has or had been increasing, terrorist activities in Northern Ireland have been on the decline.[11] From a record high of about 460 deaths in 1972, the death toll in Northern Ireland decreased to an average of 250 deaths a year during 1973 to 1976. In 1977, the number of deaths decreased to 112 and dropped further in 1978 to 81. In 1979, over 113 people were killed[12] and in 1980, only 70 died as a result of political violence.

The British government has responded to this decline in political violence by gradually withdrawing military troops to the present level of about 11,000. In 1972, there had been 21,700 British troops stationed in Northern Ireland. PIRA supporters correctly claim, however, that even though the British troop level has been declining, there has been a corresponding increase in the level of other security forces.[13] This indicates that the British government, despite troop reductions, still recognises the potentially explosive nature of PIRA activities in Northern Ireland. As one historian writes, the PIRA 'is a wind in the corridors of Irish history, a rustle in the undergrowth of Irish politics, a spark that can, if the wind blows favourably, suddenly ignite with literally napalmesque consequences'.[14]

In Italy, the indigenous terrorist threat began escalating about 1976. Terrorist attacks appeared to have reached a peak, however, in 1979. In 1975, there were 702 incidents in Italy. There were 1,353 in 1976, 1,926 in 1977, 2,238 in 1978, 2,514 in 1979 and 1,200 in 1980.[15] Unlike Spain, Turkey and Northern Ireland, indigenous terrorist activity in Italy has not caused a great many casualties, which is unusual considering the number and frequency of terrorist attacks which have taken place over the past seven years. Between 1969 and 1980, only 230 political murders took place in Italy, 90 per cent of them since 1976. Of these 230 deaths, right-wing terrorists have been blamed for about 130, 122 of which were the result of only four separate attacks.[16]

The indigenous terrorist threat in Italy, however, originates mainly from the left, which, on a daily basis, is more active and targets a broader sector of the state's representatives than rightist terrorists. The attacks of the right have been indiscriminate, caused more casualties and have involved numerous innocent civilians. The attacks by the left have targeted the 'servants of the state' — police and security officials, magistrates, prosecutors and politicians. Leading the wave of leftist political violence, which abated in 1980 and early 1981, have been the 'Red Brigades' and 'Front Line' terrorist groups. Beginning in 1980, both groups were hit hard by police arrests. In 1981, Front Line appeared to have been neutralised. With the April 1981 arrest of Mario Moretti, the alleged operational leader of the Red Brigades and the reported mastermind behind the Moro kidnapping, they were thought to have been dealt a significant tactical defeat. However, there were indications in May and June of 1981 that the Red Brigades have regrouped and still possess a significant operational capability, although it will take some time for them to rebuild to their pre-1980 level of activities. Italy, like Turkey, faces a geographically widespread indigenous terrorist threat. And, like Spain and Northern Ireland, this threat is fuelled primarily by the activities of one terrorist group. Whereas before 1980, the Italian state was not able to contain the rising level of violence, in 1980 it had begun to reduce signficicantly the number and frequency of terrorist incidents in Italy. While terrorism in general may now be manageable in Italy, the Red Brigades are not. They still play a pivotal role in defining the terrorist threat in Italy. Until the Italian authorities are able to eradicate the Red Brigades, the Italian terrorist scene will continue to be puncutated by the kidnappings, kneecappings and assassinations of the 'servants of the state'.

One major difference between the indigenous terrorist threat in Spain, Turkey and Northern Ireland, and the threat in Italy is that despite the escalating political violence there during 1976 to 1979, the Italian military as a group have not demanded sterner measures or taken an active part in the anti-terrorist campaign. This is partially explained by the fact that the Italian military has not been a significant factor in the Italian political process. Its propensity to intervene in a domestic crisis is severely limited. In June 1979 it was to provide additional security during the Italian elections, having been asked by the civilian government.[17] Another reason may be that the Italian military has not been targeted by Italian terrorists. In Turkey, members of the military have been killed by Turkish terrorists. In Northern Ireland, the British army has born the brunt of the PIRA's terrorist attacks. And in Spain, military officers there have been frequent targets of ETA-M and GRAPO. As of May 1981, over 24 field grade officers, including seven Generals, have been assassinated in Spain over the past four years. In Italy, the military has not received similar provocations.

These then are the four 'front-line' states facing serious indigenous terrorist activity in Western Europe – Spain, Turkey, Northern Irland and Italy. Northern Ireland was the first to encounter this threat in the early 1970s; Turkey and Italy followed in 1977 and Spain in 1978. By 1977, the British had begun to contain the terrorist threat in Northern Ireland. By 1980, first Italy and then Turkey made similar progress. After the attempted coup in Spain in early 1981 and what appears to be a growing involvement of the Spanish military in the counter-terrorist campaign, Spain may also be near to this goal – a dilution of the indigenous terrorist threat to social, economic and political stability. But containment does not eradicate the threat; it only makes it more manageable. It is doubtful that any of the above countries will ever completely eradicate their respective indigenous terrorist threats.

This is not a negative assessment of the political and security machinery of these countries, rather it is an acceptance of an unfortunate fact of our times, that terrorism has become ingrained into the political process.

In addition to the 'front-line' states noted above, there is a second group of Western European countries which face a more limited indigenous terrorist threat. This second group of 'border' states consists of West Germany, France and Greece. All of these countries face the potential of a serious indigenous threat. The threat in these countries is characterised by infrequent terrorist incidents and a low casualty rate. Because the threat is limited, the respective security forces in these countries are able to contain the threat without the help of military or para-military forces. On occasion, as in West Germany in late 1977 during the Schleyer kidnapping and the hijacking of a Lufthansa plane, the security forces are strengthened by supplemental financial and manpower resources and broadened legal powers. However, unlike the front-line states, which face a sustained, serious indigenous terrorist threat, the border states are confronted by a sporadic, more limited threat. Consequently, their security measures to counter this threat are temporary and limited.

In West Germany, the indigenous threat has come mainly from the left. Spearheading this threat is the Red Army Faction (RAF), a group which in the early 1970s was popularly known as the 'Baader-Meinhof Gang' (BMG). With the imprisonment and deaths (by suicide) of the early or 'historical' leaders of the BMG/RAF, a new generation of members made up the group and are now more accurately referred to as the RAF. The RAF threat in West Germany consists of two aspects. The first is the threat of infrequent high level attacks on prominent personalities by the RAF hard core (those members who live in total clandestinity and were involved in the RAF's most recent 1977 offensive).[18] The second aspect of the RAF threat consists of low-level 'molotov' attacks carried out by RAF supporters and sympathisers. A loosely knit coalition of leftist extremists who function on the periphery of the RAF hard core, these people are sometimes referred to collectively as the 'Anti-Fascist Groups' or 'Antifa'. In essence, they carry out propaganda, intelligence and logistical functions for the hard core.[19] While the hard core has been inactive in West Germany since 1978 because of increased police pressure, its 'Antifa' supporters have been increasing their activities.

In addition to the RAF threat, West Germany has also had to contend with periodic low-level bombings by the leftist 'Revolutionary

Cells' and occasional minor terrorist incidents by neo-Nazi extremists. Since 1970, indigenous terrorist groups in West Germany have been responsible for 47 deaths: the BMG/RAF for 26, the leftist 'Second of June (now basically inactive with its hard core having joined the RAF) for four, the neo-Nazi 'German Action Group' for two, a lone neo-Nazi extremist for 13 (the Octoberfest bombing in Munich in September 1980) and other right-wing groups for two.[20]

In France, the indigenous terrorist threat consists primarily of the activities of the separatist 'Corsican National Liberation Front' (FLNC). Other indigenous groups have periodically surfaced in France only to be quickly neutralised by French security forces. The more prominent ones have been the leftist, anarchist 'Armed Nuclei for Popular Autonomy', the leftist 'Direct Action Organisation', the separatist 'Front for the Liberation of Brittany' and the neo-Fascist 'Federation of European National Action' (FANE).

Only the FLNC has been able to mount a sustained, if limited, threat to the French government. The FLNC has restricted itself to date to bombings aimed at property damage. It has attempted to avoid casualties where possible. And although it has carried out periodic bombings in Paris and Marseille, it has concentrated its activities on the French Mediterranean island of Corsica, where in 1980 it claimed responsibility for half of the more than 465 bombings on the island.[21] The indigenous terrorist threat in France is less than in West Germany. In fact, more people have been killed in France over the last several years as a result of international terrorist attacks than by indigenous attacks.[22]

Greece is another country which has faced a limited indigenous threat. According to a statement by the Minister of Public Order in March 1980, since 1974 there have been six political murders, 300 bombings, 80 molotov bombings and 180 vehicle fire-bombings. Some 81 persons have been arrested for 'terrorist activities with political motives'.[23] Greek indigenous terrorist activity, like that in France, has focused on low-level bombings aimed at property damage. At present the most active indigenous group in Greece is the leftist, anarchist 'Revolutionary Popular Struggle' (ELA), which first emerged on the terrorist scene in 1975. The ELA, which is similar in tactics and motives to the revolutionary cells in West Germany, has been responsible for the majority of bombings in Greece. It has also claimed responsibility for one assassination and is suspected of three more.[24]

Although the ELA is the most active group operating in Greece, other groups have attempted to surface. Some have failed for internal reasons, others because of arrests. One recent example was the 'Popular Frontal Initiative' (PFI). A leftist group apparently founded in November 1979, the PFI was broken up by police before it could carry out any operations. This group had planned to carry out a campaign of assassinations, bombings and kidnappings against public officials, the military and certain foreign embassies (including the American Embassy).[25]

Like most Western European countries, Greece has had some problems with rightist terrorist groups. In June 1979, twelve rightist terrorists were sentenced to prison for carrying out numerous bombing attacks during 1976-8. This group was called the 'Organisation for National Resistance', and, although it caused no deaths, it was responsible for injuring eleven people when it detonated over 50 bombs in Athens on 17 December 1978. Unlike Spain, Italy, France, Northern Ireland and West Germany, Greece has not had any recent problems with right-wing terrorist groups.

The remaining Western European countries, especially the Netherlands, Portugal and Switzerland, have been faced with mere traces of indigenous terrorist activity which on occasion flares up to noticeable proportion. The Netherlands faced such a threat during 1975 to 1978 when South Moluccan extremists carried out several major terrorist attacks. They seized four Dutch establishments and an Indonesian consulate, were responsible for seven deaths and held a total of 328 people hostage, including 105 Dutch schoolchildren. This is the largest total number of hostages ever held by any contemporary European terrorist group. Since 1978, the South Moluccan extremists have been quiet, but certainly not eradicated.

In Portugal and Switzerland, occasional leftist extremist groups have carried out periodic low-level bombings. These groups have failed to develop into even a limited terrorist threat like the South Moluccan extremists. In 1980, one leftist group calling itself the 'Popular Forces of April 25' surfaced and claimed responsibility for several bank robberies, bombings, a kneecapping and an attempted kidnapping.[26] It remains to be seen whether this group develops like the revolutionary cells in West Germany or the Revolutionary Popular Struggle in Greece, or is neutralised like the Direct Action Organisation in France and Front Line in Italy. If the conditions are right in Portugal, then the April 25th group may survive and grow. What makes one country different from another is whether a particular country has the conditions necessary to nourish these groups — rampant unemployment, inflation, stagnation in the educational sector, weak judicial and prison systems, ineffective security forces, deep-rooted ethnic or religious divisions or factionalised political leadership. Given these conditions, any terrorist group has hopes for sustained development.

Supra-indigenous Terrorist Activity

A second and higher level of terrorist activity in Western Europe is supra-indigenous terrorist activity. Generally speaking this activity consists of periodic terrorist attacks carried out throughout a particular region by an indigenous terrorist group. Supra-indigenous groups are simply one step above the operational range of an indigenous group. While indigenous groups limit their operations to a single country, usually their country of origin, supra-indigenous groups supplement their indigenous attacks with periodic operations outside their country of origin. This extension of attacks outside the country of origin increases the overall terrorist threat level in a region and compounds the terrorist problem for other countries. This type of activity is found predominantly in Western Europe. It does not exist in the Far East and Africa, is infrequently found in Latin America and exists only on an occasional basis in the Middle East. At present, there are two supra-indigenous terrorist groups which operate in Western Europe — PIRA and RAF. Whether by preference, as in the case of the PIRA, or out of necessity, like the RAF, the supra-indigenous attacks by these two groups aggravate the already heightened terrorist threat level in Western Europe.

As discussed above, the PIRA has concentrated its attacks on British interests in Northern Ireland and, less frequently, in Great Britain.[27] From 1969 to 1978, the PIRA had carried out only three terrorist attacks against British interests outside the United Kingdom. In September 1973, it bombed a British Army of the Rhine (BAOR) base in Moenchen-Gladbach, West Germany.[28] Three years later it assassinated the British Ambassador in Dublin. And in August 1978 it again bombed a BAOR base in West Germany. Sometime in late 1978, a decision was presumably made by the PIRA leadership to broaden and intensify its attacks on British interests overseas.

In 1979, a year which saw the downfall of the Labour government and the election of the Conservative Party's Margaret Thatcher as Prime Minister, the PIRA dramatically increased its attacks against British interests in Western Europe. Six days before the Labour government's ill-fated vote of confidence, the PIRA on 22 March assassinated the

British Ambassador in The Hague. On the same day, it attempted to assassinate the Deputy British Ambassador to NATO in Brussels. However, in a case of mistaken identity, the PIRA killed a Belgian banker who lived near the intended target. About one week later, on 30 March, the lesser known Irish National Liberation Army (INLA) assassinated Member of Parliament Airey Neave by blowing up his car in a House of Commons garage. Neave was the Conservative Party's spokesman on Northern Ireland affairs and a close adviser to Margaret Thatcher. With the Conservative Party's victory in the 3 May elections, Neave would probably have become Secretary of State for Northern Ireland in the Thatcher government.[29]

The PIRA continued its 'supra-indigenous' campaign even after the government crisis and May elections. In July it bombed two BAOR installations in West Germany. In August it assassinated Lord Mountbatten, a British war hero and member of the Royal Family, off the coast of Ireland when it blew up his yacht. Three other people were killed in the attack, including his grandson (14 years old), a crew boy (14 years old) and the Dowager Lady Brabourne (82 years old). The same month, the PIRA bombed an outdoor stage in Brussels just before a British army band was to perform. INLA appeared to join the campaign when it bombed the British consulate in Antwerp in November.

The PIRA concluded the 1979 portion of its overseas campaign by sending letter bombs from Belgium addressed to prominent British businessmen and government officials in Great Britain. In early 1980, it continued its attacks, but focused on BAOR forces in West Germany. In February it assassinated a British army Colonel in Bielefeld. In March, in three separate incidents, it ambushed a British military patrol in Muenster, bombed a British car in Laarbrueck and wounded a British soldier near Osnabrueck. And in December, to call attention to a hunger strike by several imprisoned PIRA members in Northern Ireland, it attempted to assassinate the British European Common Market Commissioner in Brussels. Thus, during a two year period (1979-80), Irish terrorists had carried out twelve attacks (eleven by the PIRA, one by the INLA) against British interests in Western Europe.

There appear to be several motives behind this PIRA campaign. Broadly speaking, they include: publicising the PIRA's struggle in the Western European press, demonstrating a broad operational capability, stirring up British public opinon to increase pressure on the government to remove its troops from Northern Ireland and demonstrating to British troops that the PIRA will attack them anywhere, not just in Northern Ireland. All of these motives are geared towards gaining publicity and putting psychological pressure on the British public and military. Aside from such 'strategic' motives, there may also have been some 'tactical' aims to the overseas campaign.

The March 1979 attacks could have been aimed at the 18 March vote of confidence on the Labour government, i.e. to try to influence the outcome in some way, and/or the March release of the Bennett report in London which concluded that 'suspected IRA terrorists have been physically mistreated by Ulster police'.[30] After the Mountbatten assassination in August 1979, the PIRA issued a communiquè which stated that the killing was 'a discriminate act to bring to the attention of the English people the continuing occupation of our country'. It went on to say that the 'death of Lord Mountbatten and tributes paid to him will be seen in contrast to the apathy of the British Government and English people to the deaths of over 300 British soldiers . . . '[31] In essence, the PIRA was admitting that their terrorist campaign in Northern Ireland was not having the desired effect on the British government and people. The Mountbatten assassination was nothing more than an IRA shock treatment to British apathy which had been slowly building up over the previous four years. The PIRA knew that public apathy could contain, if not dilute, the effectiveness of terrorists. Its supra-indigenous campaign was partially designed to re-awaken the 'Irish problem' in the minds of the British public.

Additional elaboration on the PIRA's motives was given in February 1980. On 17 February, the PIRA assassinated a British army Colonel in West Germany. In an interview with the *An Phoblacht/Republican News*, the official newspaper of the PIRA, a PIRA spokesman explained the strategy behind the overseas campaign:

At present about half of the British army units in the North are on eighteen-month tours, billeted in places like Aldergrove and Palace barracks. The other half — those in the real frontline — are on four-month tours. Between tours all of them are either stationed in Britain or overseas and here they think they can rest from the dirty work they've been doing, and the 'hard time' they've had in Ireland. Being stationed on the Rhine is a plum job for them. Well, we intend to harass them the way they've been harassing and killing nationalist people. They think they can forget about Ireland until their next tour but we intend to keep Ireland on their minds so that it haunts them and they do something about not wanting to go back.

Overseas attacks also have a prestige value and internationalise the war in Ireland. The British Government has been successful in sup-

pressing news about the struggle in the North. With its huge propaganda machine administered by ambassadors and officials, one
example being Peter Jay when he was in America, it can spread a
rosy picture which does much to undermine the people's sacrifices
and completely ignores the people's suffering.

But we have kept Ireland in the world headlines, our struggle is
kept in the news, and sooner or later an expression of discontent-
ment probably from the English people rather than from the army,
will snowball and the British Government's ability and will to stay,
which we are sapping, will completely snap.[32]

There has been no recent evidence which would suggest that the PIRA
has altered this strategy. It is, however, logistically difficult for any
terrorist group to carry out a sustained violent campaign. It is even
more difficult when the operations are conducted outside its normal
area of operations. Since there have been no political developments
which would alter the PIRA's original motives for initiating the overseas effort, it must be assumed that as logistics are replenished and
intelligence on potential targets is accumulated and analysed, the PIRA
will continue to strike at British targets in Western Europe.

Another supra-indigenous group which contributes to the overall
terrorist threat level in Western Europe is West Germany's RAF. Although a majority of its attacks have been carried out in the Federal
Republic of Germany (FRG), the RAF has been involved in several
incidents outside the Federal Republic. Since 1975, it has been implicated in four attacks and one planned attack in Western Europe. In
1975, RAF elements seized the West German Embassy in Stockholm. When the incident was over, two German diplomats and two
German terrorists had been killed. In 1976, RAF terrorists robbed a
bank in Vienna. In March 1977, Swedish police thwarted an RAF plot
to kidnap the former Swedish Minister of Immigration. In June 1979,
RAF terrorists attempted to assassinate the then NATO Supreme Allied
Commander, Europe (SACEUR) Alexander Haig in Obourg, Belgium.
And in November of that year, RAF terrorists robbed a bank in Zurich.
During the gun battle that followed, one bystander was killed.[33]

Many of these operations outside West Germany were dictated by
increased police pressure put on the RAF at home. This pressure not
only forced the RAF to operate outside the FRG, but also forced them
to be on the run throughout Western Europe. Police pressure increased
in 1977 when the RAF carried out several major attacks in West
Germany. Prior to 1977, only six major West German terrorists were

captured outside West Germany. Since 1977, however, some 25 have been arrested and two have surrendered abroad. This is a result not only of increased police pressure in the FRG, but also of increased police co-operation in Western Europe. Since 1977, West German terrorists have been arrested in the Netherlands (3), France (7), United Kingdom (2), the United States (1), Switzerland (3), Bulgaria (4), Yugoslavia (4 — later freed) and Australia (1). And two German terrorists surrendered to the West German Embassy in Paris. In the course of these arrests, three Dutch policemen and one Swiss citizen were killed, and several Dutch and Swiss policemen were wounded. As these activities indicate, the RAF may be primarily a West German problem, but its activities also directly affect other European countries. Like the PIRA, the RAF has become a European problem.

International Terrorist Activity

A third level of terrorist activity which confronts Western Europe is 'international' terrorist activity. This type of terrorism is generated primarily by the operations of the major international terrorist groups. They carry out a majority of their attacks outside their primary targeted country and inflict additional problems and concerns on Western European countries already threatened with indigenous terrorist activity and burdened with supra-indigenous attacks. In this section, the various international terrorist groups will be consolidated into the three major and most active terrorist aggregates — Palestinians, Armenians and Croatians.[34] All three have, at one time or another, used Western Europe as a primary operational area.

At present, Palestinians and Amenians continue to operate often in Europe, while Croatians in recent years have decreased their operations in Western Eruope. None of the three have conducted any significant operations in Latin America. The Palestinians have carried out numerous attacks in the Middle East, some in the Far East, and a very few in Africa and North America. Armenians have carried out no attacks in Africa and the Far East, but some in the Middle East and North America, and one in Australia. Croatians have not carried out attacks in Africa, the Far East or the Middle East, but have conducted numerous operations (since 1977) in North America, primarily in the United States. Only in Western Europe, however, have all three carried out sustained terrorist operations or offensives.

Why the operational preference for Europe? First, there are large contingents of ethnic Palestinians, Armenians and Croatians throughout Western Europe. As a result, these terrorist aggregates have a ready-made base upon which to develop a logistical infrastructure to support their terrorist operations. Logistically, Western Europe is the ideal region for their terrorist campaigns. Admittedly, this also applies to the Middle East for the Palestinians and to the United States for Armenians and Croatians. Secondly, the primary targeted countries (Israel, Turkey and Yugoslavia, respectively) of all three aggregates are in or geographically near Europe. Thirdly, Western Europe is geographically compact, has excellent transportation facilities and cross-border movement is relatively free. Consequently, movement and escape are made easier. Fourthly, there is a preponderance of attractive targets for these aggregates throughout Western Europe — numerous Jewish establishments and prominent personalities, and Israeli, Turkish and Yugoslav diplomatic and commercial facilities and personnel in Western Europe. Target selection is broader and target availability is higher in the region. Fifthly, the publicity spotlight is brighter and more intense in Western Europe than in any other region with the possible exception of the United States. Western Europe is permeated with media exposure and access. There are more daily newspapers, magazines, radio and television broadcasts in Western Europe than in any other region.[35] Publicity, after all, is a primary tactical consideration of international terrorist groups. While other regions may have one or more of the above conditions, only Western Europe offers all of them. As a result, it has become an unfortunate magnet for international terrorist campaigns.

It is difficult to estimate accurately how many terrorist attacks have been carried out by Palestinian terrorists outside their primary targeted country — Israel. As stated previously, some attacks are never claimed, while others are carried out by 'camouflaged commandos', that is, groups using *ad hoc* names which are different from their parent organisation. Therefore, it is only possible to make a rough estimate of such attacks. Based on various chronologies containing significant Palestinian terrorist attacks from 1968 to 1980, the author estimates that various Palestinian terrorist groups have carried out some 80 or so significant terrorist attacks worldwide.[36] Sixty-six of these have taken place in Western Europe, seven in the Middle East, four in the Far East, two in Africa and one in North America. In Western Europe, the attacks took place in the following countries: Federal Republic of Germany (15), France (10), United Kingdom (6), Greece (5), Cyprus (5), Italy (5), Spain (4), Belgium (4) and Turkey, Austria, Switzerland

and the Netherlands (3 each). The targets of a majority of these attacks were Israeli commercial and diplomatic interests and Western European Jewish establishments and personalities. Other targets included Jordan (after the expulsion of the Palestinians in September 1970), Egypt (after the March 1979 peace treaty between Israel and Egypt), West Germany, Great Britain and the United States. These 66 Palestinian terrorist attacks have caused about 85 deaths. About 50 per cent of these casualties took place during four separate airport attacks in Athens (1973), Rome (1973), Istanbul (1976) and Paris/Orly (1978). Attacks on airport lounges and on passengers boarding planes has been a particularly deadly tactical trademark of Palestinian terrorist groups.

The major Palestinian groups which have claimed responsibility or have been implicated in the above attacks are: 'Fatah', the 'Black September Organization' — BSO (Fatah's terrorist arm active at least from 1971 to 1973), 'Saiqa' and its terrorist arm, the 'Eagles of the Palestinian Revolution' — EPR (Syrian controlled), 'Black June', and the 'Popular Front for the Liberation of Palestine' (the Wadi Haddad remnants, the George Habash faction, and the PFLP — General Command led by Ahmad Jabril). From 1968 to late 1971, the PFLP carried out almost all of the Palestinian attacks in Western Europe. From September 1971 until 1973, Fatah's BSO was the more active. And from 1974, when Wadi Haddad split from Habbash's PFLP, to March 1978, when Haddad died, his faction was the most active.

The activities of these groups varied depending upon events and alliances in the Middle East. The October 1973 Arab-Israeli war, the September 1970 expulsion of the Palestinians from Jordan, the Lebanese civil war, the March 1979 Egyptian-Israeli peace treaty and Arafat's diplomatic offensive in Eastern Europe, all influenced the activities, especially with regard to targeting, of the various Palestinian terrorist groups. The years 1972 to 1974 were the most active in terms of the number of Palestinian attacks in Western Europe. With the start of the Lebanese civil war in 1975, Palestinian attacks were less frequent over the next year as resources and attention were focused on Lebanon.

Attacks against Israeli and Western targets declined in 1978 as Syria, Iraq, the PLO and Black June became embroiled in an inter-Arab feud which developed into a terrorist-waged mini-war.[37] The dispute centred around the PLO and Iraq which have been on less than friendly terms since September 1970 when Jordan expelled the Palestinians and Iraq did not come to their aid. Black June, named after June 1976 when Syria fought the Palestinians in Lebanon, was an Iraqi-backed Palestinian terrorist group led by Sabri al-Banna or 'Abu Nidal'. He withdrew from the PLO in 1974 and has since been operating mostly as a terrorist arm of the Iraqi government. In this connection, his group has reportedly been used by Iraq in terrorist attacks against Syria, a historical enemy of Iraq.[38] The 1978 inter-Arab feud was apparently ignited by the 5 January assassination in London of Said Hammami, a PLO representative. The PLO suspected Black June and asked Iraq to hand over Abu Nidal. Iraq refused and the PLO retaliated. On 4 March, Iraqi embassies in Brussels and Paris were bombed. In July, there were bombings and armed attacks against Iraqi diplomatic establishments in London (twice), Brussels and Paris. In August, Iraqi interests were attacked in Karachi, Pakistan and Tripoli, Libya, while two PLO representatives were killed in Paris and a PLO office was attacked (three Palestinians killed) in Islamabad, Pakistan. On 6 September, the Camp David summit conference between Egypt and Israel began in the United States and this event apparently doused the fires of the PLO-Iraq feud. While the Arabs were fighting among themselves, their enemies were starting to unite. The attacks ceased and Western Europe breathed a temporary sigh of relief.

This brief synopsis of Palestinian terrorist attacks in Western Europe would not be complete without mentioning some of the planned operations which were never implemented because of police arrests and/or the ineptitude of the terrorists. Those attacks which have taken place are only the tip of the iceberg. There have been many instances where bombs have been defused by the police; where terrorists have been arrested at airports, border crossings or in safehouses; where terrorist attacks were not properly executed because of the inexperience, ineptitude or lack of conviction on the part of the terrorists; where luck and chance prevented more casualties; and where increased security around a facility or person deterred an attack.

To gauge accurately the Palestinian terrorist threat in Western Europe, the planned operations and the casualties they could have caused should also be considered. For example, let's look at just the year 1980. In January, Palestinian terrorists blew up part of the Mount Royal hotel in London when the bomb they were making detonated prematurely. A previously unknown Palestinian commando calling itself the 'May 15 Arab Organisation' claimed responsibility for the bomb, stating that the explosion had wounded several Israeli intelligence agents.[39] In fact, the terrorists simply made a mistake when they were preparing the explosive device. One of them was killed. The planned target of the bomb is still unknown. In March, a Palestinian terrorist mistakenly assassinated a Spanish lawyer in Madrid, who he thought was a prominent Jewish leader.[40] In April, El Al security agents in Zurich detected a bomb wired to an altimeter in a suitcase. Israeli authorities believe Palestinian terrorists were behind the attempt. In July, Swedish police arrested a group of Palestinians who had reportedly planned to assassinate Saudi Arabia's King Khalid during an official visit to West Germany and to attack an El Al crew in Copenhagen.[41] In July also, in Brussels, a Palestinian terrorist was arrested before he was able to carry out a grenade attack against El Al passengers in Brussels' airport. This planned operation was apparently timed to coincide with a 27 July grenade attack on a group of Jewish children in Antwerp.[42] In the latter attack, a man threw two hand grenades into a group of Jewish children, killing one child and wounding about 13 others. It was extremely fortunate that only one death resulted from this attack since there was a potential for mass casualties.

And in Paris on 3 October, Palestinian terrorists were apparently responsible for a bomb explosion outside a Jewish synagogue (rue Copernic), killing four people and injuring 13. At the time, French neo-Fascists were thought to be responsible. Before the bombing there had been a sharp increase in neo-Fascist attacks on Jewish establishments in France, a neo-Fascist group had allegedly claimed responsibility for the rue Copernic bombing, and there had just been neo-Fascist bombings in August Bologna, Italy which killed 85 people and in Munich at the Oktoberfest which killed 14 people. During the summer of 1980, Western Europe was facing a possible escalation of right-wing terrorism. In the case of the rue Copernic bombing, however, investigators now believe that Palestinian terrorists were probably responsible, not French neo-Fascists.[43] If this is true, then the potential for mass casualties was again present for a Palestinian terrorist attack and fortunately not reached.

Aside from the above planned and aborted attacks, there were certainly many more which were never reported in the press for fear of attracting possible Palestinian retaliation. Many Western European countries have Palestinian or other Arab terrorists imprisoned in their jails and are thus susceptible to retaliatory terrorist attacks. The Palestinian terrorist threat in Western Europe lives on unabated and, as shown above, is much more serious than many believe. As is the case for all terrorist groups operating out of the Middle East, this threat will rise and decline depending upon the shifting political winds in the Middle East. While the number, frequency and target of these attacks will fluctuate, one element remains fairly constant — the preference for Western Europe as a terrorist battlefield by Palestinian and other Arab terrorist groups.

A second terrorist aggregate which operates predominantly in Western Europe is Armenian terrorists. Operating under names such as 'The Armenian Secret Army for the Liberation of Armenia' (ASALA), 'The New Armenian Resistance' (NAR), 'The Justice Commandos for the Armenian Genocide' (JCAG), 'The October 3rd Organisation', 'The Armenian Secret Army' (ASA), etc., Armenian terrorists have been attacking Turkish diplomatic and commercial facilities and personnel in Western Europe since 1975.[44] They are ostensibly seeking revenge for the alleged genocide of some 1.5 million Armenians in 1915 by the Turkish government, and are fighting for an independent Armenian state. From 1975 to 1978, Armenian terrorists, under a dozen different group designations, carried out about 28 terrorist attacks against Turkish interests in Western Europe. These attacks were supplemented by periodic attacks in Beirut and in Turkey itself. The attacks in Western Europe consisted mainly of bombings aimed at property damage and occasional assassinations of Turkish diplomatic personnel, including three Turkish ambassadors.

The overwhelming majority of Armenian attacks from 1975 to 1978 were carried out solely against Turkish targets. In general, these attacks received little publicity and the Armenian cause remained buried under the more publicised nationalist causes of the Palestinians, Irish and Basques. During this period, at least in Western Europe, more people were generally aware of the plight and demands of South Moluccan nationalists who were seizing hostages in the Netherlands than of the Armenian cause. In late 1979, however, Armenian terrorists, primarily ASALA and JCAG, began to intensify significantly their attacks and broaden their targeting.

From 1979 to 1980, Armenian terrorists carried out some 60 attacks (28 in 1979, 32 in 1980), twice as many as in the previous three years. More significantly, beginning in November 1979, they started to target other countries besides Turkey. They bombed Western airline offices (Lufthansa, KLM, BA, TWA, Alitalia, El Al and Air France) throughout Western Europe, claiming that 'imperialism participated implicitly in the genocide of our people and the partition of our homeland'.[45] In December, they bombed an Italian transient facility which housed Armenian immigrants from the Soviet Union and demanded the closure of these refugee centres. They further threatened that, if these demands were not met, they would 'intensify the armed struggle against these regimes (the United States and Italy) and will not differentiate you from the imperialist Zionist Turkish authorities and our struggle against you will be within your borders'.[46]

In October 1980, Armenian terrorists shifted their attacks to Swiss targets. This was a result of the arrests on 3 October of two alleged Armenian terrorists in Switzerland. In previous communiqués the terrorists had warned other countries that 'anyone who interferes in the Armenian Liberation Movements will be regarded as an enemy and become consequently, a target for our fighters'.[47] This threat was implemented almost immediately in the Swiss case as a new Armenian terrorist commando calling itself the 'October 3rd Organisation' began to attack Swiss targets. During the following four months, this commando attacked or attempted to attack Swiss targets in Beirut (three times), London, Paris, Milan, Madrid, Marseille, Rome, Bern, Geneva (twice) and in Los Angeles, in order to pressure the Swiss government. The attacks stopped when Switzerland expelled the two alleged terrorists in January and February 1981.

Like the Palestinians, whose tactics they emulate and from whom they reportedly receive assistance, Armenian terrorists have demonstrated a wide operational area.[48] Although Turkey is their primary targeted country, these terrorists have carried out about 90 per cent of their attacks outside Turkey, in Western Europe, Lebanon and, more recently, in the United States and Australia. From 1975 to 1980, Armenian terrorists carried out attacks in France (14), Italy (12), Lebanon (8), Switzerland (8), Turkey (7), the United States (6), Spain (5), Great Britain (4), West Germany (4), Greece (3), Belgium (2), Denmark, Austria, the Netherlands and Australia.[49] The geographical range of these attacks implies that these terrorists have an effective logistical infrastructure. They certainly have been successful, unlike some Palestinians, in evading arrest. No Armenian terrorist has yet been caught and convicted of a terrorist attack in Western Europe. The two arrested in Switzerland were caught when a bomb they were making exploded prematurely. Another Armenian has been arrested in France for suspected involvement in an assassination attempt on the Turkish ambassador in Bern in August 1979. At the time of writing, his case is still pending. Considering the number of attacks they have carried out, their broad operational area and their ability to date to evade capture, Armenian terrorists have been the most active and successful international terrorist aggregate over the last several years.[50] They have certainly publicised their cause and in this respect they have been successful in their terrorist campaign.

The third international terrorist aggregate which has caused problems for Western Europe is composed of various Croatian *émigré* terrorist groups.[51] These groups, operating under the names 'Croatian Liberation Movement', 'Croatian Freedom Forces', 'Croatian Revolutionary Brotherhood', 'Croatian National Resistance', 'Croatian Freedom Fighters', etc., have carried out over 75 terrorist attacks (resulting in 35 deaths) against Yugoslav diplomatic and commercial establishments and personnel in Western Europe, the United States and Australia. Although they differ somewhat in tactics, ideology and operational area, they share a common goal of establishing an independent Croatian state. Currently, Croatia is one of six republics within Yugoslavia. While their primary targeted country is Yugoslavia, the majority of their attacks have taken place outside this country. This is partially a result of the tight security environment in Yugoslavia, which makes it difficult for any 'subversive' group to operate consistently there. Moreover, these *émigré* groups are seeking publicity for their cause. Since the press is closely monitored by the Yugoslav government, any terrorist attacks there would receive little, if any, publicity. Like the Palestinians in the early 1970s and the Armenians in the late 1970s, Croatian *émigré* terrorist groups have sought to publicise their cause through world-wide terrorist attacks.[52] Publicity appears to be the primary motive for these attacks since it is extremely doubtful that such attacks could force the Yugoslav government to give Croatia its independence. Like the Armenian terrorists, the Croations have so far refused to conduct their terrorist campaign within the 'homeland'. On occasion, when other countries have interfered with their activities, Croatian terrorists have not hesitated to target non-Yugoslav interests. In September 1972, they hijacked a Swedish airliner to free Croatian terrorists imprisoned in Sweden for carrying out terrorist attacks in Sweden against Yugoslav targets. In September 1976, they hijacked a TWA plane out of New York to publicise their demands and cause. In August 1978, two Croatian terrorists seized the West German consulate in Chicago in order to pressure the West German government into not extraditing a Croatian extremist to Yugoslavia.[53]

From 1962 to 1977, 60 per cent of all Croatian terrorist attacks took place in Western Europe, primarily in West Germany, Sweden, France, Austria, Norway and Belgium.[54] The remaining attacks occurred in Yugoslavia, the United States, Australia and one in Paraguay. From 1978 to 1980, 92 per cent of all Croatian attacks took place in the United States.[55] The reasons behind this operational shift from Western Europe to the United States is unclear, but it may have been dictated by increased police pressure on Croatian extremist activities in Western Europe, especially in West Germany and Sweden, where over 67 per cent of all Croatian attacks during 1962 to 1977 took place.

In 1976, the West German government outlawed several Croatian extremist groups. It was in this year also that Croatian terrorist activities escalated in West Germany and this fact, combined with the indigenous terrorist threat which confronted the government, compelled the state to institute stricter anti-terrorist legislation and forced the police to intensify their pressure on terrorist activity in West Germany. Croatian extremist groups were caught up in this anti-terrorist campaign. In Sweden, Croatian terrorist activity took place mainly during 1971-2. As a result of this activity, Sweden promulgated the core of its anti-terrorist legislation during 1973-4. Whether or not this curtailed Croatian terrorist activity there, the fact remains that the last attack there took place in 1972. Whatever the reasons, Croatian terrorist activity shifted to the United States in 1978. There continued to be periodic attacks in Western Europe, but not at the same level as before 1978. However, it seems clear that at least from 1978 to 1980, the United States became the preferred operational area for Croatian terrorists and their anti-Yugoslav campaign. In December 1980, a task force of FBI agents and New York City policemen arrested seven alleged members of a Croatian terrorist group in New York City.[56] These arrests may limit for the time being the operational capability of Croatian terrorists in the United States. Continued police pressure may compel them to redirect their activities to Western Europe.

State-directed Terrorist Activity

The fourth and final type of terrorist activity which takes place primarily in Western Europe and is a variant of international terrorism is state-directed terrorism.[57] This form of international terrorism should not be confused with governmental terrorism or repression directed at internal elements such as that which existed under Idi Amin in Uganda or in most Communist-ruled states today. The state-directed terrorist activity discussed in this section is aimed at external elements such as political exiles or other states. It should also not be confused with the term 'state-supported' terrorism which is more accurately used when discussing the logistical and operational support for an external terrorist group by a state. In this case, the state may have some input into the target selection of the terrorist group as payment for the state's support. The goals of the group, however, still take precedence over whatever input on target selection the state may offer.

In 'state-directed' terrorism, the targeting is decided by the state through one of its agencies or representatives. The targeting is tied directly to a vested interest of the state. Whether to advance national interests or simply to silence exiled political dissidents, state-directed terrorist activity significantly increased during 1980. Western Europe was its primary battleground. The most salient example of this activity was the assassinations of dissident Libyan exiles in Western Europe by the Libyan government.

This assassination campaign began in March 1980 when the body of a Libyan businessman was found in the trunk of a car in Rome. At the time, it was considered an isolated murder, possibly criminally motivated, but in succeeding months it proved to be the signal of a Libyan assassination campaign. The involvement of the Libyan government in this campaign is blatant. On 27 April, during an address to students of the military academy in Tripoli, Libya's leader, Colonel Qadhafi, bluntly stated, 'all persons who have left Libya must return by this June 10'. He further threatened, 'if the refugees do not obey they *must be inevitably liquidated*, wherever they are'[58] (author's emphasis). In London, two Libyan exiles were murdered. The Libyan embassy there called the murders an 'internal Libyan matter'.[59] In Rome, several more Libyan exiles were assassinated. In early May a 'visiting member of the Libyan People's Committee told a Rome press conference that exiles working against the government of Colonel Qadhafi would be eliminated unless they came home under a general armistice'.[60]

By the end of 1980, ten Libyan exiles had been assassinated in Rome (March), London (April), Rome (April), London (April), Rome (May), Bonn (May), Rome (May), Athens (May), Milan (June) and Manchester, Great Britain (November). There were also attempted assassinations in Rome (June), Ft Collins, Colorado (October) and Portsmouth, Great Britain (November).[61] This campaign continued into 1981. In February, Libyan gunmen, one of whom said he was a 'guerrilla of the Libyan revolution', attacked a group of Arabs and Libyans at Rome's Fiumincino airport, wounding four people.[62] In March, Colonel Qadhafi reinforced this liquidation campaign. In a speech at Sebha, he stated that the 'physical and final liquidation of the opponents of popular authority must continue at home and abroad'. He continued, 'we fear no one'.[63]

Other countries which have conducted state-directed terrorist activities in Western Europe against political exiles are Iran, Syria, Yugoslavia and Bulgaria. While some of these countries have used private citizens or, as in the case of Libya, students and mercenaries, others have unleashed their security services. Iran has targeted members of the former Shah of Iran's family and other supporters of his regime. In December 1979, the Shah's nephew was assassinated in Paris. Ayatollah Sadeq Khalkhali, the self-proclaimed head of the Iranian Revolutionary courts, claimed that his assassination squads shot and killed the Shah's nephew as part of a call by radical Moslems to 'destroy leading members of the overthrown Pahlavi dynasty'.[64] In July and October 1980 there were attempts to assassinate former Iranian Prime Minister Shaphour Bakhtiar in Paris. According to Radio Tehran, a group calling itself the 'Guardians of Islam' claimed responsibility for the July attempt.[65] In June, Khalkhali reportedly issued orders for the assassination of Bakhtiar.[66] Four days after the 18 July attempt on Bakhtiar, Ali Tabatabai, the former Press Attaché in Washington during the Shah's regime, was assassinated in Bethesda, Maryland by a man posing as a postman. Police believe that the gunman fled to Iran soon after the murder.[67] It should also be noted that there was an assassination attempt on the Shah's sister in September 1977 in Cannes, France. While this attempt cannot be attributed to the Khomeini government in power, it can be linked to the Khomeini government in exile.

Syrian political dissidents have suffered the same fate. In early July 1980, the brother of Syrian President Hafez al-Assad stated that he planned to 'liquidate all opposition inside the country and outside of it'.[68] This directive was apparently implemented on 21 July when a prominent Syrian opposition leader and former Prime Minister was assassinated in Paris. It was also reported that on the same day, a leader of the Muslim Brotherhood, an outlawed extremist opposition group in Syria which seeks to topple the Assad government, was the target of an assassination attempt in Aachen, West Germany.[69] The target was Isam al-Attar, who was apparently responsible for the co-ordination between various Muslim Brotherhood branches in Syria and Europe. Syrian President Assad reinforced his brother's threat during a speech in Damascus on 24 July when he stated that opponents of his regime are being tracked down everywhere.[70] The next attack against a Syrian opposition leader in Western Europe took place on 18 March 1981, when three gunmen burst into the apartment of Isam al-Attar in Aachen and killed his wife. Attar was not in the apartment at the time of the attack.

East European countries have also used terrorist tactics to silence their exiled political dissidents. Yugoslavia and, to a lesser extent, Bulgaria, are good recent examples of state-directed terrorism emanating from the Communist bloc countries.[71] Yugoslavia, which has been the target of over 80 anti-Yugoslav terrorist attacks by Croatian and Serbian *émigrés,* has apparently conducted a retaliatory terrorist campaign against these two ethnic groups. The exact number of victims of this campaign is unknown. According to one report, 38 Croatians have been killed in West Germany alone since 1967.[72] Some of these deaths can be attributed to criminal elements and intra-Croatian rivalries. However, 17 of these were carried out with the same type of weapon — a 7.65 mm pistol. Of these 17, ten involved a silencer. Of these ten, the same silencer was used in seven cases.[73] These 17, plus the April 1980 murder of a prominent Serbian leader in Dusseldorf (with a 7.65 mm pistol), are suspected of having been carried out by the Yugoslav secret police or their hired assassins.[74] This would bring the total to 18 (a conservative figure) in West Germany. At least four anti-Yugoslav Croatians were reportedly killed in Belgium between 1975 and 1976. Another was killed in Sweden in 1975, and one in Paris in 1978. A very conservative estimate would be that about 24 anti-Yugoslav *émigrés* have been killed in Western Europe since 1976 in circumstances which would suggest the involvement of the Yugoslav security services.[75]

Bulgaria too has used terrorist tactics against political exiles. Unlike Yugoslavia, it has not been targeted by any Bulgarian *émigré* terrorist group. On 15 September 1978, the Bulgarian Minister of Internal Affairs said: 'our enemies are not safe from us anywhere. The counter-revolution must realize that it has no safe places of asylum'. During the three weeks prior to that statement, there were two attacks on Bulgarian *émigrés* in Western Europe. In late August 1978, Bulgarian *émigré* Vladimir Kostov had a tiny poisoned pellet injected into his back as he was leaving a subway in Paris. He developed a fever but survived the mysterious attack. On 7 September, another Bulgarian *émigré,* Georgi Markov, was killed in London by an unknown assailant who used the tip of an umbrella to inject a tiny poisoned pellet into Markov at a bus stop.

There are precedents for this type of terrorist activity against Bulgarian exiles. In 1965, Bulgarian agents apparently abducted a former Bulgarian Communist Party Secretary in Vienna. In 1974, a Bulgarian refugee was kidnapped in Copenhagen. And in 1975, two Bulgarian *émigrés* were killed in Vienna. The man who shot the *émigrés* took refuge in the Bulgarian embassy, which refused Austria's extradition request. The assassin was taken to Bulgaria, sentenced to death *pro forma*, and then pardoned and released from imprisonment.[76] A Bulgarian newspaper summed up the attitude of the Bulgarian government to these activities, and in a sense probably reflected the current attitudes of Yugoslavia, Iran, Syria and Libya, when it stated rather succinctly, 'the arm of the security service is longer than the foot of the traitor'.[77]

The state of Israel has also used terrorist tactics against its Palestinian enemies outside of Israel, primarily in Western Europe. In the early 1970s, the Mossad, the Israeli secret police, was responsible for the assassinations of twelve Palestinian leaders who were allegedly involved in Palestinian terrorist activities against Israel.[78] Most of these assassinations took place in Western Europe.

In all of the above examples, states have employed elements of their intelligence and security services to assassinate those considered to be enemies of the state. In some cases, the murders were carried out by the state's secret police. In others, the secret police hired private citizens and *émigrés* for the operations. The targets were mostly exiled political dissidents who played prominent roles in the *émigré* opposition movements or simply spoke out against their former countries. In the case of Israel, the targets were Palestinian leaders who were allegedly involved in the Black September terrorist organisation which, among others, was responsible for the killing of eleven members of the Israeli Olympic team during the 20th Olympics in Munich.

While the primary motive behind Libya, Syria, Yugoslavia and Bulgaria's assassination campaigns is intimidation, Israel and Iran's operation were dictated more by revenge. As might be expected, state-directed terrorist attacks against political exiles are usually not claimed by the state or for that matter by a fictitious group. While other terrorist attacks are designed to attract publicity, the motive behind state-directed terrorist attacks precludes the desire for media publicity. The message of intimidation which the attack conveys is intended only for the respective *émigré* community. Media publicity not only causes embarrassment to the state responsible for the attack but also to the country where the attack took place. It puts the latter in a precarious diplomatic position, especially if the state responsible for the attack is an ally or major supplier of oil. Yugoslavia, Libya and Israel, however, have carried out so many attacks in several countries that the attacks developed into a concerted campaign which attracted considerable publicity.

State-directed terrorism also encompasses the use of terrorist tactics by one state against another. In the Western European context, the most prominent and recent example of this was the Iran-Iraq feud in 1980 which gradually developed into a full-scale military confrontation in September 1980. Historically at odds with each other, even more so since Khomeini assumed power in Iran, both countries in early 1980 began a slow build up of their military forces along the Iran-Iraq border. Relations between the two countries further deteriorated in April when Iraq reportedly executed an Iranian ayatollah and close friend of Khomeini, Ayatollah Mohamed Baqr-Sadr.[79] This was followed by a wave of Iranian-inspired bombings and assassination attempts against the Iraqi regime in Baghdad. Reportedly, assassins twice attempted to kill Iraqi Vice-Premier Tareq Aziz.[80]

These apparent retaliatory attacks in Baghdad by Iran signalled the start of a terrorist mini-war between the two countries — a measure short of direct military conflict. On 29 April, there was an attempted assassination of Iranian Foreign Minister Ghotbzadeh during his official visit to Kuwait. The next day, suspected Iraqi-backed terrorists seized the Iranian embassy in London. On 26 May, the Iranian airline office in Kuwait was bombed. On 4 June, the Iraqi embassy in Rome was attacked by Iranian gunmen. On the same day, an anti-tank rocket was fired at the Iranian embassy in Kuwait. On 28 June, Greek police defused two bombs in the Iranian embassy in Athens. On 27 July, the Iraqi Second Secretary in Abu Dhabi was killed and two other Iraqis were injured when a bomb exploded in one of their apartments. On 30 July, a bomb exploded near the Iranian embssy in Vienna. Two Iraqi diplomats were expelled from Austria on the next day.[81] These terrorist skirmishes were also supplemented by cross-border sabotage incidents between the two countries. The terrorist mode of the Iran-Iraq feud ended in September when the two countries engaged in direct military conflict. There continued to be occasional attacks against each other's embassies in Beirut, but the attacks in Western Europe ceased.[82]

Another example of state-directed terrorism was the apparent Iranian use of terrorist tactics to intimidate French and Italian firms which were exporting nuclear equipment and technology to Iraq. This particular terrorist campaign by Iran was just another element in the broader Iran-Iraq feud during 1980. Obviously, it was in Iran's interests (as well as Israel and Syria's) to prevent Iraq's development of nuclear energy. Ever since France signed a formal agreement with Iraq in November 1975 to equip Iraq with a nuclear research centre, it has been criticised by Iran and Israel.

There has been speculation that Israel may have gone beyond words and resorted to terrorism in an attempt to prevent France from helping Iraq develop a nuclear capability. In April 1979, a French factory near Toulon, which was constructing two nuclear research reactors for Iraq, was heavily damaged when five explosive charges were set off by unknown saboteurs. It was estimated at the time that the damage caused by the bombs would set back by at least eighteen months the delivery of the two reactors to Iraq. A French ecological group initially claimed responsibility for the attack but French authorities 'doubted that environmental protestors had the knowledge, sabotage skills, and technical atomic information that was needed for the highly professional and successful operation'.[83] Speculation centred on Israeli commandos with probable inside help at the factory.[84] There certainly were Israeli precedents for such actions. The 'Wrath of God' hit teams in the early 1970s and the December 1969 'expropriation' of five missle-launching patrol boats from a port in Cherbourg, France are other examples of the Israeli philosophy of placing the survival of Israel above international law.[85]

In 1980, Iran also attempted to prevent Iraq from developing a nuclear capability. On 7 August, a previously unknown group calling itself the "Committee for Safeguarding the Islamic Revolution' claimed responsiblity for planting a bomb which exploded outside the home of a bookshop owner in Paris. The man had the same last name as a French nuclear scientist with ties to Iraqi nuclear projects. The terrorists had obviously made a mistake in gathering intelligence on their intended target. In claiming responsibility for the bombing, the group stated that the nuclear scientist 'had been decorated for helping Iraq make nuclear weapons'.[86] On the same day, the same group bombed the offices of the Italian firm SNIA-Techint in Rome and also attempted to bomb the home of the firm's director. The group said it bombed the firm's offices because of the support it is giving to the 'oppressive Iraqi regime'.[87]

On 11 August, five French companies participating in the construction of a nuclear research reactor in Iraq received threatening letters from the above group.[88] Then, on 25 August, this group sent a letter to the Reuter News Agency in which it threatened six French and five Italian firms allegedly helping Iraq develop nuclear energy. The letter stated that the 'governments of Italy and France have taken a very dangerous course in taking a decision to arm the dictatorial regime of Iraq with atomic bombs'. It went on to state that the 'goal of the Islamic revolution is to put an end to the interference of imperialism in the internal affairs of Iran . . . '.[89] There have been no additional attacks or threats against French or Italian firms since August 1980.[90] The September military conflict between Iran and Iraq may have diverted, at least for now, Iran's attention away from this issue. However, it still remains in the long-term interest of Iran, and Israel for that matter, to hamper, if not prevent, the Iraqi development of nuclear energy. The 7 June 1981 Israeli air attack on the Osirak nuclear reactor outside of Baghdad is testament to the lengths Israel will go to preserve its security. This attack will also ease Iran's anxiety for now.

Iran has also attempted to pressure France into cancelling the delivery of French Mirage fighter planes to Iraq. The delivery was scheduled to take place during the Iran-Iraq military conflict and could have been misinterpreted. Once again Iran resorted to terrorist pressure. On 26 December 1980, an anti-tank rocket was fired at the French embassy in Beirut, and a French embassy car was bombed there also. The next day, a group calling itself the 'Forces of Struggling Ranks' claimed responsibility for the attacks. A spokesman for the group said that 'it would continue to strike against French interests if Paris supported Iraq in the war against Iran'. He went on to say that the group would attack again 'if France went ahead with the planned sale of Mirage fighter planes to Iraq'. And finally, the spokesman demanded that France no longer allow Shapour Bakhtiar, the Iranian Prime Minister under the former Shah, to live in Paris.[91] France refused to stop delivery of the Mirages and in February 1981 started the delivery to Iraq.[92] It has been reported that the French embassy in Beirut then received threatening letters in April from 'pro-Iranian Palestinian groups'.[93]

More recently, another possible example of state-directed terrorism has occurred. Like Iran's terrorist attacks and threats against French and Italian firms, this recent example concerns the export of nuclear technology and equipment to another country. On 20 February 1981, the home of an engineer of the Swiss firm, Cora Engineering AG, was bombed in Zizers, Switzerland. The firm was involved in the delivery of equipment for a nuclear installation in Pakistan. Apparently, other Cora executives received additional threats should the firm continue to export nuclear-related equipment to Pakistan. On 19 March, the Cora firm announced that it was halting all deliveries to Pakistan. A Cora spokesman said that the threats came from a 'foreign organisation'.[94] This mystery was further amplified on 18 May when a bomb exploded in the offices of the West German Waelischmiller Company in Markdorf, West Germany. The director of the company also received a death threat if his company continued to export nuclear-related equipment to Pakistan. The anonymous caller who made the threat said that he 'represented a group trying to prevent the spread of nuclear weapons to South Asia'.[95] He also claimed that his group was responsible for the attack on Cora in Switzerland.

The motivating force behind this alleged group remains unknown. If it is an independent terrorist group, then it is a rare philanthropic one. Such broad, regional interests are usually associated with states, as was the case in the previously mentioned Israeli and Iranian examples. The question would then arise as to which state's interests are involved? Since the attacks so far have been aimed at Pakistan, countries like India and Afghanistan come to mind. One could even speculate further and consider the Soviet Union since its interests are tied to India and Afghanistan.

As in most cases concerning the suspected involvement of a state in directing terrorist activities against external elements, it is usually difficult to trace the attack directly back to a particular state. This is obviously intended on the part of the state involved. In cases where leaders or officials of a particular state (Libya, Syria and Iran) have openly sanctioned such activities, or where states have employed their intelligence services (Yugoslavia and Israel) and have been caught, the link between the state and the attacks are fairly obvious. As the above examples suggest, there has been an increasing tendency on the part of certain states to ignore international law and the laws of other states by sanctioning the murder, kidnapping, bombing and physical intimidation of their perceived enemies while residing in other states. It has also been shown that some states use terrorist tactics in an attempt to influence the foreign policy of other states. In this sense, terrorism has become an instrument of foreign policy for those countries which have shown a preference for bullets over diplomatic notes.

Conclusions

Political terrorism, in its various forms, can be found in almost every region of the world. Some regions, however, receive a larger share of the burden than others. This applies in particular to Western Europe, Latin America and the Middle East, which together since 1968 have accounted for 75 per cent of all terrorist activity. Of these three, Western Europe since about 1977 has had the most active terrorist environment in the world. This is a direct result of Western Europe's unique confrontation with multi-tiered terrorist activity encompassing *indigenous, supra-indigenous, international* and *state-directed* attacks.

From the regional perspective, the terrorist threat in Latin America stems from the indigenous level, and much of this proceeds from classic insurgency conditions. Cross-border operations by indigenous Latin American groups are rare. International terrorist and state-directed attacks seldom occur there. In the Middle East, the terrorist threat arises from the cross-border operations of various Palestinian and Arab terrorist groups which because of the mercurial political environment in the region frequently change patrons and shift targets. Many of the political feuds between the Middle Eastern countries are fought in the terrorist mode at the international level. In the majority of cases, these feuds are fought on the terrorist battlefield of Western Europe. A corollary problem of these activities for Western Europe is that they have a tendency to foment interaction (mostly logistical) between European indigenous and supra-indigenous groups and Palestinian terrorist groups. International terrorist logistical and operational activities in Western Europe spin a web which naturally attracts or catches certain indigenous groups. Whether osmotic or symbiotic, these relationships are facilitated by the operational preference for Western Europe by these international groups.

The indigenous terrorist threat in Western Europe has brought down one government (Turkey), shaken another (Spain), challenged the political fibres of two more (Northern Ireland and Italy) and strained the bilateral relations between four (Ireland and the United Kingdom; France and Spain). Since 1977, indigenous terrorism has been responsible for over 6,100 deaths in Western Europe. It has siphoned billions of dollars away from social and educational programmes as countries have increased their protective security and law enforcement expenditures to counter the indigenous threat. It has compelled many Western European democracies to curtail the civil rights of its citizens as these countries enact strict anti-terrorist legislation. It has forced these countries to develop special counter-terrorist forces to combat the indigenous threat. The crux of the problem is that indigenous terrorism has forced many countries in Western Europe to divert state resources, both material and human, from potentially positive programmes (new schools, roads, health facilities, etc.) to defensive, negative programmes (anti-terrorist laws, special counter-terrorist units, protective security hardware, damage compensation payments and increased expenditures for security and police forces). It causes human casualties and suffering, generates public fear and contributes to the erosion of the public's confidence in the state's ability to protect them and their property. If the above political, financial and psychological effects of indigenous terrorism are permitted to intensify over a period of time, they will eventually destabilise the state.

When combined with the indigenous threat, the activities of supra-indigenous, international and state-directed terrorism only compound the security problem for many Western European states. Security and law enforcement agencies in say Paris, London, Rome, Madrid or Brussels, must not only concentrate their attention and resources on their respective indigenous terrorist groups, but also on the Provisional Irish Republican Army, West Germany's Red Army Faction, various Armenian, Croatian and Palestinian terrorist groups, Arab terrorist groups and the state-directed hit teams of Libya, Iran, Iraq, Yugoslavia, Bulgaria, etc. These terrorist problems do not exist to the above extent for their counterparts in the Middle East, Latin America, the Far East, Africa or in North America.

Unfortunately, there are no concrete indications at this time that these problems will go away in the immediate future. While one country (Turkey) contains an indigenous threat, it flares up in another (Spain). While one indigenous group is neutralised (Front Line in Italy), another springs up somewhere else (April 25th Group in Portugal). While one indigenous group reduces its activities (South Moluccans), another will escalate (ELA in Greece). While one leader of an indigenous group is captured (Curcio of the Red Brigades in Italy), another takes his place (Moretti, until 1981). While one international terrorist group reduces its operations in Western Europe (Croatians), another intensifies its attacks (Armenians). And each time there is an inter-Arab or intra-Palestinian feud, or a shift in a Middle East political alliance, Western Europe seems to feel the terrorist repercussions of these events. For all of these reasons, Western Europe has the most active terrorist environment in the world. It is unfortunately a magnet for ethnic, religious and political conflicts fought in the terrorist mode.

Notes

*The paper represents solely the opinions of the author and should not be interpreted in any way as representing the views or policies of the Office of Security or the US Department of State. It was completed in June 1981.

1. Statistics based on the Central Intelligence Agency's File on International Terrorism Events (FITE), which contains information on over 6,714 terrorist incidents since 1968.

2. Charles A. Russell, 'Europe: Regional Review', *Terrorism: An International Journal*, vol. 3, nos. 1-2 (1979), p. 158 and 'Latin America: Regional Review', *Terrorism: An International Journal*, vol. 4, nos. 1-4 (1980), p. 278. Russell's statistics are based on a Risks International, Inc. (Alexandria, Virginia) terrorist data base consisting of over 6,000 'significant terrorist incidents'.

3. These levels or typologies of terrorist activity are based primarily on the operational area of a terrorist group, i.e. whether a particular group has a limited or broad operational area. A secondary consideration is the targeting emphasis of the group. Does the group consistently target one country or nationality or several? Is this targeting temporary or sustained? Less objective and functional factors such as ideology and motivation are not considered essential in the following typologies. While these factors are important in understanding the origins and goals of a group, they are less significant in assessing the operational capability of a group – a primary consideration in threat assessment.

For purposes of this article, *indigenous* terrorist activity consists mainly of the attacks or offensive operations of a terrorist group which carries out all of its attacks within the primary targeted country, most often the country of origin of the group. These attacks may be directed at personnel or facilities of the targeted country or at foreign interests within that country. From an operational perspective, the threat from an indigenous terrorist group is geographically limited to a single country. Consequently, indigenous terrorist activity is considered to be the lowest or most basic level of terrorist activity in Western Europe.

Supra-indigenous terrorist activity consists solely of the attacks by terrorist groups which carry out periodic attacks outside their primary targeted country. These groups, which are simply a variant of indigenous terrorist groups, have a tendency to restrict their operations to a single region. The majority of their attacks are carried out within the primary targeted country, but, unlike indigenous groups, they supplement these attacks with external operations. Due to the regional impact of their attacks, supra-indigenous activity is considered to be at a higher level than indigenous activity.

International terrorist activity consists of the attacks of terrorist groups which carry out a majority, in most cases an overwhelming majority, of their attacks outside their primary targeted country. Because of the trans-regional impact of such attacks, this type of activity is considered to be at a higher level than indigenous and supra-indigenous terrorist activity. At this level, one finds groups which target more than one country or nationality. This contrasts with the attacks by indigenous and supra-indigenous groups which generally concentrate their attacks on their primary targeted country. The preference for multinational targeting by the international groups is facilitated by their expanded operational area. It is also at the international level that one finds the preponderance of joint and commissioned terrorist attacks.

State-directed terrorist activity is the highest level of terrorist activity found in Western Europe. This type of activity is directed by a state against external elements (usually political exiles, other states or nationalities) beyond its own boundaries. This type of terrorist activity has no geographical limits. It differs from international terrorist activity in that state-directed terrorist activity is directed by a state, backed by all the resources of a state, rather than by a sub-national group. As such, its impact is potentially more severe than the previous three levels of terrorist activity.

For another 'functional' approach to the classification of terrorist groups, see the excellent article by Ariel Merari, 'A Classification of Terrorist Groups', *Terrorism: An International Journal*, vol. 1, nos, 3-4 (1978), pp. 331-46. See also, Richard Schultz, 'Conceptualizing Political Terrorism: A Typology' in Alan D. Buckley and Daniel P. Olson (eds), *International Terrorism: Current Research and Future Directions* (N.J. (Avery Publishing Group, N.J. 1980), pp. 9-14.

4. It is the author's belief that a good portion of the 'indigenous' terrorist activity in Latin America, the Middle East and Africa is carried out by guerrilla movements which employ conventional military tactics involving, at the least, squad-level operations designed for occasional face-to-face engagements with the

security forces. This is in sharp contrast to indigenous terrorist groups in Western Europe which (1) refrain from conventional military tactics; (2) rarely employ more than two or three people in each operation; and (3) avoid face-to-face engagements with the security forces. As a result, the political violence which is taking place in El Slavador, Lebanon, Uganda, South Africa, Ethiopia and the Western Sahara equates more to civil war and insurgency conditions than to the acts of indigenous terrorist groups.

5. *Washington Post*, 13 August 1980; *Milliyet* (Istanbul), 2 September 1980; and *Cumhuriyet* (Istanbul), 7 June 1980.

6. Reuter News Agency, 16 September 1980.

7. From September 1980 to April 1981, more than 25,000 people were arrested for suspicion of terrorist or extremist activity. *Washington Post*, 17 April 1981.

8. *New York Times*, 15 March 1981.

9. United Press International (UPI), 12 March 1979.

10. Data based on author's files. For a good estimate of the financial cost of maintaining peace in Northern Ireland to the British government, see Ed Moloney, 'The IRA', *Magill* (Dublin), September 1980, p. 16.

11. The hunger strike campaign by imprisoned Irish terrorists will probably temporarily reverse this trend. From 1 March 1981, when the hunger strike began, to late May, four hunger strikers died in the Maze prison outside of Belfast. The provisional IRA has promised retaliation for these deaths. [Ed. note: This hunger strike ended in September 1981. Ten Irish terrorists died during this strike.]

12. Reuter, 31 December 1979; and *New York Times*, 28 August 1979.

13. *An Phoblacht/Republican News* (Belfast), 18 October 1980, p. 9. Although this newspaper is a PIRA propaganda organ, the figures were based on the official figures compiled by the *Belfast Telegraph*, 30 August 1980.

14. Tim Pat Coogan, *On the Blanket: The H-Block Story* (Ward Press Review, Dublin, 1980), p. 31. This recent book is an excellent, fairly objective study of the IRA's political and military use of the prisons and prisoners to further the IRA's cause.

15. Statistics from Vitorfranco S. Pisano, 'The Red Brigades; A Challenge to Italian Democracy', *Conflict Studies* (London), no. 120 (July 1980), p. 2, and *Washington Star*, 10 January 1981.

16. Right-wing or neo-Fascist terrorists killed 16 people when a bomb exploded in a Milan bank in 1969; twelve people in the bombing of a train near Bologna in 1974; nine people in a bomb attack during a demonstration near Brescia in 1974; and 85 people in the Bologna bombing in August 1980.

17. The decision to use the military to supplement the police forces during the June elections was taken by the Ministers Committee for Security on 9 May 1979. A 3 May terrorist attack on the Christian Democrat Party headquarters in Rome in broad daylight is believed to have provoked the decision to employ the military See the 9-10 May 1980 issues of *Paese Sera* (Rome) and *Il Messaggero* (Rome).

18. In 1977, RAF elements were responsible for (1) a planned kidnapping in April of the former Swedish Minister of Immigration in Stockholm; (2) the April assassination in Karlsruhe, West Germany of the Federal Prosecutor Siegfried Buback; (3) the July murder (an apparent aborted kidnapping) in Frankfurt of Juergen Ponto, the Chairman of the Board of the Deutsche Bank; (4) the August attempted rocket attack (a 'Stalin organ') on the Federal Prosecutor's office in Karlsruhe; and (5) the September kidnapping and subsequent October murder of Hanns-Martin Schleyer, President of the German Industries Federation and a close adviser to Chancellor Helmut Schmidt. 1977 remains the high watermark for West German terrorists.

19. *Die Welt*, 16 June 1980; *Die Zeit*, 20 June 1980; and *Der Spiegel*, 16 March

1981, p. 36-42.

20. The West German Ministry of Justice reported on 3 April 1981 that left-wing terrorists have been responsible for 30 murders, 110 attempted murders, 100 injuries and have taken 163 hostages. Currently, 102 leftist terrorists are in custody. Right-wing terrorists have killed 17 people, attempted to kill two more and have injured 221. At present, 33 right-wing terrorists are in jail. UPI, 3 April 1981.

21. From 1954-71, there was a total of 109 terrorist incidents on Corsica committed by groups demanding autonomy. In 1972, there were twelve, 1973 – 42, 1974 – 111, 1975 – 226, 1976 – 296, 1977 – 350, 1978 – 480, 1979 – 400 and 1980 – 465. From 1976, when the FLNC was founded, to the present, the majority of the above attacks, primarily bombings, can be attributed to the FLNC. Beginning in 1979, the FLNC started to carry out more and more attacks on the French mainland, especially Paris. For background information on the FLNC, see *Le Figaro* (Paris), May 1980; *Le Monde* (Paris), 25 April 1980, 13 January 1981 and 11 February 1981; *Paris Match*, 6 July 1979; *L'Express* (Paris) 23 August 1980; and Reuter, 18 April 1981.

22. According to Reuter, 22 July 1980, twelve people have been killed in France over the last two years as a result of Middle East related political violence. This is certainly more victims than indigenous groups have been responsible for over the same period. As of April 1981, the author's files indicate that the above total is now 21.

23. *Athens Post* (Athens), 2 March 1980.

24. A group calling itself the '17th of November' group has claimed responsibility for the December 1975 assassination of Richard Welch, the First Secretary of the US embassy, the December 1976 assassinations of two Greek policemen and the January 1980 murder of the deputy chief of the Greek anti-terrorist police and his chauffeur. Police suspect that the '17th of November' group may be a branch or commando of the ELA. See the following Greek newspapers of 22 February 1980 – *Vema, Nea* and *Messimvrini*.

25. *Acropolis* (Athens), and the *Athens News* (in English), various issues from 16-20 February 1980.

26. For additional information on the April 25th group, see *The Times* (London) 22 April 1981 and Reuter, 14 May, 6, 13 October 1980 and 26 March 1981.

27. According to Reuter, 3 December 1980, from 1970 to 1980, 48 people have been killed and 750 injured in Great Britain by bombs planted by Irish terrorists. Assassinations by Irish terrorists in Great Britain are rare. INLA's murder of Airey Neave in March 1979 was the most high-level assassination in Great Britain since the IRA killed Sir Henry Wilson in 1921. Over the last several years, it has become increasingly difficult for Irish terrorists to operate in Great Britain as British authorities have continued to disrupt PIRA's logistical infrastructure on the mainland.

28. The attack was apparently part of a PIRA letter-bomb campaign carried out through August and September. During this campaign, letter-bombs were sent to British officials in Great Britain, the United States, Gibraltar, Zaire, Portugal and Belgium. Most of those sent overseas were detected and defused, but two caused injuries in the United States and Zaire.

29. 'Airey Neave was assassinated by us because he was a militarist . . . he demanded the strengthening of the UDR [Ulster Defence Regiment], more SAS [Special Air Services] men in the north and the re-introduction of internment. It was Neave's ambition . . . to intensify repression and thereafter to impose a political solution. Thus, he was a prime target but in addition we felt that it was time the Westminster armchair militarists suffered directly the conse-

quences of their polices.' 'Why We Killed Airey Neave — the INLA', *Magill* (Dublin),April 1979, p. 4. As for the timing of the attack, INLA stated, 'the final decision was taken after the no confidence vote in the House of Commons on the night previous to the assassination'.

30. *Washington Post*, 14 March 1979.

31. Associated Press (AP), 30 August 1979.

32. *Republican News* (Belfast), 23 February 1980.

33. Other incidents outside West Germany involving German terrorists (not directly linked to the RAF) include: December 1975 — two German terrorists (2JM) working with Carlos and the PFLP attacked an OPEC Ministerial meeting in Vienna; January 1976 — two German terrorists (RZ) working with the PFLP planned to shoot down an El Al airliner in Nairobi, Kenya with a surface to air missile; June 1976 — two German terrorists (RZ) working with the PFLP hijacked an Air France plane to Entebbe; and November 1977 — four German terrorists (2JM) working with two novice Austrian terrorists kidnapped an Austrian million-aire (Michael Palmers) in Vienna. German terrorists have been involved in more 'joint operations' than any other terrorist group (excluding of course the Pales-tinians). The Japanese Red Army (JRA) ranks second. Moreover, again excluding the Palestinians, it appears that more German terrorists have been captured outside their primary targeted country than any other terrorist group.

34. Many of the groups which operate within these aggregates frequently use different names in carrying out an attack to confuse the authorities and/or to commemorate a signifcant event or comrade. Thus, within the Palestinian aggre-gate, there have been groups like the 'Black September Organisation', 'Black June and 'Black March'. While Armenian terrorists have used names like the 'October 3rd Group' and the 'May 28 Armenian Organisation'. In some cases, no group will claim responsibility for an attack. For example, in December 1980 a bomb exploded in a Jewish-owned hotel in Nairobi, Kenya killing about 18 people (British, Italians, Americans and Kenyans). No group has claimed responsibility for this attack, yet the police believe 'Arab terrorists' were involved, specifically the Popular Front for the Liberation of Palestine (PFLP). (See *Washington Post*, 8, 9 January 1981.) The PFLP has denied any involvement. In other cases, like the June 1979 attempted assassination of the then General Haig in Belgium, several groups will claim responsibility. After the Haig attack, about five groups, three of which were previously unknown, claimed responsibility. Moreover, initially, the PIRA, which was not among the five, was strongly suspected. Needless to say, all of the above makes it difficult for analysts to monitor the activities of the various groups. As a result, rather than discuss all of the individual international terrorist groups which have operated in Western Europe, this section will focus on the three major and most active terrorist aggregates mentioned previously.

35. Based on the author's admittedly superficial survey of data as compiled by the *1981 Almanac, Atlas, and Yearbook* (Simon and Schuster, New York), pp. 139-40. The exception was in number of daily newspapers, where the United States had 1,812 as opposed to 1,191 for all of Western Europe. South and Central America combined only had 752, while the Middle East had 120.

36. This figure excludes attacks in Jordan and Lebanon because these countries have been or are being used as major operational bases for Palestinian terrorists. The September 1970 clash between Jordan and the Palestinians, and the 1975-6 civil war in Lebanon also make it difficult to extract the terrorist attack from the numerous conventional guerrilla encounters which existed in these countries at the time. Aircraft hijackings have also been excluded since they take place in mid air; although, it should be noted that the majority of Palestinian hijackings have taken place on US and Western European aircraft over Western European air space. Finally, the author admits that the limiting adjective

'significant' is subjective in nature. Significant attacks in this section includes assassinations, attempted assassinations, bombings which produced casualties or extensive property damage, hostage seizures, embassy attacks, use of anti-tank rockets and attacks at airports. The chronologies used were: (1) 'Palestinian Guerrilla Operations Outside Israel 1968-1978', found on pp. 10-11 of 'Through the Barrel of a Gun', *The Middle East* (July 1980); (2) a US government publication entitled 'Significant International Terrorist Incidents: 1970-1980'; and (3) the author's files for incidents from 1978 to 1980.

37. For background on this 1978 feud, see the *Christian Science Monitor*, 1, 8 August 1978 and *Newsweek*, 14 August 1978.

38. For background on Black June and Abu Nidal, see *The Middle East*, July 1978, pp. 26-8 and February 1978, p. 44.

39. Reuter, 17 January 1980.

40. UPI, 3 March 1980.

41. UPI, 15 July and 13 December 1980; *Expressen* (Stockholm), 18 December 1980; and *Dagens Nyheter* (Stockholm), 19 July 1980. In January 1981, Sweden ordered the expulsion of four Palestinians for terrorist activity. These arrests apparently broke up a PFLP-GC cell in Uppsala, Sweden.

42. *The Times* 30 July 1980; *Washington Post*, 28 July and 2 August 1980; and UPI, 28 July 1980. In April 1979, a Palestinian group calling itself 'Black March' (after the March 1979 Israeli-Egyptian peace treaty), carried out an unsuccessful grenade attack on an El Al plane at Brussels airport. The terrorists panicked and began to fire on innocent bystanders in the lounge area.

43. AP, 26 March 1981. No Palestinian terrorist group has as yet claimed responsibility for this bombing or the one in Nairobi in December 1980.

44. For some background on these groups, see *Le Figaro* (Paris), 5 March 1981; *Panorama* (Milan), 1 September 1980, pp. 62-5; *Paris Match*, 20 March 1981, pp. 78-9; *The Middle East* (London), June 1981 pp. 21-8; *Los Angeles Times*, 25 January 1981; and *Armenian Weekly* (Boston), 16 August 1980. Most of the information on Armenian terrorists comes from the Western European press. *Armenian Weekly*, an English language Armenian-American newspaper, and *Armenian Reporter* (New York), publish reports on and communiqués of Armenian terrorist groups. In mid-1980, ASALA began to publish a magazine called *Armenia* which contained information on their attacks and motives. It is published in Beirut, Lebanon. Two issues of this magazine were published in 1980, and six as of June 1981. This is a valuable primary source document on ASALA terrorist activities.

45. New Armenian Resistance communiqué no. 9, released in Paris on 21 April 1980.

46. ASALA communiqué released in Rome, dated 23 December 1979. For additional information on this threat, see *Panorama*, 1 September 1980, which contains an interview with an ASALA spokesman.

47. New Armenian Resistance communiqué no. 9.

48. *Los Angeles Times*, 25 January 1981. *Paris Match*, 20 March 1981 and *Armenian Weekly*, 16 August 1981. The ASALA campaign to force the Italian government to close down those emigration centres which process Armenian refugees is reminiscent of a Palestinian terrorist attack in Marchegg, Austria on 28 September 1973 in which some Jewish refugees from the Soviet Union were seized. Saiqa, the Palestinian group involved, demanded the closure of a Soviet Jewish emigration processing centre at Schoenau Castle in Austria.

49. All statistics on Armenian terrorist attacks were taken from a soon-to-be-published research paper on contemporary Armenian terrorism by Andrew Corsun of the US Department of State's Office of Security Threat Analysis Group.

50. Since 1975, Armenian terrorists have been responsible for over 80 terrorist attacks including 16 assassinations, six attempted assassinations and two anti-

tank rocket attacks. The remaining attacks were primarily bombings.

51. Some Serbian *émigré* groups have also engaged, albeit on a limited basis, in anti-Yugoslav terrorist activities. See for example, Reuter, 20 February 1979; *Washington Post*, 2 September 1977 and *Toronto Sun*, 30 August 1977. Like the Armenian aggregate, little has been written on Croatian terrorist activity.

52. For some general background on Croatian terrorist activity, see Stephen Clissold, 'Croat Separatism, Nationalism, Dissidence, and Terrorism', *Conflict Studies*, no. 103 (January 1979); *The Times*, 22 October 1978 *New York Times*, 21 June and 18 September 1976, 22 June 1979 and 24 March 1980; *Washington Post*, 12 September 1976 and *International Herald Tribune*, 8 November 1978.

53. For additional information on these attacks on non-Yugoslav targets, see *New York Times*, 15 June and 21 July 1977; *Washington Post*, 13 September 1976 and 25 July 1979; and *Chicago Tribune*, 18, 19 August and 1 December 1978 and 1 January 1980.

54. All statistics on Croatian terrorist attacks were taken from an unpublished research paper on anti-Yugoslav terrorist activity by Lisbeth Renwick of the US Department of State's Office of Security Threat Analysis Group.

55. Their most publicised attacks in the US have been (1) the hijacking of a TWA plane out of New York in September 1976; (2) the seizure of the Yugoslav UN mission in New York City in June 1977; (3) the seizure of the West German consulate in Chicago in August 1978; (4) the hijacking of an American Airlines airliner out of New York in 1979; and (5) the bombing of the Statue of Liberty (minor damage) in June 1980. There have also been several plots and planned operations which never materialised. See, for example, *Cleveland Press*, 13 September 1980; *Washington Post*, 16 June 1979; and *New York Times*, 13 May 1981.

56. *New York Daily News*, 12 December 1980; and Reuter and UPI, 12, 13 December 1980. On 25 June 1981, nine members of the hierarchy of the Croatian National Resistance (OTPOR) were arrested in New York City and Ontario, Canada and charged with at least two murders, three arsons, more than 50 acts of extortion, four conspiracies to commit arson, four conspiracies to commit murder and four actions of interstate transportation of explosives. For additional details, see *Washington Star*, 25 June 1981.

57. See, for example, Jacques de Vernisy, 'The New International Terrorism', *World Press Review* (November 1980), pp. 23-5.

58. UPI, 10 May 1980.

59. Ibid.

60. Reuter, 10 May 1980.

61. The attempt in the United States is suspected of having been carried out by a former member of the US army's Green Berets. For additional information on this particular incident and the other connections between US citizens and Libyan terrorist activity, see *New York Times*, 24 May 1981, *Rocky Mountain News* (Denver), 24 April 1981; *Denver Post*, 23 April 1981; Stephen Kurkjian and Ben Bradlee Jr's article, 'The Americans Who are Training and Supplying Libyan Terrorists', in the Outlook Section of *Washington Post*, 22 March 1981, p. D1; and 'Libyan Aide Denies Country Aids Terrorism but Differs on Definition', in *Washington Post*, 30 May 1981.

62. *Daily American* (Rome), 27 February 1981.

63. *Washington Post*, 11 March 1981.

64. UPI, 9 December 1979.

65. Reuter, 21 July 1980.

66. Reuter, 18 July 1980. On 13 May, Khalkhali gave a news conference in Tehran in which he said that the deposed Shah and his family were under a death sentence and that anyone who assassinates them would be carrying out the

people's verdict. He also mentioned Shapour Bakhtiar. (*Washington Post*, 14 May 1980.) Two days later, he invited the PLO to execute the former Shah. He also quoted an alleged message from Ayatollah Khomeini in which the Iranian leader stated that 'anyone, Iranian or Palestinian, Moslem or non-Moslem or even from the Bahamas [at the time, the Shah was staying there], was free to execute Shah Mohammed Pahlavi', (UPI, 15 May 1980). One Iranian newspaper even offered an all expense paid trip to the holy city of Mecca to anyone who killed the Shah (Reuter, 17 May 1980).

67. *Washington Star*, 18 April 1981.

68. Vernisy, 'The New International Terrorism', p. 24.

69. *Washington Post*, 22 July 1980. According to the Syrian government, about 300 Baath Party members, government officials and ordinary civilians have been assassinated by the Moslem Brotherhood. The victims included 'three or four Soviet experts'. *The Times*, 28 February 1981. Thus, the Soviet Union may also have a motive for eliminating Moslem Brotherhood exiles in Western Europe.

70. Reuter, 24 July 1980. There have also been reports that the infamous Carlos was hired in April 1981 by the Syrian intelligence services to 'mastermind special operations in Europe against President Hafez Assad's political opponents'. See *Economist Foreign Report* (London), 7 May 1981, pp. 5-6. This issue of the *Foreign Report* also states that Syria and Libya have 'decided to set up a joint command for their secret services, to co-ordinate their covert foreign operations and, as part of the joint effort, to move the centre of their European operations from Bonn and Paris to London'.

71. Other East European countries, including the Soviet Union, have carried out similar operations against their political exiles. Most recently, in February 1981, two Romanian exiles in Paris and one in Cologne, West Germany, received identical book bombs hidden in books written by Nikita Khruschev and mailed from Spain. All three exiles had taken part in a press conference in Madrid in November 1980 on human rights in their country. *The Times*, 5 February 1981 and *Washington Post*, 5 February 1981.

72. *Die Welt*, 25 February 1980.

73. Ibid.

74. On the murder of Dusan Sedlar, an anti-Yugoslav Serbian leader, see *Die Zeit*, 18 April 1980.

75. For additional information on Yugoslav retaliatory terrorist attacks against Croatian and Serbian exiles, see Clissold, 'Croat Separatism', pp. 12-15, *Washington Post*, 16 August 1979; *The Times*, 22 October 1978; *Stern* (Hamburg), 8 June 1978; *The Manchester Guardian* 14 January 1979; *Die Welt*, 30 December 1977; and UPI, 18 October 1978.

76. With the exception of the Kostov and Markov incidents, all of these accounts were taken from *Der Spiegel*, 9 October 1978, pp. 152-5.

77. *Otchestven Front*, 24 September 1974, as quoted in *Der Spiegel*, 9 October 1981.

78. For background on Israel's 'Wrath of God' hit teams, see Christopher Dobson, *Black September: Its Short, Violent History* (Macmillan Publishing Co, New York, 1974), pp. 89-133 and David B. Tinnin, *Hit Team* (Little, Brown, Boston, 1976). In *Black September*, Dobson, on page 68, states that Prime Minister Golda Meir, speaking to the Knesset one week after the Munich Olympic massacre, said Israel would fight Arab terrorists wherever possible. 'We have no choice but to strike at them.'

79. *The Times*, 24 25 July 1980.

80. *Washington Post*, 24 September 1980.

81. These incidents can be found in *Kuwait Times* (Kuwait), 5 July 1980; Reuter, 26 May 1980; *Arab Times* (Kuwait), 5 July 1980; and *The Times*, 31 July 1980.

82. For example, on 2 October anti-tank rockets were fired at the Iranian and Iraqi embassies in Beirut. These attacks were probably part of the Iran-Iraq military conflict. Beirut is frequently used to 'settle scores' among the various Palestinian elements and between other Arab countries.

83. From an unpublished research paper by Stefanie Stauffer entitled 'Iraq's Quest for Nuclear Capability' for Dr Duncan Clarke at the American University's School of International Service (autumn 1980), p. 7.

84. *Washington Post*, 7 April 1979; Reuter, 14 April 1979; and UPI, 9 April 1979.

85. At the time of the Cherbourg incident, the delivery of the patrol boats was being blocked by the French government. In another interesting 'unsolved' incident, an Egyptian nuclear scientist who was assisting the Iraqis with their nuclear programme was assassinated in Paris in June 1980. (*The Times*, 11 July 1980). No group claimed responsibility. Keep in mind that most of the attacks carried out by Iranian elements were always claimed by a group.

86. Reuter, 7 August 1980.

87. UPI, 7 August 1980. See also *Economist Foreign Report*, 4 February 1981, p. 4.

88. *The Times*, 13 August 1980.

89. Reuter, 25 August 1980. The last two quotes are from a copy of the communiqué.

90. In April and October 1980, bombs were discovered near the nuclear equipment factory 'Framatome' near Chalon-sur-Soane, France. *The Times*, 21 October 1980.

91. Reuter, 26, 27 December 1980.

92. On 1 February, the Iranian embassy stated that the 'Iranian people will never forget this act by the French government'. It should be noted that since the start of the Iran-Iraq military conflict, France had not delivered any military equipment to Iraq. France saw the Mirage delivery as 'special' since they were ordered and presumably paid for before the start of the war. Iraq is France's second largest oil supplier and also one of its best customers for arms (*The Times*, 2 February 1981). Ironically, considering the Israeli position in 1975, France has refused to give a delivery date to Iran for the three remaining missile patrol boats near completion in a Cherbourg shipyard (*The Times*, 4 February 1981).

93. *Le Point* (Paris), 13 April 1981, p. 73.

94. AP, 21 March 1981; and *La Suisse (Geneva), 16 March 1981*.

95. Reuter, 18 May 1981; and *Washington Post*, 19 May 1981.

4 THE EUROPEAN COMMUNITY AND TERRORISM: POLITICAL AND LEGAL ASPECTS

Juliet Lodge with David Freestone

Nothing in the Treaty of Rome establishing the European Economic Community (EC) obliges its signatories to pursue or adhere to a common policy regarding the suppression of terrorism. Indeed, terrorism is outside the jurisdiction of the EC's institutions. Nevertheless, the events of the late 1960s and 1970s impressed upon many states and notably those in the EC with contiguous borders, the need to act in concert and to make common arrangements if terrorist offences were to be countered effectively. The two principal European forums within which steps have been taken to realise these aims are the Council of Europe and the EC.

The Council of Europe took the lead in 1973 in working towards the adoption of anti-terrorist measures by its members; but the EC did not seriously begin concerted appraisal of anti-terrorist measures until 1976. The impetus for EC action has emanated largely from the European Parliament and draws inspiration from the Council of Europe's Convention on the Suppression of Terrorism (ECST). Yet, for various reasons, some EC members have been unwilling to see a comparable EC agreement drafted and enforced. This may seem paradoxical in view of the fact that EC member governments must in part have been motivated to explore the adoption of common principles in this area by the inadequacy of existing international provisions and by a desire to intensify co-operation among themselves on the matter.

However, the delays in achieving agreement on EC action against terrorism relate to a number of considerations. Apart from political factors and difficulties borne of the differences between civil law states like France and common law states like the United Kingdom, it must be realised that the adoption of a common EC 'policy' on terrorism has important implications not simply for the jurisdiction of the member states and the nature of their mutual and reciprocal obligations, but that it would be tantamount to an extension of the EC's competence to a sphere hitherto the prerogative of the member states, and hence imply that EC law in this area would be binding and assume precedence over national law, as in other areas covered by EC legislation. As has been amply demonstrated in other policy areas in the EC, the compartmentalisation of policy is replete with difficulties since the integration of one or more sectors has ramifications for others. This was one of the considerations underlying the French proposal to deal with terrorism in the EC not by EC legislation *per se* but through the creation of a common judicial area (un espace judiciare européenne). Differences of opinion over the advantages of either approach complicated attempts within the EC to concert action against terrorism.

This paper begins by outlining the key features of the European Convention on the Suppression of Terrorism. The EC's attempts to adapt and implement it are then scrutinised, and the problems associated with the creation of a common judicial area explored.

The European Convention on the Suppression of Terrorism

The European Convention on the Suppression of Terrorism (ECST)[1] attempts to avoid the more obvious pitfalls bedevilling earlier international endeavours at co-operation in the suppression of terrorism which date back at least to the two conventions sponsored by the League of Nations in 1937 — neither of which was ratified by sufficient members to come into effect.[2] The ECST does not attempt the notoriously difficult task of defining terrorism, nor does it try to set up an international tribunal with criminal jurisdiction. It seeks to tread a less controversial path, although it has been criticised by all sides of the political spectrum. The regime it establishes between signatory states (which are limited to the member states of the Council of Europe) is grafted onto existing extradition arrangements.

Its prime purpose is to modify existing bilateral and multilateral extradition arrangements between signatory states, so as to exclude the use of the so-called 'political defence' in relation to certain specified offences of violence which might loosely be classified as 'terrorist' offences. The 'political defence' is the most obvious means by which fugitive terrorists have been able to escape extradition and, hence, trial. The earliest record of its inclusion is in a Belgian treaty of 1833, but the 'political defence' in its various manifestations can be found in the overwhelming majority of national extradition laws and international extradition treaties.[3] It is, for example, included in the European Convention on Extradition, a multilateral treaty concluded under the auspices of the Council of Europe in order to rationalise extradition arrangements between member states.[4]

The European Convention on Extradition excludes from extradition fugitives accused of a 'political offence' or 'an offence connected with a political offence'. Not surprisingly, there is no definition of these terms, for national extradition laws vary considerably over the circumstances in which the 'political offence' is allowed as a defence. The Federal Republic of Germany (FRG), France and Italy, for example, give pride of place to the subjective motives of the offender. While in the Netherlands, the nature of the interests affected by the alleged crime must be considered also.[5] The English courts combine consideration of the offender's motives with an increasingly restrictive view of the circumstances in which it is possible to commit an 'offence of a political character'.[6]

The aim of the ECST is to deprive the fugitive offender, accused of one of the listed offences,[7] of the right to plead, in extradition proceedings between signatory states, that her/his offence should be regarded as a 'political offence' or as 'an offence inspired by political motives'. This, it has been argued, abolishes the 'right of asylum', and is why the Convention has been so stridently criticised.[8] In fact, this effect of the Convention is severely restricted by two other provisions. First, article 5 (included at the instigation of the United Kingdom) permits a state to retain the right to refuse extradition for a listed offence if it has 'substantial grounds for believing that the request for extradition . . . has been made for the purpose of prosecuting or punishing a person on account of his race, religion, nationality, or political opinion, or that that person's position may be prejudiced for any of these reasons'. This is, in fact, the second leg of the traditional 'political defence', and it concentrates on the circumstances of likely trial or punishment rather than on the motives of the offender. It is intended to prevent persecution but is a highly sensitive issue as it imputes bad faith to the request of a signatory (and, *ex hypothesi*, friendly) state for extradition in respect of terrorist offences.[9]

Secondly, article 13 of the ECST allows signatories to register a reservation permitting them to reject a request for extradition on the grounds that the offence is of a political character, notwithstanding the fact that a listed offence is involved. This provision appears to negate the ECST's object and has itself been vigorously criticised as severely weakening the Convention and its efficacy.[10] However, the reservation was included to meet political requirements of potential signatories. But it should be noted that the effects of the reservations under article 13 are in turn circumscribed by other important provisions. First, any such reservation must be accepted on the basis of reciprocity — thus any state making such a reservation may have it invoked against itself.[11] Secondly, such states are obliged, when deciding whether to invoke their reservations in a particular case, to take into account the following factors:

any particularly serious aspects of the offence, including whether
(a)   it created a collective danger to the life, physical integrity or liberty of persons;
(b)   whether it affected persons foreign to the motives behind it; or
(c)   whether cruel or vicious means have been used in the commission of the offence.

These are, in fact, the terms of the 1974 Resolution (74) 3 of the Committee of Ministers on International Terrorism of the Council of Europe.

Thirdly, should a state decide not to extradite an offender covered by the Convention (for example, either by invoking an article 13 reservation or because it decides to use its rights under article 5), then the principle of *aut dedere aut judicare* – extradite or try – comes into play. Article 7 obliges such a state to 'submit the case, without exception whatsoever and without undue delay, to its competent authorities for the purposes of prosecution', where the decision to prosecute should be taken in the same manner as it is with any serious national offence. To reinforce article 7, states are also obliged to amend their rules of criminal jurisdiction to allow them to try such an offender (provided that they recognise the principle of jurisdiction upon which the requesting state has based a request for extradition).[12] Finally, the ECST is subject to a compulsory arbitration clause which in the event of a dispute over its interpretation or application can be invoked by either party, failing a friendly settlement.[13]

Despite the initial approval and signature of 17 of the members of the Council of Europe, the ECST cannot be said to have been an outstanding success. The 'extradite or try' principle is intended to prevent terrorists finding refuge and, hence, the ECST's success must in the first instance be judged by the number of states that are party to it. To date it has been ratified by only ten states: Austria, Cyprus, Denmark, the FRG, Iceland, Leichtenstein, Norway, Spain, Sweden and the United Kingdom.[14]

Doubt may be also expressed about the provisions which oblige states to prosecute for offences committed outside their territory, with all the concomitant problems of collecting evidence and witnesses. In 1975, Eire and Northern Ireland concluded a similar arrangement which permitted each to prosecute offences committed in its neighbour's jurisdiction.[15] To date only one prosecution has been started under this arrangement, in Dublin in 1979, and that resulted in an acquittal for lack of evidence.[16] Even conceding the unique character of the Irish situation, this is not an encouraging precedent. This issue is particularly important because of the number of states which have already indicated their reservations about the demise of the 'political offence'. Sweden, Denmark and Norway have made reservations under article 13, and France, Italy and Portugal made declarations in similar terms when initially signing the ECST. Failure to extradite political offenders, it will be remembered, gives rise to the obligations under article 7 to submit them to prosecution locally.

France is the most notable of the states which have failed to ratify the Convention because it was an initial signatory and initiated action on the 'espace judiciare européenne' proposals within the EC. Apparently, the French government made its ratification of the ECST dependent on the success of the latter. However, such proposals require unanimity among EC member states and it has been alleged by *Le Monde* that they had been blocked by the Dutch, in retaliation for the failure of Dutch proposals on the desalination of the Rhine.[17] In addition, the election of the Socialist President Mitterrand in May 1981 seems to preclude future French ratification of the ECST. This is because the French left has traditionally opposed the extradition of political offenders, and one of Mitterrand's early presidential acts was to stop the extradition to Spain of Basque ETA member, Tomas Linaza, to face charges of murder, after a French court had ruled it could go ahead.[18]

Moreover, Ireland has consistently refused even to sign the ECST, arguing that article 29 of its Constitution prevents the extradition of political offenders. Article 29 provides that 'Ireland accepts the generally accepted principles of international law as its rule of conduct in its relations with other states'. The interpretation which consecutive Irish governments have put upon this article has been a matter of considerable academic and political controversy. In practice, the non-extradition of political offenders appears to be a matter of state discretion and, hence, if it is a rule of international law at all, then it is permissive rather than obligatory. Furthermore, rigid adherence to the principle of not extraditing political offenders represents 'a narrow conception of the nature of international law and the process of its growth'.[19]

The ECST's impact has been small. There are, as yet, no reported cases of trials under the Convention. Even if its main impact could be seen as a symbolic gesture of solidarity — a pact to prevent terrorists from finding refuge in European states — then the small number of ratifications shows even this to be a limited success.

The European Community

Not until July 1976 did EC Ministers discuss terrorism. However, the European Parliament — which had exercised its rights to issue opinions on all matters of topical interest during the 1970s — had been active before this, and remains committed to promoting the conclusion of anti-terrorist measures that will close loopholes in existing conventions to which some or all EC member states are party. EC consideration of measures to combat international terrorism embraces six main elements and has been extended as necessary. The six elements concern attempts to secure agreement among the member states:

(1) to approve and accept measures, to apply to the EC as a whole, similar to and adapted from the Council of Europe's Convention on the Suppression of Terrorism;

(2) to adopt, in the EC, a common system for the extradition of terrorists;

(3) to consider creating a common judicial area (un espace judiciare européenne) to assist the EC's members in combating criminal offences;

(4) to encourage the study of problems associated with terrorism; including the abuse of diplomatic bags;

(5) to impress upon countries, notably in the Arab or Third World, which have given havens to terrorists perpetrating offences on EC members' 'territory', that trade and political relations with the EC are, thereby, likely to be infringed;

(6) to act to promote more adequate firearms' control in further-ance of the European Convention on the Acquisition of and Possession of Firearms.

All give rise to numerous difficulties in the EC and, moreover, raise a number of legal niceties as to the legal basis for any EC action in these areas since — with the arguable exception of the sixth element listed above — they fall outside the scope of the EC's competence as delineated by the Rome Treaty. However, the spate of terrorist activities either indigenous to an EC member state or commenced or committed in an EC country and/or involving their aircraft, embassies, diplomatic personnel or nationals throughout the 1970s led the European Parliament's delegated, and latterly its elected, Members (MEPs) to press for the adoption of measures to combat terrorism. (They have considered and been vigilant of the potential abuse, by governments, of existing national anti-terrorist and anti-subversive measures (such as the FRG's Radikalenerlass – the Radicals' Decree) but these are outside the scope of this paper.) Furthermore, concern with respect for human rights has featured in deliberations over trading relations with the Lomé (African, Caribbean and Pacific countries) and Arab countries, and has an external dimension relevant to the discussion of terrorism at the supranational level.

EC member governments themselves have adopted a cautious attitude towards this question. This is due both to fears as to the impact of any common EC legislation on existing national measures, and to concern that the sovereignty of individual member governments in this sensitive area should not be compromised. While EC Ministers of the Interior and Justice have periodically met to discuss terrorism, the results have been slow and limited. This is not surprising since at the ministerial and officials' level, action proceeded within the framework of Foreign Ministers' meetings, European Political Co-operation and European Councils (summits) – that is, outside the EC's formal, supranational decision making process. Moreover, while MEPs can pass motions and resolutions on terrorism, there is no commensurate obligation on or freedom for EC Ministers to act to further MEPs' wishes.

The liberation of the Entebbe hostages in 1976 led to all the party groups in the Euorpean Parliament on 6 July 1976 adopting and approving a resolution to combat international terrorism. The resolution not only called on the EC's institutions to act, but advocated action in respect of Third World countries. In addition, it referred to the need for greater EC cohesion in international organisations considering terrorism.[20]

Eleven days before the Council of Europe's Committee of Ministers signed the European Convention on the Suppression of Terrorism, MEPs pressurised EC member governments to ratify the Convention immediately.[21] The all-party resolution to this effect was designed to underline their conviction that the EC's credibility in this area would be enhanced by common co-ordinated ratification of an international agreement by the EC member governments.[22] This time the resolution was transmitted to the EC's member governments and parliaments. Even so, it had no discernible effect: member governments felt neither legal nor moral obligations to respond positively to MEPs' resolutions.

During 1977, while continuing to press for stronger national and supranational action to suppress terrorism and to ensure that the perpetrators of terrorist offences in the EC be duly tried, the European Parliament began considering the wider aspects of terrorism. Its Political Affairs Committee studied terrorism and reported to Parliament on 14 November 1977.[23] On 11 October 1977, both the Socialist and Christian Democratic groups tabled motions for resolution on terrorism in the EC.[24] The two motions are interesting in that both go beyond restatement of concern that terrorists should be brought to account. Both embody the sixth element of EC action on terrorism by calling for EC arms control. The Socialists were concerned that anti-terrorist measures should be kept to a minimum; that traditional liberal democratic rights, values and practices should not be infringed by member governments; and that they should not be encouraged to introduce measures antithetical to them by the extent of the terrorist problem. Underlying this, of course, is anxiety that any terrorist claims, notably in the FRG, that the government itself was anti-democratic and a source of state violence against the individual, should not appear to be bolstered by the nature, scope, duration, provisions and application of anti-terrorist measures especially if these could be shown to violate basic constitutionally guarded civil liberties, freedoms and rights.

By contrast, the Christian Democratic, Liberal and Democratic and European Progressive Democratic motion emphasised the need for joint efforts in the EC 'to provide effective protection for all citizens and to safeguard democracy in the European Community'.[25] It stressed the need for further preventive measures to combat terrorism, expected the EC Council of Ministers to adopt measures to strengthen supranational co-operation in combating crimes of violence and terrorism in the EC,[26] and called upon it to encourage the conclusion of international agreements on anti-terrorist measures.[27] This was an allusion to the failure of all member states to ratify the European Convention on the Suppression of Terrorism; to the slow progress in the UN towards the conclusion of a Convention against the taking of hostages; and clearly expressed the conviction that the EC's members should be pressurised at the EC-level to take more positive, harmonised, and concerted action in international bodies seeking to combat terrorism.

The Christian Democratic, Liberal and European Progressive Democratic motion for resolution shared the Socialists' concern to condemn terrorism, but went further in outlining measures to supplement those already in force or under consideration. While the Socialists had also noted the need for EC action to control the sale of arms, the Christian Democratic, Liberal and European Progressive Democratic motion recommended that the Council of Ministers should consider the following:

(a) the setting up of a permanent conference of Ministers responsible for the internal security of the individual member states;
(b) the harmonisation of legal and administrative provisions on internal security;
(c) the harmonisation of identity card and registration measures;
(d) the harmonisation of arms legislation;
(e) the establishment of an integrated system of investigation within the Community;
(f) the extension of mutual legal assistance between the member states in the Community.[28]

Both motions for resolution were referred at the European Parliament's sitting of 12 October 1977 to the Political Affairs Committee which was instructed to report to the House at its November part-session. On 20 October 1977, Mr Fletcher-Cooke (European Conservative: United Kingdom) was appointed rapporteur. The Committee considered a motion for a resolution the same day, and adopted it unanimously on 2 November 1977. This motion embraced aspects of both the Christian Democratic, Liberal and European Progressive Democratic and Socialist motions, but was less specific than either in advocating new measures. No mention of arms control was made.[29] Why was a more dynamic role for the EC not advocated? Why was there no willingness to encourage the EC to take the lead in international efforts to combat terrorism? Had the Committee simply assumed that the political climate made such efforts impossible?

When Mr Fletcher-Cooke presented the Committee's report to the European Parliament on 15 November 1977, he admitted that the Political Affairs Committee had chosen deliberately to draft a short report devoid of novelty in the hope that this would guarantee that the report would 'gain the maximum degree of assent'.[30] Moreover, existing anti-terrorism conventions had yet to be used. The Committee also regarded the European Convention on the Suppression of Terrorism as the most significant of such conventions given its intention to ensure that terrorists should not be above the law, especially in view of the internationalisation of terrorism. Terrorism was to be regarded as a crime 'similar to, if not worse than, the old international crime of piracy',[31] and one that, like piracy, should be dealt with differently from other crimes.

Although EC Ministers of the Interior had discussed ratifying and using existing anti-terrorist instruments, they had not been successful in realising their objectives. The Political Affairs Committee, therefore, urged them to intensify their collaboration in concert with the Commission, and to enforce existing international anti-terrorist measures. This meant that the European Parliament was being advised to do no more than pressurise member governments in respect of existing conventions; and was, to some degree, an admission of defeat. Nevertheless, the resolution was welcomed at least as an expression of the EC's resolve to resist terrorism by constitutional means. MEPs also discussed improved co-ordination of police efforts to combat terrorism,[32] the creation of an international prison under international supervision[33] for the detention of terrorists and the suspension of EC trade agreements with third countries providing shelter to terrorists.[34]

The Commission and Council of Ministers spokesmen, however, advocated caution especially as member states had still to ratify the relevant existing conventions to ensure that their legal positions conformed with each other.[35]

The Commission, lacking the right to initiate proposals in this sphere, could do little more than support the Parliament and affirm the responsibilities of and possibilities for concerted member governments' actions. While some MEPs advocated a tough line towards terrorists, including the reintroduction of the death penalty,[36] others insisted that ultimately the fight against terrorism would be won 'by refusing to resort to emergency laws, and by rejecting the hysteria which cynical elements or unwitting proponents of chaos who exploit events seek to foster among the public in order to turn one nation against another at a European level'.[37] Calling for anti-Fascist measures to combat terrorism – a 'combination of security and tolerance, a national respect for truth, and a constant appeal for the unity of our citizens, enabling them to renew their faith in democracy and eradicate this evil which today threatens democracy itself in some of our countries and at a European level' – Mr Sandri (Communist: Italy) appealed, above all, for political co-operation to locate terrorist power centres and to establish the links between their financial backers and instigators.[38] For the Commission, Viscount Davignon indicated that the Commission urgently wanted the creation of a legal instrument to cover all the EC's member states, and advocated the ratification of all existing conventions to eliminate differences between the Nine.[39]

The resolution eventually adopted by MEPs did not appreciably advance EC-wide inter-governmental co-operation on combating terrorism. Bilateral co-operation continued, but supranational-level concertation and harmonisation seemed to depend on the commission of terrorist acts in the EC. Tragically, a stimulus for greater government co-operation on terrorism was given by the kidnapping in March 1978 of Aldo Moro, President of the Italian Christian Democratic Party.

On 17 March 1978, the European Parliament unanimously agreed to an all-party motion condemning the kidnapping of Aldo Moro.[40] This was followed by the EC Heads of Government meeting in Copenhagen at the European Council on 7-8 April which similarly condemned Mr Moro's kidnapping and declared solidarity with the Italian government and people.[41] The European Council adopted a declaration on combating terrorism and expressed concern lest increased terrorism undermine the functioning and principles of society in the EC. The European Council agreed to give high priority to intensified co-operation to defend the EC against terrorism; to conduct studies of the problems of terrorism, including the abuse of diplomatic bags;[42] and decided that the relevant Ministers should increase their mutual co-operation and submit their conclusions as soon as possible on the proposed creation of a European jurisdictional area.[43] Mr Fellermaier (Socialist: FRG) deplored the nebulousness of this term.[44] However, discussion of its implications was postponed until the ensuing debate on legal questions, although it was noted that aspects of an EC policy on terrorism may conflict with national laws regarding, for example, the search of houses and, therefore, not be acceptable to some states.[45]

During the debate on terrorism, Mr Sieglerschmidt (Socialist: FRG) advocated greater police liaison and a simplification of procedures to facilitate police co-operation.[46] Shortly thereafter, during Question Time, he raised the question of EC co-ordination of the sale and supply of arms by EC member states to countries which, others pointed out trained and financed terrorists. The Danish President-in-Office of the Council of Ministers, Mr Andersen, argued that a common arms procurement policy was not possible and evaded the question.[47] Over and above stating that the EC's Ministers of Justice had not met since 1974, Mr Andersen argued against the EC duplicating efforts of the Council of Europe and in favour of good contact and a sensible division of labour with it.[48] He did not, therefore, meet objections that a common jurisdictional/judicial area, first mooted by President Giscard d'Estaing, was intended simply to cover terrorism rather than criminal and civil law. Instead, he simply underlined the differences between the member states, implying that not only was harmonisation impossible but that it was not worth pursuing.

Moreover, similar arguments were advanced during the debate when the issue of special citizens' rights was discussed – again, to little effect.[49] However, what is clear is that by the spring of 1978, and following Moro's murder,[50] thinking – notably in the European Parliament – about EC action to combat terrorism had gone well beyond concern with the enforcement of a common undertaking to extradite terrorists, and encompassed the related issues concerning the search for and arrest of terrorist suspects, police liaison, arms supply, procurement and sales, the maintenance of EC citizens' democratic rights and a common judicial area. Indeed, in May, during Question Time, Commission President Jenkins agreed with the need for concerted action to combat terrorism in general and arms smuggling in particular. He assured the Parliament that if the Commission lacked the necessary power to take action, it would use its influence to persuade national governments to co-operate closely.[51]

The problem of arms control was to become a preoccupation of the European Parliament during the second half of 1978. This can be attributed both to the realisation that combating abuses in arms procurement, supply and sales was an essential facet of the attempt to curb terrorism, and to parallel developments in the Council of Europe where, on 28 June 1978, the Committee of Ministers presented the European Convention on the Control of and the Acquisition and Possession of Firearms by Individuals for signature (endorsed by the United Kingdom, Ireland, Denmark and the FRG).[52] While the Commission favoured EC action on this front, it was powerless and uncertain about the legal basis for any action over and above the co-operation, outside the EC's framework, of EC Ministers of the Interior which had begun in 1976.[53] Davignon hinted that Commission action might be possible if the Nine agreed that article 235 of the Rome Treaty should be the basis for action. Failing this, the Commission might have recourse to article 100, although action would be difficult to justify since this article concerned the approximation of laws in so far as it was necessary to the functioning of the common market. Article 36, which provides for member states to take measures restricting free trade on a number of grounds, including public policy ('ordre public'), public safety or security, could possibly be invoked. Even so, action in this area was difficult.

While it is true that the legal basis for Commission action in this sphere was open to dispute, the problem lay with the unwillingness of EC member governments to compromise their national provisions on this and other matters relating to terrorism in the name of EC harmony. Their failure even to endorse the European Convention on the Suppression of Terrorism led to further pressure in 1979 from the European Parliament, and notably from its directly elected MEPs. At the same time, some progress towards a common EC attitude on combating and prosecuting terrorists was achieved, after a great deal of haggling, by the EC's Ministers of Justice using greater leeway than the Council of Europe in the interpretation of what acts constituted political offences justifying a refusal to extradite providing the case was referred to the appropriate national authorities for prosecution. In addition, to overcome French objections, the member states supported a Belgian compromise to follow up French proposals for a common EC judicial or legal zone (un espace judiciare européenne) where, *inter alia*, anti-terrorist measures would be tightly enforced.[54] Henceforth, discussions about arms control, anti-terrorist measures based on EC accord regarding the extradition of terrorists, and the creation of a common judicial area proceeded *in tandem* with the broader and equally controversial debate concerning defence and a common arms procurement policy for the EC. This issue was complicated by the fact that not only was defence explicitly excluded from the Rome Treaty but Ireland was not a member of NATO, France had a special relationship with NATO, and the FRG's access to nuclear weaponry know-how remained contentious.

In 1979 and 1980, EC initiatives against terrorism reflected external stimuli and, as before, largely translated themselves into pressure from the European Parliament on the EC's member governments.

Following the murder of Lord Mountbatten in August 1979, the whole issue of terrorism and EC action to combat it was debated, often acrimoniously, at the September session of the European Parliament following the tabling of a question by Lady Elles on behalf of the European Democratic Group addressed to the Foreign Ministers concerning the nature of progress towards a common system of extradition.[55] Lady Elles noted that terrorist crimes invariably involved a cross-national element and, therefore, made EC harmonisation crucial. She advocated greater police co-operation, a common policy on extradition or prosecution and common extradition procedures; and noted that states seeking accession to the EC must be kept informed of the contents of any EC agreement on extradition (such as that under consideration at the time by the Nine) and apprised of their obligation to ratify it upon accession.[56]

Before debate on extradition and Lady Elles' remarks could proceed, Mr Skovmand of the Danish People's Movement against the EC tried to persuade the House against debating the issue on the grounds that it fell outside the EC's competence; that any EC agreement would infringe national sovereignty, and extend terrorist activity to those countries such as Denmark which, he asserted, did not suffer terrorism by virtue of their greater tolerance relative to their neighbours.[57] Mr Skovmand failed in his attempt. Mr Gendebien (a 'non-attached' Belgian MEP), alluding to the Council of Ministers' opinion of 30 July 1979 supporting the view that the issue fell outside Parliament's competence, argued that since the Council of Ministers had agreed to reply to Lady Elles' question, it recognised the Parliament's competence; that, moreover, Parliament was 'automatically competent in any matter discussed by the Council of Ministers'.[58]

Although MEPs agreed on condemning terrorism, they differed over the question of extradition for political offences. Lady Elles dismissed fears articulated about the treatment afforded suspects of political/ terrorist offences in different member states on the grounds that the Nine were signatories to the European Convention on Human Rights which, she maintained, represented a sufficient guarantee of offenders' rights.

Clearly, at the root of this issue was the question of respecting human rights guaranteed by either the European Convention or national constitutions or provisions and whether comparable guarantees existed in each member state. Since the EC had failed, in spite of pressure from the European Parliament, to promote a citizens' charter, the member states shared only commitment, in this respect, to the Convention. However, Lady Elles reminded the House that the whole legal basis of the EC as expressed in the EC Court of Justice was founded on the rule of law and recognition of the human rights and fundamental freedoms of EC citizens. Posing a rhetorical question, she asked how the living and working conditions of all the peoples in the EC could be constantly improved as stated in the Rome Treaty's preamble if people lived in a state of terrorism and instability caused by terrorism.[59]

The main body of the debate focused on the question of establishing and securing EC acceptance of the principle of 'extradite or try'. Replying to Lady Elles' question, Mr Andrews, the Irish President-in-Office of the Foreign Ministers, explained that the Nine were considering measures to intensify co-operation among themselves in a number of areas of criminal law, including extradition. In accordance with under-standings reached at the fifth, sixth and seventh European Councils, a group of senior officials had contemplated two measures to this end. The first was an agreement between the member states to apply the European Convention on the Suppression of Terrorism; the second, a draft convention on co-operation in criminal matters between the Nine and studied in the context of proposals for the creation of an 'espace judiciare européenne'. He explained that the aim of the former was to apply the European Convention on the Suppression of Terrorism within the EC by regulating each member state's position while taking into account whether or not a member state had signed or ratified the Con-vention, and whether or not a state had made or intended making a reservation to the Convention. This was to be accomplished in such a way as to avoid infringing any member state's constitutional require-ments.

The draft convention on co-operation in criminal matters is, similarly, mainly concerned with extradition and applies to 'terrorist-type offences' and 'a broad range of offences of a certain gravity'.[60] Its objectives are to require member states to submit cases to their competent authorities for prosecution in certain circumstances where extradition has been refused, and to ensure that they have the jurisdic-tional competence for this; and to establish simplified procedures. The draft is considered as but a first step in the creation of 'un espace judiciare européenne'.[61]

When MEPs debated the issues raised by Lady Elles' question and Mr Andrews' reply, not only were exchanges between Irish and Northern Irish MEPs particularly acrimonious, but many MEPs clearly doubted whether either the European Convention on the Suppression of Terrorism or the draft EC agreement on its application in the Nine could be effective instruments against terrorism given the number of reservations expressed by individual member states.[62]

Most MEPs were primarily concerned with measures to combat terrorism although some raised the question of dealing with the causes of terrorism. In spite of their reservations that extradition was but a partial step towards accomplishing this, and that any EC agree-ment concerning the principle of 'extradite or try' might be tantamount simply to a modification of the basic notions behind the European Con-vention on the Suppression of Terrorism making them compatible with the most restrictive provisions of individual constitutional require-ments, they endorsed current efforts to deal with the problem notably by political as opposed to repressive means.[63]

Such objections notwithstanding, the Nine — having established a group of legal experts to draft a criminal convention as a first step in establishing (un espace judiciare européenne)[64] finalised their first efforts to agree on the application of a common policy on the extradition of terrorists in the EC. Following the Dublin European Council in November 1979, the EC Ministers of Justice endorsed an agreement[65] to apply the broad terms of the European Convention on the Suppression of Terrorism to the EC. The agreement must be, and remains to be, ratified by all the nine (as there then were) EC member states before it can come into force (article 6(2)) as the agreement, issued from political co-operation arrangements rather than from normal decision making processes under the Rome Treaty, does in fact provide a legal basis for action on terrorism and is therefore controversial. Various articles may provide such a foundation, and include article 48 *et sequentia* on the Free Movement of Persons. Some have argued that all such agreements could, and indeed *should*,[66] be based upon the Rome Treaty, by the use of article 235 which provides that:

If action by the Community should prove necessary to attain, in the course of the operation of the common market, one of the objectives of the Community and this Treaty has not provided the necessary powers, the Council shall, acting unanimously on a proposal from the Commission and after consulting the Assembly, take the appropriate measures.

By acting on the basis of a Treaty article, agreements by member governments' ministers, such as the Dublin Agreement, would derive their binding force from European Community law, rather than from general international law as is the case with the Dublin Agreement. Without this, however, the force of such agreements derives from general international law.[67] As such the Dublin Agreement represents an unusual and interesting experiment. In essence, the EC member states agreed to apply the ECST among themselves notwithstanding the fact that a number of the member states are not parties to it (for example, France, Italy, Luxembourg, Belgium and the Netherlands) and that Ireland has not even signed it.

The agreement works in two main ways. First, EC member states accept that in extradition proceedings between two member states the European Convention will apply in full (i.e. without reservation) *even if* one or both of the states are not party to it, or if one or both have made the 'political defence' reservation permitted by article 13 (see above). Secondly, the agreement seeks to restrict still further the effect between EC member states of such reservations. Hence, where member states party to the European Convention have made 'article 13' reservations, those reservations will not apply in extradition proceedings between EC member states unless a further declaration to that effect is made under article 3 of the agreement (addressed to the Department of Foreign Affairs of Ireland, with whom instruments of ratification etc. must be deposited). Also under article 3 those member states that are not party to the European Convention because they have not signed it (e.g. Ireland), or have signed it but not yet ratified it, are required to indicate by declaration if they wish to retain the 'political defence' in extradition proceedings between EC member states. So far Italy, France and Denmark have made declarations under article 3.

Since November 1979, MEPs' efforts to combat terrorism have again been largely responses to terrorist incidents, and especially to the worsening situation in Northern Ireland. Significantly, at its April 1980 session, the European Parliament called upon the Commission and Council to offer such assistance as appropriate to defuse the situation in Northern Ireland, and politicians in the United Kingdom also called on the British government to consider whether EC intervention might not help to realise a settlement.

Conclusion

Since the summer of 1979, the European Parliament's concern with terrorism and MEPs' motions on the topic have related to three main areas. First, the continuing debate both on EC action to combat terrorism and to provide for a common system of extradition. Secondly, MEPs' preoccupation with the creation of a European judicial area. Thirdly, repeated motions condemning the occupation of the US embassy in Teheran by Iranian students, advocating EC action to pressurise, in full consultation with the USA and other NATO members, Iran to release the American hostages, and calling upon EC member governments to contemplate the suspension of diplomatic relations between Iran and the EC's members. This third issue illustrated more graphically, perhaps, than the others the manifold problems besetting any EC action to combat or respond to terrorism. MEPs themselves could do little more than call upon the EC's Foreign Ministers acting within the framework of political co-operation (that is, on an intergovernmental rather than supranational basis) to concert their responses and to formulate a common policy.[68]

The other areas, however, also showed how EC action could be stymied by recalcitrant governments, or by members wanting to exploit the issue in order to gain leverage on other, non-related, issues. It would, moreover, be erroneous to suppose that MEPs universally welcomed the Dublin Agreement on the Suppression of Terrorism. While many MEPs favoured the Agreement and called on the Nine's parliaments and governments to ratify it forthwith,[69] others were anxious lest the Agreement endanger rather than safeguard democracy in the EC.[70] The latter felt it ended the right of asylum, and opposed what they saw as the 'implicit disappearance of this fundamental freedom'. They considered it 'unacceptable that under the guise of a European judicial area a repressive Europe should be built up', condemned 'this retrograde step in respect of human rights', and invited the Nine's governments 'to make use of the declaration . . . under Article 3 of the Agreement activating the reservation mentioned in Article 13 of the European Convention [providing] for protection at law to be restored in political cases'.[71] The same group of MEPs had already expressed fears in September 1979 about the establishment of a European judicial area by means of a common system of extradition. They felt that it would 'reduce the degree of discretion left to judges',[72] endanger democracy by providing for greater state power, and so play into the hands of terrorists arguing that the state wielded excessive, illegitimate and increasingly repressive authority.[73]

Clearly, many MEPs felt it essential to guard against the possibility that states might abuse anti-terrorist legislation.

Interestingly, also, the question of a European legal area and the Dublin Agreement surfaced in another guise when MEPs discussed and affirmed the need for a minimum EC standard regarding compensation to victims of acts of violence. As in the case of action to suppress terrorism, inspiration was drawn from the Council of Europe. What MEPs wished to ensure was that reciprocity in compensation awards existed among EC states, and that individuals should not be denied compensation because such reciprocity did not exist or because compensation is awarded in their own country only if the crime occurred on national territory. Moreover, there are widely divergent practices. In Italy, for example, compensation provisions are governed partly by regional laws and, for victims of terrorism, by another law.[74] While the question of compensation for victims of terrorism is obviously relevant to MEPs' deliberations, their concern stemmed from the spate of disparate and relatively new pieces of national legislation introduced by some member governments. These, it was argued, were discriminatory and, therefore, neglected the Rome Treaty's articles prohibiting discrimination on the grounds of nationality (article 7) and guaranteeing freedom of movement (articles 48, 52 and 59). The principle at issue was to ensure that the possible benefits of new laws were not restricted to nationals of a given member state in areas related or subject to EC action.

What is becoming increasingly apparent is that by attempting to adopt a common position on combating terrorism, additional areas have been opened for scrutiny, some of which can and should be dealt with via normal Commission-Council decision making processes, others of which require deliberate acts of intergovernmental co-operation within or outside existing intergovernmental bargaining arrangements such as the European Councils (summits), and Conference of Foreign Ministers meeting in political co-operation.

Notes

1. European Treaty Series, no. 90.
2. See M.O. Hudson (ed.), *International Legislation,* 9 vols. (Carnegie Endowment for International Peace, Washington DC, 1931-50), vol. 7, pp. 862, 865. For a brief review of attempts by the international community to control terrorism, see R.A. Friedlander, 'Terrorism and International Law: What is Being Done?', *Rutgers Camden Law Journal*, vol. 8 (1977), pp. 383-92.
3. For a detailed discussion of state practice in relation to political offenders, see I.A. Shearer, *Extradition in International Law* (Manchester University Press, Manchester, 1971) pp. 166-93 and M.C. Bassiouni, *International Extradition and World Public Order* (Sijthoff/Ocean, Leyden/Dobbs Ferry, 1974) pp. 368-426. For a general discussion of extradition in the context of the ECST, see D. Freestone, 'Legal Responses to Terrorism: Towards European Cooperation?' in J. Lodge (ed.), *Terrorism: A Challenge to the State* (Martin Robertson, Oxford, 1981) pp. 199-210.
4. European Treaty Series, no. 24. The Convention came into force on 18 April 1960. On 1 March 1981 it had been ratified by 14 members of the Council of Europe. The United Kingdom is not a signatory. Israel and Finland are also parties.
5. Hudson, *International Legislation* and Friedlander, 'Terrorism and International Law'.
6. Note, for example, the classic case of *re Castioni* [1891] 1 Queen's Bench (QB) 149; *re Meunier* [1894] 2 QB 415. More recently, see *Cheng* v. *Governor of Pentonville Prison* [1973] Appeal Cases (AC) 931 and (in relation to Ireland) *R.* v. *Governor of Winson Green Prison, ex parte Littlejohn* [1975] 3 All England Reports (All ER) 208.
7. Listed offences are, by article 1:

(a) an offence within the scope of the Convention for the Suppression of Unlawful Seizure of Aircraft, signed at The Hague on 16 December 1970;

(b)   an offence within the scope of the Convention for the Suppression of Unlawful Acts against the Safety of Civil Aviation, signed at Montreal on 23 September 1971,

(c)   a serious offence involving an attack against the life, physical integrity or liberty of internationally protected persons, including diplomatic agents;

(d)   an offence involving kidnapping, the taking of a hostage or serious unlawful detention;

(e)   an offence involving the use of a bomb, grenade, rocket, automatic firearm or letter or parcel bomb if this use endangers persons;

(f)   an attempt to commit any of the foregoing offences or participation as an accomplice of a person who commits or attempts to commit such an offence.

In addition, by article 2, a Contracting State may decide not to regard as a political offence or as an offence connected with a political offence or as an offence inspired by political motives a serious offence involving an act of violence, other than one covered by article 1, against the life, physical integrity or liberty of a person; or a serious offence involving an act against property, other than one covered by article 1, if the act created a collective danger for persons.

8. See J.J.A. Salmon, 'La Convention européenne pour la repression du terrorisme: un vrai pas en arrière', *Journal des Tribunaux* (24 September 1977), p. 497 and G. Soulier, 'European Integration and the Suppression of Terrorism', *Review of Contemporary Law* no. 2 (1978), pp. 21-45.

9. The English courts, for example, have been very unwilling to do this in the past. See *Government of Greece* v. *Governor of Brixton Prison* [1971] AC 250; *Atkinson* v. *USA Government* [1969] 3 All ER 208.

10. P. Wilkinson, 'Problems of Establishing a European Judicial Area', (AS/Pol/Coll/Terr (32) 16), report to *Conference on Democracy against Terrorism in Europe: Tasks and Problems* (Strasbourg, 12-14 November 1980) p. 4.

11. Article 13(3). But note that the United Kingdom has indicated that it does not intend to invoke such a right.

12. Article 6. The implications of this provision are complex. The United Kingdom implementing legislation, Suppression of Terrorism Act, 1978, c.26, s.4, extends 'territorial' jurisdiction to the territories of all the contracting states. For a more detailed discussion of this, see Freestone, 'Legal Responses to Terrorism', pp. 201ff.

13. Article 10. Note that the ECST also provides for the widest measure of 'mutual assistance in criminal matters' relating to offences under articles 1 and 2 (article 8). This too is subject to the same political exclusion as extradition. Norway has made such a reservation, and Italy has declared its intention to reserve the right to refuse assistance in relation to 'political offences'.

14. The Convention came into force on 4 August 1978. On 1 March 1981 it had been signed by all the member states of the Council of Europe except Malta and Ireland. Parties (with dates of ratification) are: Austria (11 August 1977); Cyprus (26 February 1979); Denmark (27 June 1978); FRG (3 May 1978); Iceland (2 July 1980); Liechtenstein (13 June 1979); Norway (10 January 1980); Spain (20 May 1980); Sweden (15 September 1977); United Kingdom (24 July 1978).

15. As a result of an Anglo-Irish Commission that reported in May 1974 (HMSO, Cmnd 5627). See A. McCall-Smith and P. Magee, 'The Anglo-Irish Law Enforcement Report in Historical and Political Context' *Criminal Law Review* [1975], p. 200. Implemented by Criminal Law Act, 1976, no. 14 (Eire) and

Criminal Law Jurisdiction Act, 1975, c.59 (UK).

16. *Guardian*, 6 October 1979. For comment, see J. Kelly, 'Problems of Establishing a European Judicial Area', (AS/Pol/Coll/Terr (32)8, report to *Conference on Democracy*, p. 7.

17. Kelly, 'Problems', p. 4.

18. *Guardian*, 10 June 1981.

19. A.E.Evans, 'The Apprehension and Prosecution of Offenders: Some Current Problems' in A.E. Evans and J.F. Murphy, *Legal Aspects of International Terrorism* (Lexington Books, Lexington, Mass., 1978), p. 499.

20. *European Parliament Working Documents*, 222/76 (6 July 1976): Motion for a resolution tabled by Mr Aigner, Mr Behrendt, Mr Berkhouwer, Mr Bersani, Mr Blumenfeld, Mr Boano, Lord Castle, Mr Cousté, Lord Gladwyn, Mr Lange, Mr de la Malène Mr Normanton and Mr Patijn with a request for debate by urgent procedure pursuant to Rule 14 of the Rules of Procedure on measures to combat international terrorism: PE 45.394.

21. *Debates of the European Parliament* (DEP), no. 211 (January 1977), pp. 188, pp. 203-5.

22. *European Parliament Working Documents*, 513/76 (13 January 1977): Motion for resolution tabled by Mr Fellermaier on behalf of the Socialist Group, Mr Bertrand on behalf of the Christian Democratic Group, Mr Durieux on behalf of the Liberal and Democratic Group, Mr Cointat on behalf of the Group of European Progressive Democrats, Sir Peter Kirk on behalf of the European Conservative Group, Mr Sandri on behalf of the Communist and Allies Group with request for debate by urgent procedure pursuant to Rule 14 of the Rules of Procedure on the European Convention on the Suppression of Terrorism: PE 47.528.

23. *European Parliament Working Documents*, 372/77 (14 November 1977): Report drawn up on behalf of the Political Affairs Committee on acts of terrorism in the Community: PE 50.974/fin.

24. *European Parliament Working Documents*, 327/77 rev. (11 October 1977) and 328/77 rev. (11 October 1977) respectively.

25. *European Parliament Working Documents*, 328/77 rev. PE 50.777/rev. (11 October 1977) Clause 5, p. 2.

26. Ibid., Clause 6.

27. Ibid., Clause 8.

28. Ibid., Clause 7.

29. *European Parliament Working Documents*, 372/77 (14 November 1977) p. 5.

30. *DEP*, no. 223 (15 November 1977), p. 67.

31. Ibid., p. 68.

32. Ibid., p. 72.

33. Ibid., p. 73. This was done with German war criminals after 1945.

34. Ibid., p. 70.

35. *The Sittings* (November 1977), p. 9.

36. *DEP*, no. 223 (November 1978), pp. 79, 86.

37. Ibid., p. 80.

38. Ibid.

39. Ibid., p. 86.

40. Ibid. (March 1978), p. 23.

41. *European Parliament Working Documents*, 50/78 (10 April 1978).

42. *The Sittings*, no. 9 (November 1978), p. 15 gives a summary of Tam Dalyell's question about this.

43. See *DEP*, no. 229 (April 1978), p. 115. This was the second time that the European Council had mentioned a 'jurisdictional area'.

44. Ibid., p. 120.

45. Ibid., pp. 142-3.

46. Ibid., p. 139.

47. Ibid., pp. 149-52.

48. Ibid., pp. 164-5.

49. Ibid. Also see, *The Sittings* (April 1978), p. 15.

50. For a summary of Parliament's tributes to Moro, see *The Sittings* (May 1978), p. 15.

51. Ibid., pp. 15, 20.

52. *European Parliament Working Documents*, 284/78 (31 August 1978): Oral Question 0-41/78: PE 54.137.

53. *The Sittings* (September 1978), p. 5.

54. *Financial Times*, 11 October 1978.

55. *European Parliament Working Documents*, 1-288/79 (12 September 1979): Oral Question O-19/79: PE 59.182.

56. *DEP*, no. 245 (September 1979), pp. 170-1.

57. Ibid., p. 172.

58. Ibid., p. 182.

59. Ibid., p. 172.

60. Ibid., p. 173.

61. Ibid.

62. Ibid., pp. 179-80.

63. *Bull:EC* 9-1979, point 2.3.15.

64. *The Week*, 12-16 November 1979, p. 14. Also see the *Annual Report to Parliament on Political Cooperation* presented on 24 October 1979 by Mr O'Kennedy, Chairman of the Conference of Foreign Ministers of the Member States meeting in political co-operation, in *Bull: EC* 10-1979, point 3.4.1., p. 137.

65. For text, see HMSO, Cmnd 7823.

66. See I.E.Schwartz, 'Article 235 and the Law Making Powers in the European Community', *International and Comparative Law Quarterly*, vol. 27 (1978), pp. 614-28.

67. For a full discussion of the legal status of decisions and agreements adopted by the Representatives of EC Member States, see H.G. Schermers, *Judicial Protection in the EC* 2nd edn (Kluwer, Deventer, The Netherlands, 1979) pp. 126-8, and sources cited there.

68. See the motion for a resolution tabled on 15 April 1980 on behalf of the European Democratic Group, European People's Party and the Liberal and Democratic Group on the plight of the Americans held captive in Teheran, *European Parliament Working Documents*, 1-89/80/rev. II (15 April 1980).

69. See *European Parliament Working Documents*, 1-603/79 (14 December 1979).

70. See *European Parliament Working Documents*, 1-593/79 (12 December 1979).

71. Ibid.

72. See *European Parliament Working Documents*, 1/370/79/rev. (27 September 1979).

73. For example, statement on 27 May 1981 by Mr Vandemeulebroucke (MEP) urging the European Parliament to ask the Council to what extent it intended to follow the resolution adopted by the European Parliament in its May session (9 May, after the death of Bobby Sands the H-block hunger striker). Although he urged a European solution to the Northern Irish problems he questioned the compatibility of the European legal area proposals with such a solution. See *Agence Europe*, 28 May 1981.

74. Report drawn up on behalf of the Legal Affairs Committee on compensation for victims of acts of violence, *European Parliament Working Documents*, 1-464/80 (13 October 1980). This details the various provisions, pp. 9ff.

5 THE RED BRIGADES AND THE ITALIAN POLITICAL TRADITION*

Richard Drake

Swift's assertion, that 'Language is the archive of history' illuminates the historical meaning of a salient linguistic development in Italy during the past decade, the addition of a new word to the Italian language: *bierre*. The word is formed by pronouncing the letters 'br', for *brigatisti rossi* or Red Brigades, and it signifies a shocking new concatenation of violence and ideology, producing gruesome consequences for a thoroughly traumatised society. From 1969, the year of the Piazza Fontana massacre in Milan, to 1980 there have been 12,690 episodes of left- and right wing terrorist violence in Italy: 362 people have been killed; 4,524 have been wounded.[1] In no other contemporary European society have so many people been maimed and killed as sacrificial victims to the tyranny of both left- and right-wing ideology.[2] However, on the whole in recent years the left has been perceived as the greater threat to Italian democracy, with the Red Brigades generating the most notoriety of all the left terrorist groups.[3]

Some pressing questions arise here. Where does Red Brigadism come from? Who are its exponents and who supports them? What do they hope to achieve and at whose expense? Since we are only in the midst of this bloody progression and there is no science of the future, the definitive study of the Red Brigades must wait upon events. Nevertheless, even now it is possible and necessary for historians to look at the terror unfolding in Italy from a perspective uniquely their own; certainly not to demonstrate the utility of history in an obviously practical way, as Clio's Merlin waving a magic wand over events, but rather to suggest that politics, like history, is process, or to use Fernand Braudel's phrase 'slow but perceptible rhythms', as well as personalities, events and immediate economic forces, or *histoire événementielle*.[4] In other words, the past imposes a set of possibilities on the present, which, in certain revolutionary situations may not be adequate for the political needs of the moment. Still, whatever is new in the political equation only comes into existence in conflict with the old, making tradition, i.e. history, indispensable in political analysis, and it is the absence of this historical perspective that makes so much of the writing on the Red Brigades positively misleading.

Americans have an especially difficult time grasping what to them are the peculiar nuances of Europe's heavily ideological political tradition, and this difficulty exists for reasons pointed out by Richard Hofstadter more than thirty years ago in *The American Political Tradition*. In this book Hofstadter argued that American political life has been and remains essentially the struggle between two competing forms of liberalism. Federalists and Jeffersonian Democratic-Republicans, Whigs and Jacksonian Democrats, Republicans and modern-day Democrats have contested elections more or less peaceably — save for the grisly exception of the Civil War — within the liberal tradition. Americans have divided over political issues, not over political ideologies. There has been a remarkable ideological consensus of 'shared convictions' in the American political tradition, and few leaders or spokesmen of national prominence have arisen to question the liberal fundamentals of the country's system.[5] Freedom of the individual, freedom of association, equality before the law, consent of the governed and intellectual freedom are not the issues in American politics, as they all too frequently are in Europe; they are, to a degree seldom realised anywhere else, the accepted ends of political discourse.

It would be a crude error for us to draw smug conclusions from these facts, however. As Maurice Merleau-Ponty tellingly remarked, at about the same time that Hofstadter was explaining the American political tradition, liberalism cannot be judged solely by the ideas it espouses, at least not while recollections of genocidal policies towards American Indians and the lynching of untold numbers of black people remain vivid in the historical memory.[6] Yet on the level of ideas, where ideology operates, American politics traditionally have become vitriolic at the point when people begin to argue over how liberal ends should be achieved and, more precisely, what the role of the federal government should be in this process. The bitter struggle in Washington's administration between Alexander Hamilton and Thomas Jefferson over the National Bank was a prophetic symbol of the country's political course. It surely would be excessive to argue that both of those men would feel comfortable in American politics today, but they would recognise the present system as a direct consequence of what has gone before.

The European political tradition generally and the Italian political tradition in particular possess very different characteristics. America effectively missed feudalism whereas the modern European political tradition arose as a response to feudalism. If the American Revolution was less violent and bloody than the French Revolution, it was because the French revolutionists had more numerous and forbidding obstacles to overcome. Whereas the American revolutionists opposed a tax system of recent origin, their French counterparts had to grapple with the root and branch of a social and cultural hegemony that was a thousand years in the making. The kinetic force of a millennium of history is not easily redirected, let alone stopped. The Declaration of the Rights of Man and Citizen was a death sentence on the feudal system of France, but to implement the declaration a generation of Frenchmen suffered and caused the world to suffer the destruction of war, only to have those lofty sentiments bloodily perverted by Robespierre in the Terror and systematically caricatured by Bonaparte in the Empire. Other Europeans did not even have benefit of the caricature, and in the end the peoples of Spain, Italy and Germany revolted against their French oppressors. The modern Italian political tradition begins with this revolt.

Here, too, I think, are to be found the origins of Italy's modern political torment, of which the most recent infliction has been Red Brigade violence. First, however, some brief remarks about the Red Brigade phenomenon itself, what Braudel calls 'the history of events: surface disturbances, crests of foam that the tides of history carry on their strong backs'.[7]

I

In a land where geometric progression appears to be an axiom of politics, the Red Brigades constitute only one of 597 terrorist groups of both the left and right.[8] This particular left-wing terrorist group achieved an eminence in Italy and in the outside world because it abducted and killed a former prime minister. The March 1978 'Black Thursday Massacre', ending in the murder of Aldo Moro, was an unsurpassed public relations triumph, and today when the world thinks of Italian terrorism it thinks primarily of the Red Brigades.[9]

Moro's murder woke up the world to something of which Italy had long been painfully aware. The Red Brigade movement evolved out of the Metropolitan Collective of Milan, an organisation founded on 8 September 1969 by dissident student and worker groups: Renato Curcio was the leader of the students; Corrado Simioni and Franco Troiano represented the workers. Curcio seems to have enjoyed precedence almost from the beginning. On 20 October 1970 their *Foglio di lotta di sinistra proletaria* announced the creation of the Red Brigades: 'Against the institutions that administer our exploitation, against the laws and the justice of the bosses, the most decisive and conscious part of the proletariat in struggle has already begun to fight for the construction of a new legality, a new power.'[10] They defined themselves as 'autonomous worker organisations (*Brigate Rosse*) that indicate the first moments of proletarian self-organisation to fight the bosses and their henchmen on their terrain with the same means that they utilise against the working class . . .'[11]

Other Red Brigade manifestoes and propaganda statements soon followed under the sign of the five-pointed red star, always with a vociferous call for revolution, a vehement rejection of reformism in the Italian Communist party (PCI) and a dire warning about the imminence of a right-wing coup (*un golpe bianco*) led by the more conservative elements of the Christian Democratic party (DC) in alliance with the extreme right-wing Movimento Sociale Italiano (MSI) at the behest of the 'superpadroni imperialisti', Nixon and Kissinger.[12] Their first violent attacks, beginning with the firebombing of cars and theatres and with armed robberies – called 'proletarian expropriations' for the financing of revolution – occurred in November and December 1970; their first kidnapping, on 3 March 1972, of Idalgo Macchiarini a director at Sit-Siemens. Prior to blowing himself to bits on 15 March 1972 on a terrorist raid in Segrate, near Milan, the outlandish millionaire publisher, Giangiacomo Feltrinelli, helped to finance the Red Brigades, and he influenced them by his personal example as well.[13] None the less, up to this point the activities of the Red Brigades, including those of the recently established Rome branch, amounted to a totally ineffective campaign to convert the masses to revolutionary Marxism through a series of audacious acts. Curcio's followers remained isolated and uninfluential, seemingly a piece of ideological flotsam left over from the euphoria of *sessantottismo*, or the existential utopianism that had been the special intellectual product of Berkeley and Paris in the late 1960s.

Only in 1973 did the Red Brigades begin to attract concerned and widespread attention. Even before then the Communist Party had begun to move towards the 'historic compromise' with the Christian Democrats, but in the autumn of that year a policy of accommodation tending towards collaboration was openly announced. In a series of sensational articles, published in *Rinascita* from 28 September to 12 October 1973, Communist Party leader Enrico Berlinguer made it clear that the PCI believed in class collaboration. The working class, he claimed, could not triumph without the help of other classes. Political isolation had been the fatal mistake of Italian Socialists in 1922 and, incidentally, of Chilean Communists in 1973. Berlinguer's ideas crystallised around the party's new theme of complete independence from Moscow in search of 'the democratic way to socialism' by means of 'a strategy of reform'. Therefore, the party would work with all 'popular forces', including Catholics as well as Socialists.[14]

The Red Brigades had already rejected this position out of hand, in a January 1973 theoretical statement, published in *Potere operaio* on 11 March of that year, claiming that the party was following 'a strategy exactly opposed to ours'.[15] A furious propaganda war broke out on the left, with extremist groups, such as the Red Brigades, picking up added support or, at least, tolerance from Communists who expressed disenchantment with their party's moderation. Many Communists — mostly of the younger generation — were left ideologically homeless by the revisionist shifts within the PCI. Among such disillusioned leftists the Red Brigades would find both recruits and a sympathetic audience.

Meanwhile, social and economic factors contributed massively to the further radicalisation of Italian politics. The migration from countryside to city and from south to north continued at a prodigious rate (8.3 million from 1951 to1971), far faster than industrial growth, leaving an enormous and constantly widening gap between the job rate and the need for employment, with 300,000 unemployed in Naples alone.[16] The double effect of this epic migration has been to injure Italian agriculture seriously and to create an enormous *lumpenproletariat* in the cities. Thus, the Italians suffer from the worst of all possible situations for an industrial power — an economy totally dependent upon imported oil, iron and coal together with a growing dependence upon imported grain. As Alberto Ronchey noted in a 1973 book, *Atlante ideologico*, the Italian solution to the problem of modernisation has left the countryside dangerously depopulated, the cities tremendously overpopulated, with the net result that Italy, more than most of her neighbours, is darkened by 'the eclipse of Europe'.[17]

At the same time the country's university system collapsed under the weight of more than one million students, three times the number enrolled in British universities and financed by a national budget less than the amount spent on the University of California system alone.[18] Unemployment and underemployment are chronic problems for these students, and the cost of their instruction has been estimated to be 1,075,000 lire per year for every student, prompting the philosopher of science, Francesco Barone, to observe that: 'Socially, therefore, an enormous machine is constructed to produce nothing or, worse, desperation.'[19] Many of these students are not willing to lead lives of quiet desperation. The historian, Rosario Romeo, has described the 'young proletarian committees' at the University of Milan: 'They occupied the university, stopped all teaching and research, and went on a rampage, destroying books, documents, scientific instruments, as well as wrecking the premises.' When the rector was asked why the police were not called in, he replied that to have done so would have provoked 'more serious incidents which might have included loss of life'.[20]

The case of Walter Alasia, a Red Brigadist killed on 15 December 1976 by the police in Sesto San Giovanni (known as the Italian Stalingrad), has become a classic illustration of what Sabino Acquaviva and M. Santuccio describe in *The Social Structure of Italy* as the tragedy of Italian education: 'People come to the end of their studies equipped with an out-of-date culture that proves an anomaly in the society in which they have to earn their living.'[21] Actually, Alasia, the son of nominal PCI parents, did not live long enough to experience this disillusionment. He was a student at the neighbourhood Istituto Tecnico Industriale Statale, once a prestigious technical school whose graduates seldom failed to obtain lucrative jobs, but by the early 1970s ITIS was paralysed by the open admissions rot that afflicted Italian universities generally. Now everyone had to be let in, but as a rule no one, with a mind sullied by the rudiments of education, could be let out. Those who did persevere made progress in spite of the system rather than because of it, and certainly in Alasia's case, as his biographer, Giorgio Manzini, remarks, the school 'became a factory of malaise, of desperate frustration'.[22] Alasia and other radical students at ITIS, alienated by the reformist tendencies of the PCI and inspired by Lotta continua, Potere operaio, Avanguardia operaia and other dissident groups promoting the myth of revolution on the extraparliamentary left, made up lists of proscribed teachers, i.e. those elitists who were hard graders. The angry revolutionaries disrupted the school by running through the halls during classtime with megaphones, inciting other students to overthrow the reactionary educational system. When Alasia and his cohorts did deign to attend a class it was only to provoke the teacher, either by turning their backs on him or by moving their chairs out into the hallway, chanting revolutionary slogans as they left. ITIS and Alasia are microcosms of Italy's educational disaster, amply justifying Ronchey's images of the entire system as 'an anthropological parking lot',' a 'reservation for Metropolitan Indians' and, more ominously, 'a sanctuary for guerrillas'.[23]

A constantly expanding economy would have enabled the Italians to meet the challenges of migration and education, but beginning with the 'hot autumn' of 1969 Italy entered a new era of bitter labour strife, characterised by an ever increasing number of strikes and lost man-hours.[24] The generally weak economy of the early 1970s became severely enfeebled in the mid-1970s. Violent inflation and deepening recession, exacerbated by the oil crisis of 1973, thoroughly transformed Italy's economic miracle from a reality to a distant and embittering memory. The progress of the 1950s and 1960s had led to ever rising expectations for continued economic betterment in Italy. When the decline began, it occurred while Italy was only in the middle of indus-trialising its society; the timing could not have been worse, and the Italians were suspended between backwardness and modernity.[25]

It was against this background of economic and social disintegration that a new form of terrorism enigmatically appeared, making Italian life, in the words of Morris West, 'a series of sinister absurdities punctu-ated by moments of pure horror'.[26] There were 467 terrorist attacks in 1975, 685 in 1976, 1,806 in 1977, 2,725 in 1978, 2,139 in 1979 and 833 in 1980.[27] The sharp decline in 1980 is deceptive because in that twelve-month period more people were killed by terrorists, 135, than in any previous year; until then the annual record for terrorist deaths was 38, in 1978.[28] The terrorist strategy was to strike at the head of the establishment by eliminating 'eminent personages'. Estimates about the number of actual combatants vary, but 3,000 is a common figure, roughly equivalent to the number of Italian partisans who fought from September 1943 to March 1944.[29] Moreover, the number of Italians sympathetic to the terrorist movement is shockingly large, especially in the huge and directionless university world.[30]

As the Italian social and economic crisis worsened in the mid-1970s the terrorist organisations of the left, notably the Red Brigades, became bolder and more confident in their attempts to detach the working class from the existing system. In so doing the terrorists moved into the vacuum created by the reformist tendencies of the PCI. When, on 18 April 1974, the Red Brigades kidnapped Judge Mario Sossi in Genova, the writer, Leonardo Sciascia, reasoned: 'the action of the Red Brigades has been understood and explained in every way except the most obvious one, and that is as a means of preparing and of beginning to make a revolution'.[31] He also suggested how the point of departure for the terrorists was the realisation that the official left actually did not want a revolution, that it long ago had become a posturing and hypocritical part of a system it only pretended to condemn.

More than anything, however, the escalation of terrorist violence revealed the alarming impotence of the Italian state. Indro Montanelli's blistering indictment of 'how all state defence services are blind and deaf' did not appear to be excessive.[32] Many examples could be cited here, but one will do. Late in 1974 Curcio, public enemy number one, was captured and incarcerated in the country's most dilapidated prison, in Casale, at complete liberty to go anywhere on the institution's premises, to make unlimited telephone calls outside and to have full and unregulated visitation rights. The journalist, Giorgio Bocca, observed, 'More than a prisoner, Curcio resembled a terrorist on sabbatical.'[33] The parallel between this case and that of Hitler following the Munich beer hall *putsch* is striking, but Curcio did not stay in jail long enough to write a contemporary Italian left-winger's version of *Mein Kampf*. On 18 February 1975 his wife, Mara Cagol, and three other Red Brigadists walked into the prison, overwhelmed 17 guards without incident, and spirited Curcio away.[34] Unfortunately, this *opera buffa* episode is not typical of the relationship between the Italian government and the Red Brigades; the government's inability to cope with the problem of terrorism more often leads to violence and death.

Scarcely less pitiable have been the attempts of the PCI to deal with terrorism or, until quite recently, even to recognise the Red Brigades as a problem of the left.[35] From 1972 to 1977 the Communist press tended to dismiss the Red Brigades as an extension of the *trama nera*, or Fascist conspiratorial network. The *agent provocateur* is a stock figure on the Italian political stage, and 'Away, away servants of the CIA' long passed for analysis of the Red Brigade problem. If the official PCI position was dismissive, a large portion of the left charitably regarded the Red Brigades as 'comrades who erred', but perhaps less than the party now that it was enmeshed in the toils of the Christian Democratic Party through the historic compromise. Only when Communists and left-wing sympathisers themselves began to fall victim to terrorist violence did this attitude change. The maiming of Communist Party member Carlo Castellano, with eight bullets in his legs and one in his abdomen, on 15 November 1977, shocked the left into a new awareness of what the Red Brigades represented in Italian political life. In explaining their reasons for punishing Castellano, the Red Brigades called him 'the Berlinguerian par excellence' who wanted 'to lull the working-class to sleep and to integrate it into capitalist development'.[36] Such a person would be the very most dangerous enemy of true Com munism.[37] The growing threat to its left caused the PCI to take a harsher stand against the terrorists. On 20 January 1978 *Rinascita's* Fabio Mussi wrote: 'Today we must recognise that in the 1970s there was formed in Italy a terrorism of the left.'[38] In the same article Mussi acknowledged that there had been too little 'self-criticism on the left' and that this would have to change.

Two other clamorous events in 1977 intensified the party's concern over the problem of terrorism. On 17 February of that year Luciano Lama, the Communist secretary of the Confederazione Generale del Lavoro (CGIL), was insulted, physically attacked and whistled out of a hall at the University of Rome by the students of the 'new Roman left' when he tried to explain the reasons for the party's so-called *svolta sindacale*, or policy of moderating wage demands and accommodation with industry.[39] These ardent youths were in no mood to listen to the secretary's pleas for realism. In the past the party had always said 'not yet' to militant cries for revolution; now it appeared to be saying 'never'. As so often for the younger generation of Italian Communists, Chairman Mao had scored a telling point when he had asked: 'Who will persist in listening to the words of a general who has never won a battle?'[40]

Later that same month a youth insurrection in Bologna, the Communist showplace city, fully revealed the pitfalls in the party's eurocommunist position. With three or four thousand militant Marxist students at the University of Bologna alone, it was quite useless for the cultivated and aristocratic Communist mayor of the city, Renato Zanghieri, to call upon the rioters to keep the peace. Anyone with a taste for irony will want to savour this appeal for a moment: a Communist leader imploring Communist revolutionaries to cease and desist from their disruptive activities in the name of law and order.[41] Whose law and order was he invoking? Six months later, in September 1977, an even larger though more peaceable demonstration of ten thousand at Bologna's Palasport answered the city authorities and the PCI with a thunderous roar: 'Viva Curcio!'

By 1977, however, Curcio was no longer the paramount chief of the Red Brigades. On 6 June 1975 his wife died in a shootout with police near Monferrato, a place since hallowed by Red Brigade propagandists as the 'Battaglia di Arzello'. The death of Mara Cagol transformed the Red Brigades, according to Giorgio Bocca, into an organisation 'more ferocious, more theoretical, more numerous, more tied to plans of international terrorism, more mysterious'.[42] Curcio himself experienced capture a second time, on 18 January 1976, but new leaders emerged to take his place, notably Giorgio Semeria and Mario Moretti. Only in 1976 did systematic executions begin, although earlier, in 1974, the inadvertent murders of two Padova *missini* had happened during a Red Brigade raid. Meanwhile, the Red Brigades had become renowned for their infamous 'kneecappings' (*azzoppamenti* or the less elegant *'gambizzazioni'*).[43] Thirty-six of these occurred in 1977, but the terroriest event of the year was the 16 November Red Brigade murder of Carlo Casalegno, the deputy editor of *La stampa*, who had been a hero in the Resistance.[44]

Moro's turn came five months later. In the background of the former prime minister's kidnapping loomed the Turin trial of Curcio and other Red Brigade defendants — called by one journalist, 'the historic nucleus' of the movement.[45] The trial had begun in May 1977, but at that time the presiding judge found the people of Turin strongly disinclined to participate in the proceedings as jurors. No lawyer wanted to touch the case, especially after 28 April when the Red Brigades assassinated the 75-year old president of the Turin Lawyers' Association, Fulvio Croce. Only on 8 March of the following year could the trial go forward, and then Turin was a city dominated by fear, its people literally immobilised in a state of siege. Eight thousand armed police and *carabinieri* stood guard around the old Lamarmora barracks' courthouse, but they were powerless to prevent the assassination of Marshall Berardi, the head of Turin's political police. A fresh shock occurred one week later with the abduction of Moro, and it seemed, quite wrongly as events proved, that nothing worse was possible. The state's legal machinery chugged laboriously along until 22 June when the accused received sentences ranging from five to fifteen years. By then, however, the headlines were dominated by the national reaction to Moro's tragic fate.

At the time of Moro's kidnapping his five-member security guard had been massacred in a terrorist action of such matchless precision that many analysts refused to believe that it could have been the work of Italians. Bocca observes that 'Italian pessimism toward the nation is such that any action of excellence is automatically attributed to strangers'.[46] The same author adds that Italian marksmen have won gold and silver medals at the Olympics, although admittedly not in shooting at moving targets. Once again and with more dismal results than ever before, the Italian police groped helplessly in the dark with their terrorist opponents. The most gigantic police operation in Italian history proved entirely useless. Moro was tried and found guilty in the 'People's Court', and then on 9 May the authorities, acting on a telephone tip from the terrorists themselves, discovered Moro's body in Via Caetani, right in the middle of downtown Rome. In an obliterating indictment of 'the stupidity inherent in the mechanism of Italian public life' Ronchey allowed that the police had been abysmally inefficient, but: 'Why should they have revealed themselves to be efficient, any different than the minsters, the post office, the telephone service, the hospitals, the schools, the state industries?'[47] How ironic, Sciascia observed in *L'affaire Moro*, for the government to be impotent in everything else, but to affect a show of strength in refusing to negotiate with the Red Brigades for Moro's life. That refusal was not the least tragic decision 'in this terrible country that Italy has become'.[48]

Red Brigade violence did not diminish after the Moro affair. Indeed, during the early months of 1979 terrorist violence and beatings reached levels of intensity and ferocity not seen in Italy since the days when Balbo's blackshirts clubbed the opponents of Fascism into submission.[49] There was a lull after that, as the Red Brigades suffered personnel and tactical losses. Nevertheless, the dramatic kidnapping of the American general, James L. Dozier, on 17 December 1981, affirmed that the group was far from being moribund, contrary to the optimistic predictions of some analysts in 1980 and 1981. The general's spectacular rescue, on 29 January 1982, was certainly a severe blow to the Red Brigades, but only a rash prophet would undertake now to say whether or not it was a decisive setback.

II

The boldness and tactical brilliance of the Moro kidnapping astonished the imprisoned Curcio as much as anyone, and he remarked at the time, 'we did not do things in such grand style'.[50] His statement underscores the great change that occurred in the Red Brigades around 1975; until then the movement retained a romantic, post 'flower child' character, at least in comparison with its later actions. The murders began on a systematic basis only in 1976 when Curcio was in prison and others had taken hold of the movement's reins. The names of Semeria and Moretti have already been mentioned, but another name must be mentioned now: Antonio Negri, a political science professor at the University of Padua and, at the request of Louis Althusser, a guest lecturer at the Ecole Normale Supérieure.

The precise nature of Negri's relationship with the Red Brigades is not completely clear. This question has been the subject of a complicated legal since Negri's arrest on 7 April 1979, and given the ponderous character of Italy's court system, in all probability the matter will not be fully resolved for some time.[51] The legal point, however, is not the most important consideration here; the intellectual one is, for whatever the nature of Negri's direct involvement in Red Brigade actions his indirect involvement, through his books, has been enormous.[52] In short, Negri provides a leftist rationale for sabotaging and terrorising the capitalist state. This rationale is revealed most unambiguously in a short work entitled *Il domino e il sabotaggio: sul metodo marxista della trasformazione sociale* (1978).

Negri begins his analysis by protesting that he does not want to give an anarchist interpretation of Leninism but at the same time he insists on the necessary connection between 'destabilization and destructuralization' in all revolutionary Marxist thought, i.e.: 'To destabilize the regime cannot be a thing distinct from the project of destructuring the system.'[53] For the authentic Marxist, then, there cannot be any question about the 'strategy of tension' in the war against capitalism. The struggle between capital and labour has not, in its essentials, become any more complex or less implacable since Marx's time: what is good for the capitalist state is bad for the worker. To put this another way, the Communist revolutionary should no more compromise with this state than a God-fearing Christian should compromise with the Devil.[54] Good lies on the side of those who work for the 'self-valorization' of the proletariat; evil is done by anyone who directly or indirectly maintains 'the process of capitalist production'. 'Self-valorization of the proletarian class,' he writes, 'is above all the destructuralization of the enemy totality.'[55] There can be no compromise, no dialogue, no commerce of any kind with the representatives of the money system. In the capitalist world, the state structures and the workers destructure; that is all.

Naturally, Negri cannot find a single redeeming feature in the present-day eurocommunist policies of the PCI. In eurocommunism he is overwhelmed by the stench of reformism, for 'reformism radically negates this sense of rapport [between self-valorization and destructuralization]; it affirms instead the coherence of self-valorization and structuralization.'[56] In his mind this is nothing other than the *Evolutionary Socialism* (1899) heresy of Eduard Bernstein and of all the other 'soft' Marxists who in their cowardly longing to avoid a fight end up as prisoners of the enemy system.[57] Today the leaders of eurocommunism, elsewhere referred to by Negri as 'the grandchildren of Giolitti', raise the banner of this tiresome doctrine, serenely proclaiming that socialism can be had without tears or blood.[58] What a cruel deception this 'ideologia di merda' is, Negri writes with characteristic vehemence.[59] Eurocommunism cannot work because it rests on an assumption which Marx himself specifically denounced, which is expressed in Negri's idiom as the monstrous synthesis between proletarian self-valorisation and capitalist valorisation. Whatever eurocommunism might be it is not Marxist, but Negri adds it is certainly 'ugly, evil, untenable', and 'worse than a tragedy'.[60]

'Reformism is infamous', Negri writes in the section of the book entitled 'Worker Sabotage', and he concludes that at the present time worker self-valorisation and worker sabotage must be regarded as interchangeable terms.[61] In an interview with Beniamino Placido for *La Repubblica*, Negri had claimed that Italian workers were in the same position occupied by black slaves on American plantations 130 years ago.[62] Such a system could not be reformed; it could only be brought down with the utmost violence. Dostoyevsky's fanatical Verhovensky had articulated this revolutionary position in *The Possessed* a century earlier: 'an incurable invalid will not be cured whatever prescriptions are written for him on paper'.[63] But Negri alights on the same point in *Il dominio e il sabotaggio* with a sense of discovery: shooting, sabotage, strikes, absenteeism, deviant behaviour, criminal behaviour and the refusal to work — all contribute to the destabilisation of the political regime and, inevitably, to the destructuralisation of the capitalist economy.[64] Wherever capitalist valorisation breaks down, proletarian valorisation is augmented: 'And no pity for the enemy.'[65]

Negri lacks Marx's scruples about random violence. Here the Italian is very close to anarchist practice, although he always insistently denies any merit in anarchist ideas. If anything he surpasses Marx's invective, an extraordinary feat, in dismissing the anarchists as witless charlatans; the talk of Bakunin and Kropotkin about individual freedom coming to pass after the destruction of the state is simply Arcadian nonsense as far as Negri is concerned. Freedom for Negri, as for any totalitarian philosopher, is a much overused word. He asks, freedom for what, and the answer must be freedom for the self-valorisation of the working class. Next to this larger class freedom, freedom for the individual loses all real meaning. He accepts the proposition that true socialism can only come about through a dictatorship of the proletariat, but not along the lines of the Russian model. In *Marx oltre Marx: quaderno di lavoro sui Grundrisse* (Feltrinelli, Milan, 1979), based on his 1978 lectures at the Ecole Normale Supérieure, he calls for a Communism that is not capitalism by another name, i.e. one that completely does away with all systems of surplus value, instead of, as in Russia, augmenting them and making them even more oppressive than they are in the West. However, in the capitalist interim properly politicised violence fosters the ultimate good of mankind, an assessment which accounts for the strong outward similarity between revolutionary anarchism and Negri's Autonomia movement of loosely connected revolutionary student and worker groups.[66]

Thus, there is much of Bakunin's spirit in Negri's plans for Italy, at least on the tactical level. Bakunin, to Marx's intense disgust, had urged the anarchists 'to learn from the criminals' in waging war on bourgeois society, for the criminal 'is the implacable enemy of the state and the whole social and civil order set up by the state'.[67] The criminal, Bakunin asserted, has the technique that the anarchist needs, the anarchist has the theory that the criminal needs; together these two forces could destroy the oppressive state. To overturn 'the great centralist state' was the goal of Bakunin's revolutionary programme, thereby permitting, in his own phrase and one with the most profound interest for students of Negri's thought, 'the federation of local autonomies'.[68]

Negri's own refusal to endorse the Soviet model — indeed he has publicly expressed revulsion at Solzhenitsyn's ghastly revelations in *The Gulag Archipelago* — appears to be based primarily on a fear of the centralising power, at least as it evolved in Russia; this is very plainly a twentieth century projection of Bakunin's own fears regarding state power, even in a country that called itself Communist.[69] Negri is ever at pains to urge his fellow Communists not to repeat the mistakes of the Bolsheviks, i.e. allowing the political mode of transition to become institutionalised and therefore corrupt. In this manner the ineffable hopes of 1917 ended in the antithesis of proletarian humanism under Stalin. 'Our problem,' he explained in *Dall' operaio massa all operaio sociale*, 'is the organisation of an adequate force for this transitional phase.'[70] His thought, therefore, represents an exhilarating advance over the typical Marxist response to the problem of power, which is vastly to underestimate its seriousness.

Marx, for instance, had absolute faith in the integrity of a ruling elite of workers and exhibited only scorn for Bakunin's prescient rejoinder in *Statism and Anarchy*: 'Indeed, but with your permission, of former workers, who once they become only representatives or rulers of the nation will cease being workers . . . and will begin to look on all the common workers from the "state-military heights"; they will no longer represent the nation . . . Whoever is capable of doubting this knows nothing about human nature.'[71]

It would seem, then, that Negri, along with Orwell, learned at least one of the lessons that Bakunin had to teach; and perhaps one other, that a few hundred dedicated militants could start the revolutionary process, though not win it. Hence, as he had written earlier in *Proletari e stato*, 'the necessity of a militant avant-garde force, capable of deepening . . . and continuing the crisis and of blunting . . . the violence of the bosses'.[72] That Negri had no aversion to including politicised criminals in his avant-garde force became clear at his judicial hearing.[73] He further borrowed from Bakunin by insisting that the university world, with its disaffected students and marginal intellectuals, would be teeming with would-be revolutionaries, and Negri successfully transformed the University of Padua from a quiet provincial school into a hotbed of Potere operaio and, then, Autonomia activity.[74] Angelo Ventura, a professor of history at the University of Padua, has described the intimidating tactics, including hammer attacks, used by Autonomia against other professors at Padua, even Socialist and Communist professors. Himself a shooting victim of the terrorists, Ventura emphatically states; 'I am convinced that Potere operaio first and then Autonomia are the central axis of Italian terrorism.'[75] Severino Galante, a PCI member of working-class origins and an assistant professor of political science at the University of Padua, has vividly portrayed what it is like to be terrorised by Autonomia: to see his name spray-painted on the walls of the city as one marked for revolutionary punishment; to receive death threats by telephone at night; to search the faces of students in the Piazza dei Signori — looking for the one with the mission to kill or maim him.[76]

Negri's incendiary rhetoric and exhortations to violence move multitudes on the radical left in Italy, and his middle-class social situation makes him a perfect example of Karl Mannheim's principle, enunciated in *Ideology and Utopia*, that the fanaticism of radicalised intellectuals 'bespeaks a psychic compensation for the lack of a more fundamental integration into a class and the necessity of overcoming their own distrust as well as that of others'.[77] The exact connection between books like *Il dominio e il sabotaggio* and the Red Brigades cannot yet be established with certainty. We are much too close to these events to make definite, final judgements. However, this much can be said now: Negri's arguments appear to be the theoretical primer of Red Brigadism. More graphically and with greater acrimony than anyone else on the left, Negri has expressed the militants' disenchantment with the PCI — 'a dead loss', he calls it — and why a new organisation is needed to revivify the Marxist programme which has been betrayed by the 'borghesia burocratica piciista'.[78] Enter his Autonomia movement, founded in 1973 following the demise of Potere operaio that year.[79]

After the Moro affair Negri denounced the Red Brigades as 'paranoid', 'confused' and 'stupid'.[80] He may have meant it. Hannah Arendt's point in *The Origins of Totalitarianism* — 'There is an abyss between the men of brilliant and facile conceptions and men of brutal deeds and active bestiality which no intellectual explanation is able to bridge' — is well made.[81] Nevertheless, at Negri's hearing it was shown that he had met often with Curcio.[82] Moreover, Autonomia has never retracted its policy of diffuse terrorism. Although the Moro affair provoked a crisis in the relations between Autonomia and the terrorist bands, it is extremely difficult to determine exactly where the Red Brigades have failed to heed the strident call for 'destabilisation and destructuralisation'. There was for some time an unmistakable unity between Negri's theory and the practice of the Red Brigades. Negri may have changed his mind lately, but, in Thomas Sheehan's phrase, 'the professor cannot put the blood back'.[83]

III

In a famous essay, 'The Modern Prince', Antonio Gramsci called upon the PCI to play the same role in twentieth-century Italian society that Machiavelli had urged Lorenzo de' Medici to assume in the sixteenth century, but for many in the 1970s it appeared that the party had done no better with its opportunities than the ineffective Florentine duke had done with his. Negri, for example, accused the party of sacrificing working-class goals in the name of 'unity and program generalities'.[84] This abnegation had made the PCI compliant and contemptible because neither Marx nor 'even the most elementary categories of Marxist discourse' were any longer present in the party consciousness.[85] In Negri's view Palmiro Togliatti, the leader of the PCI for more than 30 years, was responsible for the sorry condition of the party as 'a totally unfit force' in representing working-class interests.[86] In a fatal reformist spirit of accommodation with the capitalist structure, he had dropped the word 'class' from the Italian Communist vocabulary, 'except on liturgical occasions'. Under Togliatti's leadership, the PCI had adopted an ideology of 'synthesis at any cost, of compromise at any cost', and things had become progressively worse under Longo and Berlinguer.

The perceived failure, bankruptcy and betrayal of the PCI, given such mordant expression in *Il dominio e il sabotaggio*, is the outstanding development in Italian left-wing politics of recent years. If it were not for this perception, the Red Brigades would have about as much significance in Italian political life as the Weathermen and the Symbionese Liberation Army had in America, which is to say about as much as the media deigned to give them. The Red Brigades are not a fringe group in anything like the same sense that their would-be American counterparts were even at the height of the turmoil in the United States brought on by the Vietnam war. To understand how a numerically small group of ideological fanatics could play such a large role in Italy's political consciousness, even bringing national life to an absolute stop seemingly at will, two fundamental points must be kept in mind. First, unlike the Weathermen and terrorist groups in other Western nations, the Red Brigades possess a definite social base, among the students and the *emarginati*, the so-called '*lumpenborghesia*' and the *lumpenproletariat*. Secondly, the process of Italian history has legitimated a peculiar version of utopian politics, distinguished by a strong millenarian character, and has produced a radical tradition that is in and of itself an active force on the country's political scene.[87]

The legitimation of radical politics as an acceptable element of Italy's social character demonstrates in a concrete way the insight of a further point adumbrated by Gramsci in 'The Modern Prince', i.e. 'to write the history of a party means in fact to write the general history of a country from a monographic point of view'.[88] His injunction, while sensible, is daunting, particularly in a single essay. Gramsci's 'monographic point of view', which I take to be a precocious formulation of Braudel's 'middle-term' plane of history, can only be hinted at here, but even in its barest outlines the Italian political tradition is distinct for its chiliastic aspects.

A political tradition is a body of national experiences, usages, customs and beliefs which enable a people to make sense of the present in an historical context. For the Italian people the one national experience they nearly all had in common, beginning in 1495 with the Battle of Fornovo and lasting until unification in 1860, was foreign domination. First the French, then the Spanish, later the Austrians and sometimes all three, invaded Italy and subjected the Italians to various forms of exploitation and tyranny. The country's intense regionalism, a product of the rugged Apennine mountain chain and of the long-term success, unusual in Western Europe, of the city-state economy and culture, was massively reinforced from the outside by the politics of invasion. By the end of the eighteenth century Italy, long an inert bone of contention among the warring powers of Europe, was sunk in an abyss where the masses wallowed in poverty, ignorance and superstition while the upper-class culture of the time found its most memorable symbol in Goldoni's fawning Venetian *cicisbei*.

Napoleon appeared on this scene in an explosion of energy which blew the old Italy apart. Thereafter, the entire peninsula became subjected to French republican institutions, in the name of the most advanced principles of the day: liberty, equality, fraternity. These words possessed a special charm for Italian intellectuals, exiguous though influential, who welcomed the French with great expectations, although not for long.

Even at the outset of the French hegemony in Italy signs were not altogether missing that something quite apart from the promotion of revolutionary brotherhood had begun, such as the absorption of the entire Kingdom of Sardinia and all of Liguria by France. French fortunes rose and fell in Italy during the next several years, according to the outcomes of Napoleon's interminable wars, but by 1814 he had been in power long enough for a definite impression to be made, and it was not one that the Italians cared to prolong. Experience showed that the Italian republics and then, in Napoleon's imperial phase, the Kingdom of Italy served merely as puppet states whose main function was to provide the French war machine with money, men and foodstuffs. During the seventeenth century Italy performed similar services for Spain — minus the revolutionary cant. In 1814, with their economy enfeebled and retarded by the restrictions of the Continental system, most politically conscious Italians were aware that, despite the utopian slogans, the fundamentals of the Italian situation *vis-à-vis* the outside world had changed hardly at all.

Napoleon fixed the essential terms of Italy's intellectual politics. He appealed to the idealism of the country's politically active intellectuals and then made a mockery of that idealism, at the same time generating new ideals in the minds of outraged Italians. A form of this cyclical process, with a bewildering change of names and ideas, has been going on ever since. Carbonarism, Mazzinianism, Anarchism, Socialism, Nationalism, Communism, political Catholicism, Fascism — the Red Brigades — fit into a peculiarly Italian pattern of right and left despair with existing reality.

It has been the tragic misfortune of Italian liberalism to be judged as the embodiment of that reality from the inception of the country's national history. As Italy's first prime minister, Cavour had as much of an impact on the history of that office as George Washington had on the office of the presidency of the United States: both men established precedents that would endure in scarcely altered form right up to the present day, and in Italy the liberal political tradition, with its Historic Left and Historic Right factionalism, is the almost unrelievedly sad story of government leaders vainly trying to equal the sagacity, the energy and the will of the man Denis Mack Smith calls 'the most considerable personage in modern Italian history'.[89]

Yet not only the liberals fell into factional dispute: the entire political spectrum has always been on the point of dissolution, perhaps more for the socialists than for any other single group. Indeed, the maximalist/minimalist divisions within Italian socialism have only been papered over from time to time during periods of the least turmoil in the party's history, never truly eliminated. The Libyan War, World War I, the disastrous post-war period — all revealed the depressing truth behind the party's impressive façade of popular and intellectual favour. Socialist power in Italian politics was enormous, but unpredictable and irresponsible, as the triumph of Fascism in 1922 convincingly demonstrated.[90]

The rise and generation-long success of Fascism is the outstanding development in twentieth-century Italian history, reverberating with epochal significance for the history of the world. In terms of Italian politics, Mussolini's success can only be compared with Cavour's; although the *duce*'s regime ended in total collapse, Fascism was a political masterpiece, brought to perfection when its protagonist outwitted and completely defeated all his opponents.[91] Precisely because he so thoroughly understood — and despised — the Italian political tradition, resplendent in rhetorical brilliance but with a poor record of actual achievement, Mussolini could play with consummate skill the dual Machiavellian role of lion and fox; only when he left what for him was the sure ground of Italian politics did he run up against the iron obstacles for which political life in Italy had given him no preparation whatsoever.

Mussolini had won the post-war power struggle in Italy because his party enjoyed more unity than all the others and he alone knew, or at least he alone acted on the knowledge, that a new and fluid political situation had been created in Italy as a result of the outcomes on the Western Front, in the Russian Revolution and at Versailles. Enrico Corradini's Nationalist Party contributed the right-wing syndicalist doctrine which ultimately would constitute Fascist ideology, but a history of Fascist ideology would make very light reading. Fascism, in Ernst Nolte's succinct phrase, was its history, and that history took its theme from a series of tactical victories over liberalism and socialism and from the continuing efforts of Mussolini to ensure his triumph: these efforts were always at the heart of his domestic and foreign policies. When Fascism itself went down to a more complete defeat than any it ever administered to its liberal and socialist opponents, the very negative character of the movement — its lack of genuinely positive content — permitted liberalism and socialism to resurface in Italian politics, playing much the same roles that they had played before 1922.[92]

Of course liberalism and socialism had undergone profound internal changes. The old liberal transformist party of Giovanni Giolitti, Italy's outstanding pre-war prime minister, was nothing more than a memory of the *belle epoque*. The Christian Democratic Party of the post-World War II era, led by Alcide De Gasperi, began pretty much as a Church party in the tradition of Don Sturzo's post-World War I Popolari, but with the accretion of power and influence the DC became increasingly secular and more of an organised means to regulate the country's spoils system than an ideologically based party, i.e. it has come to serve many of the same political functions in contemporary Italy that the Liberal Party served 70 years ago. *La Repubblica*'s Rodolfo Brancoli is right to insist that the DC, with its large and faithful following, is more than merely a system of distributing political spoils: it does rest on a solid base, and it represents fundamental Italian interests and values.[93] Nevertheless, 35 years of unbroken power has subjected the DC to temptations which no political organisation could have resisted, and it now seems problematic at best, despite the attempted *rifondazione* under Benigno Zaccagnini's leadership, that the party can emerge from the morass of corruption and venality which the shocking scandals of 1976 fully revealed to be its natural habitat.[94]

Cold War pressures induced the United States to spend huge sums of money directly subsidising the DC hegemony, not counting the 75 million dollars from 1948 to 1976 earmarked for CIA anti-Communist campaigns during Italian elections or the 46 to 49 million dollars that Exxon contributed for the same purposes between 1963 and 1972.[95] The return on these investments has been a blackening of America's image in Italy as a meddlesome, hypocritical and bungling overlord. Only on rare occasions has Washington's Farewell Address warning about 'entangling alliances' been more prophetic than in this scandal-ridden relationship between the United States and the Christian Democrats. Still, tainted as the DC has been, it would be superficial for us to attribute the present Italian crisis to the corruption and the moral collapse of one party. We should remember, too, that American administrations did much to bring about these deplorable conditions.

Meanwhile, the energy that Italian socialists did not spend wielding national power was lavished with a connoisseur's delectation on the careful refinement of sectarian rivalries. Nothing new there in Italian politics, but since the price of this indulgence was Fascism, it is a pity that someone in authority on the left did not have the foresight, the courage and the power to refuse to pay it.[96] Actually, in the years after World War I Filippo Turati tried to play the peacemaker; however, in a party of such raucous younger spirits as Amadeo Bordiga, Giacinto Menotti Serrati and Antonio Gramsci the elder statesman's diplomatic gestures had little chance of success and, indeed, were vehemently rejected. The schism of 1921 produced a Russian-inspired Communist Party, a Socialist Party bled white by defections, and a Fascist triumph — in that order. The irony of this schism is that today the PCI finds itself the object of the same radical critique so clamorously put forward by the founding Communist fathers as they exited in high dudgeon from the Socialist Party. Despite the brilliant legacy of Gramscian humanist Marxism, the PCI has not been able to speak with an authoritative voice for all party factions since the death in 1964 of Gramsci's lieutenant and then leader of the party in his turn, Stalin's favourite, Togliatti.[97] In fact, the very attempt of the party to abandon its Stalinist past by accepting Italy's pluralist system and by working within it has caused volcanic materials to be built up around a vent in the party's crust; the volcano has become active with the eruption of the Red Brigades.[98]

IV

The Italian political tradition has resulted, up to this point, in a confrontation between a Balkanised DC and a PCI which is in constant danger of losing its left wing. Smaller parties and factions continue to proliferate in the Italian political arena, but they derive their chief importance according to how they influence DC/PCI relations.[99] The Red Brigades are no exception to this rule, and the group's principal tactical objective has been to block the historic compromise between the PCI and the DC. As the chief architect of that compromise strategy Aldo Moro became enemy of the people number one on the Red Brigade proscription list. He was kidnapped on the very day when the PCI formally became a member of the DC parliamentary coalition, and later it was an act of the highest political symbolism for Moro's Red

Brigade killers to place his corpse in Via Caetani, approximately 300 yards from the DC headquarters and 200 yards from the headquarters of the PCI. This was their ceremonial way of simultaneously taunting the helpless Italian police and explaining why Moro's death was an act of revolutionary justice.

The Red Brigades have appeared at a moment of maximum disorder in the Italian political tradition, a confusion worse confounded by a cultural crisis of revolutionary magnitude. Since the end of World War II, the traditional left and centre parties, with their Marxist and Christian origins, have been faced with an enemy infinitely more threatening to their principles than Fascism ever was: consumer society. Camus once remarked that the greatest threats in the contemporary world are Soviet totalitarianism and American consumerism; in Italy the latter has wrought a revolution more far-reaching than any envisioned by Marx.[100] Nothing less than the annihilation of the country's traditional Marxist and Christian values has occurred in the aftermath of the post-war boom, and, as Pier Paolo Pasolini noted in a famous article, no other values have appeared to take their place. Italy, according to him, has experienced an 'anthropological mutation', leading to the *'borghesizzazione'* of the entire country, a process based 'on the hedonistic ideology of consumerism and of the consequent modernist tolerance of the American type'.[101] Alberto Moravia offers a similar view, adding that twentieth-century terrorists have one thing in common with nineteenth-century terrorists: the fight for liberation — in the nineteenth century from tyranny, in the twentieth century from fetishism, hedonism, corruption, alienation and materialism.[102] We should be aware, however, and thanks to *Rinascita*'s Alberto Minucci we are aware that the Fascists also promised 'to scrub the bourgeois sewer'.[103] We would all do well to contemplate the consequences of Italy's last attempt to terrorise the country into liberation from plutocratic corruption.

The religious crisis has been particularly acute, and the Church, while far from powerless, has never been weaker among the young than it is today. If Church attendance figures and public opinion polls are any indication, the attempt of the Second Vatican Council to streamline and modernise the Church has apparently not succeeded in winning back the young, but has succeeded only too well in thoroughly confusing the old. For the most ardent of the alienated Catholics it is a short psychological step from a spiritual eschatology to an eschatology of social ideals, resulting in a Catholic-Marxist dialogue that neither group could ever have with people in the liberal centre. For example, Negri began his intellectual career as a pious philosophy student in Catholic Action. Curcio had a traditional Catholic education and was, up to within two years of his conversion to revolutionary terrorism, a devout and practicing Catholic.[104] On 1 August 1969 he and Mara Cagol, who had spent her youth in the least progressive Catholic circles of the north, were married in a Church ceremony.[105]

However, it was at the University of Trento that Curcio and Cagol, in the words of Ronchey, 'became converts to that post-religious ideology in which absolute values are transferred from transcendental faith to sanctified social conflict'.[106] The Sociology Faculty there became the cradle of Italy's student movement, with the first sit-in occurring from 24 January to 10 February 1966, and out of such dissident activities an unprecedented student revolutionary consciousness evolved.[107] Curcio emerged as a leader among the student activists and edited, in collaboration with Mauro Rostagno, *Proposta di foglio di lavoro*, which called for a new university radicalism in the war against capitalism.[108] They wanted to create an *università negativa* – a university offering *controcorsi* that would negate the evil capitalist hegemony. By this time the Christian activist in him had vanished and a new kind of Marxist revolutionary was struggling to be born.

No less than idealistic Catholics, idealistic Marxists have watched the modern world pass them by, as consumer society heads in a direction never prophesied by Marx. In its relentless search for votes, the PCI has shown a tolerant willingness to jettison Marx himself, and the embarrassing Soviet model has been quietly stored in the deepfreeze, out of sight and – it is hoped at PCI headquarters – out of mind. None of this has happened smoothly. Thousands of the party faithful have looked on in shock and dismay as the PCI has shifted towards new positions which only a short time ago would have been unthinkable. In *Unsettling Europe*, Jane Kramer depicts the disturbed surprise of San Vincenzo's aged communists when no one sang the 'Internazionale' at the local Festa dell'Unità.[109] It had always been sung before. Why not now? The answer, of course, is that the party no longer maintains a revolutionary profile; it is now collaborating with industrialists and Catholics. For those fundamentalist pro-Stalin Marxists in San Vincenzo the party's about-face is nothing less than a sacrilege, and their reaction is typical of that of many Communists in the country for whom Marxism traditionally has been an evangelical faith.[110]

Hardly less astonished was the American news correspondent, Martin Agronsky, in a September 1977 interview with the Communist leader, Giorgio Napolitano, who blithely confessed that the PCI saw nothing wrong with NATO.[111] Agronsky thought that the Italian had mis-spoken himself and asked for a clarification. Napolitano then added, 'if there were an attack by the Warsaw Pact against NATO, naturally we would be obliged . . . to defend our country. We are determined to defend our country against any external attack.'[112] A perplexed Agronsky ventured to say that: 'The gentlemen in the Kremlin will be amazed when they hear this.' Probably not — if they had read Gramsci, who theorised that since the Italian Communists had different problems than those faced by Lenin it would be necessary for the PCI to adopt a different, more supple, strategy, one suitable for the peculiar contours of the national situation. It is nevertheless true that for decades the PCI maintained its identity on the left as the upholder in Italy of the Soviet model, and *Rinascita*'s hagiographic eulogy for Joseph Stalin in March 1953 documents the tremendous Soviet influ-ence on the PCI until well into the post-war period. Only with Hungary, even more with Czechoslovakia, and then, in a *coup de grâce*, with Afghanistan was the old pro-Russian faith overthrown in the name of polycentrism. As for Poland in late 1981 and early 1982, Washington can only wish that the West German reaction and that of some of its other NATO allies equalled the PCI's passionate condemnation of General Wojciech Jaruzelski's martial law regime. Moscow felt com-pelled to react to this condemnation with a shrill editorial in *Pravda*, denouncing the PCI for giving 'direct aid to imperialism'.[113]

The PCI is now seen, correctly, as the heir of Turati, not of Bordiga or even of Gramsci; surely Gramsci could not have abided pluralism as a permanent condition which the PCI now claims it is willing and even eager to accept.[114] The need for the party to win new votes and to establish effective political alliances with other parties overshadows other considerations now. Even though the DC has been cool towards the PCI since Moro's death, it is unlikely that Berlinguer's fundamental strategy will change in the near future.[115] At great risk, he has led the party on a forced march towards the vital centre of the political spec-trum, and it would be difficult to imagine where else he can go now. Thus, the PCI has travelled in the direction of the major social demo-cratic parties of Europe, but not without alienating those fervent spirits among its members who only want to discard the parliamentary system, not to conquer it at the polls.

Those fervent spirits on the extraparliamentary left want to dis-card the old morality as well. One of the most important social devel-opments in Italy during recent years has been the emergence of, in Christopher Lasch's words about contemporary America, a culture of narcissism growing out of a campaign for personal liberation, particularly in sexual matters. A recent political cartoon in *Autonomia operaia* called for 'space to organise ourselves, to struggle, to amuse ourselves', to establish 'autonomy of struggle and of sexuality', as well as 'to transform interpersonal relationships'.[116] Manzini's biography of the Red Brigadist, Walter Alasia, is extremely valuable for this kind of detail, e.g. the students' favourite radical review at ITIS was *Il pane e le rose*, the very title of which attempts an unimaginable fusion of Gramscian and D'Annunzian elements; the review ran a regular column under the question, 'Are you satisfied with your sex life?'[117] Traditional Marxists, with their puritanical devotion to the work ethic, are as much at a loss and in some ways more at a loss to understand what the new left is talking about than almost anyone else in Italy — ironically because new left rhetoric presupposes a Marxist vocabulary. This is what Ronchey means when he writes that on the level of morality the extra-parliamentary left represents something completely new in Italy: to the old-fashioned Communist working-class concerns this new left has added the hedonism of the post-industrial West.[118] The upshot is a form of cultural schizophrenia that has torn the left into a thousand pieces, leaving the DC more firmly in control, despite appearances, than it has been in 20 years. Nevertheless, it exercises control over a system that is on the verge of disintegrating, much as the old Italian city-state system disintegrated shortly after the French invasion of 1494. A sudden deepening of the present socio-economic crisis is, as Gianfranco Pasquino suggests, 'the major risk' facing the DC today.[119]

The erosion of the once venerated ideological certainties in the highly variegated Marxist and Catholic traditions occurs just as giant fissures appear in the Italian social structure, no doubt contributing massively to that erosion. This social crisis underlies everything that we have been considering so far about the Red Brigades. Earlier we saw how the problems of migration, of education and of the economy continually plague Italian politics, but these are only aspects of the deeper structural problem of society itself. In the simplest terms, Italy has never managed to overcome the social difficulties inherent in the dual model of northern industrialism and southern agrarianism; instead of complementing each other, the two corrupted each other to such a degree that over the last hundred years a large percentage of intelligent Italians in every generation has desired revolution. This seems to be the fundamental explanation for the enormous popularity of socialism among Italian intellectuals almost from the movement's inception and the irresistible appeal now of Marxism to a broad cross section of the population, an appeal which must strike every foreign observer as one of the distinctive characteristics of Italian life.[120]

Moreover, while the present base for revolution is large and growing among the students and the *emarginati*, support for the ruling hegemony crumbles as the people at the top become alienated from the system that they are paid to run.[121] A new managerial class has arisen since 1945, giving Italy such modern tone as it possesses, and precisely for this reason it is despised throughout the country with 'a totally implacable execration'.[122] Acquaviva and Santuccio write of these managers as the saving remnant in a society swarming with parasites, most of them with government jobs and displaying 'a remarkable capacity for reproducing themselves quite spontaneously'.[123] As the two authors of *Social Structure in Italy* see it, the producing business class is fighting a losing battle against two enemy groups: the intellectuals whose Marxist-inspired visions are never free of fantastic elements, completely lacking Marx's own realism and careful attention to detail; and the horde of government officials, whose particular art is the corruption of public life. The government is the most tormenting of these two antagonists, for it creates the atmosphere in which radical change must be actively desired by every mentally alive Italian.[124]

In such an environment, with the country's traditional Catholic and Marxist cultures unravelling in a vacuum, the wonder is that the Red Brigade phenomenon has not caused an even greater upheaval. It might yet because the elements which created the present crisis are still active and, if anything, potentially more explosive at the start of the 1980s than they were ten years ago when the Red Brigades came into existence. As J. Bowyer Bell has recently noted, 'Italy faces not so much a terrorist problem as a need to restructure its society' – a prescription which has not changed at all since Cesare Lombroso wrote *Gli anarchici* (1894): 'We suffer above all from our defective economic order.'[125] This is not to dismiss the possibility of outside interference in Italian domestic affairs. Claire Sterling asserts, in *The Terror Network*, that the KGB has played a much larger role in the terrorism of the 1970s than has been generally recognised.[126] Yet the remarks of Bell and Lombroso point to a deeper truth: the ingredients of terrorism are present in the Italian social situation, and without them an organisation like the KGB would have nothing to exploit.

Karl Mannheim observed in *Ideology and Utopia* that the cultural and political traditions of every country exercise a decisive influence on its present, to the extent that in each generation intellectuals inherit a cultural and political situation which they either maintain in its received state or modify by thinking further what other people have thought before them.[127] Both of these traditions in Italy are best summed up, I think, by Ignazio Silone in *Bread and Wine*:

> The race to which we belong is distinguished by the fact that it begins by taking seriously the principles taught us by our own educators and teachers. These principles are proclaimed to be the foundations of present-day society, but if one takes them seriously and uses them as a standard to test society as it is organized and as it functions today, it becomes evident that there is a radical contradiction between the two. Our society in practice ignores those principles altogether. It is this discovery that leads one to become a revolutionary.[128]

In other and poorer words Italy, a country of exalted Classical-Christian-Marxist ideals, faces a degraded reality of ignorance, poverty and superstition with a degree of public venality and malversation approaching Latin American standards. It is not difficult to understand how this disjunction between the ideal and the real would produce politically aberrant behaviour, on the right as well as on the left, and this, in fact, has been the country's political destiny from the Carbonari to the present day.

The Red Brigade phenomenon is in many ways unique, but in others it belongs to the left-wing apocalyptic strain of the Italian political tradition. Apart from the broad Italian setting, including Italian history, Red Brigadism would appear as a kind of diabolical phenomenon, much like Edmund Burke's image of the revolutionary Jacobins as 'those hellhounds called terrorists'.[129] This is graphic enough as description – and one must not, in Juan Linz's words, minimise the 'sublimated expression of criminal impulse, aggression, brutality, and sadism' – but for a serious political analysis of either Jacobins or Red Brigadists a more vivid sense of history is required.[130] It is one thing to say, with Swift, 'There is nothing so extravagant and irrational which some philosophers have not maintained for the truth'; it is another thing, and a more important thing, to say why this should be so. In the Italian case the authors of *Social Structure in Italy* seem to be on to something of fundamental importance when they write: 'Long after Socialism had spread throughout the rest of Europe, it remained little known in Italy where, nevertheless, the spirit of rebellion was strong, with armed gangs leading insurrections, as well as pursuing a general strategy of terrorism and assassination — the stiletto being the favorite weapon.'[131] Sciascia adds a necessary coda to the same point by insisting that more than anything else the Red Brigades, despite their fanciful claim of descending from the Resistance, resemble the Mafia.[132] The *azzoppamenti* and the assassinations are hardly more than variations of practices employed by the rural Mafia. The vaunted efficiency of the Red Brigades is comparable in the popular mind to the efficiency of the Mafia, and the psychological objective of both organisations is to make people fear the invisible *mafioso* or *brigatista* more than the visible *carabiniere*. Negri himself is reported to have said that: 'The problem is to construct an informal but iron organization capable of a mafia-like productivity.'[133]

This is not to say that Italians have a peculiar penchant for violence. Surely the Italians need not be embarrassed in the company of Americans on the general subject of violence, not as long as violent crimes in the United States are anywhere from two to ten times higher than in any Western European country, including Italy.[134] Nevertheless, the political violence that we have seen recently in Italy, with literally thousands of politically motivated attacks every year, has achieved the condition of an art form, the special product of a fateful conjunction between that country's tragic history and the crisis of contemporary Italian society. It is this conjunction that we have sought to illuminate.

History never repeats itself on the level of detail, but the Red Brigades fit into the classical pattern of revolutionary group formation in Italy. This involves, first, the development of an alternative conception of the world, or a counter-hegemony in opposition to the class and cultural hegemony of the ruling elite. In the case of the Red Brigades that intellectual development has been exceedingly complex, originating in the late 1960s when disillusioned leftist students attempted to promote a revolutionary movement based on the utopian sentiments then enjoying a widespread popularity among young people the world over. It is impossible to answer here the comparative question of why those sentiments proved ephemeral elsewhere, but not in Italy; however, the uprooting of traditional agricultural society and the simultaneous destruction of traditional urban life in favour of a new mass society cannot have been negligible factors, particularly in view of the dense eschatological atmosphere in Italy to begin with.[135] From Curcio's student populism to Negri's sophisticated neo-Marxist analysis is a quantum leap, but the link between the two has been their shared resentment towards the PCI for its betrayal of revolutionary ideals. Still, on the strength of their ideas alone, the Red Brigades would never have distinguished themselves from all the other organisations of the revolutionary left in Italy. Negri's theories have an all-purpose value for the Gruppi d'Azione Partigiana, the Nuclei Armati Proletari and Prima Linea, as well as for the Red Brigades.

The second phase in the pattern of revolutionary group formation involves political propaganda, i.e. spreading the new conception of the world by means of widening the revolutionary base. Autonomia operaia is the primary engine of this extraparliamentary revolutionary campaign, and though the movement repudiates any attempt to connect it with the Red Brigades in fact the terrorists do serve a complementary function, as agents for the propaganda of the deed, leading eventually, they hope, to the third phase of the revolutionary group formation process, armed revolt. This has been an enormously successful strategy so far and here the the Red Brigades have cut a striking figure on the left, pushing Italy into a transitional stage between individual acts of terror and genuine guerrilla warfare.[136] The use of anarchist tactics by the Red Brigades is an ironic note in the story, given the historic enmity between Bakunin and Marx. The murders and the maimings are offered as sacrifices on Marx's altar, but to the student of the Italian political tradition a proper inscription for the Red Brigades might be: 'C'est la revanche de Bakunin.'

Notes

*With the support of grants from the American Philosophical Society and the Princeton University Committee on Research in the Humanities and Social Sciences

1. Mauro Galleni (ed.), *Rapporto sul terrorismo: le stragi, gli agguati, i sequestri, le sigle 1969-1980* (Rizzoli, Milan, 1981). See tables on pp. 49, 86 and 114.

2. Angelo Ventura analyses 'the singularity of the Italian case' on the question of terrorism in 'Il problema storico del terrorismo italiano'. *Rivista storica italiana*, March 1980. Ventura, a member of the PSI and a professor of history at the University of Padua, was wounded in a terrorist attack by Fronte comunista combattente on 26 September 1979.

3. In August 1980 Italian neo-Fascist terrorism reclaimed the headlines as a result of the Bologna railway station explosion that killed 85 people and wounded 200 others. This event should remind us of an old truth, that the political extremes, steeped in traditions of violence, provoke each other to the excesses characteristic of Italian political life. However, in the 1970s the left overshadowed the right in the perpetration of political violence. For more on the terrorism of the right, see Giorgio Bocca, *Il terrorismo italiano* (Rizzoli, Milan, 1978), especially Chapter IV, 'Il Terrorismo Nero', and the relevant chapters in Galleni, *Rapporto sul terrorismo*.

4. Fernand Braudel, *The Mediterranean and the Mediterranean World in the Age of Philip II* (Harper and Row, New York, 1972), vol. I, pp. 20-1. In this single article I could not very well deal with the '*forces profondes*' of the timeless or long-term historical dimension, so dear to the *Annales* School, but that dimension does exist, and it is best summarised by Alberto Ronchey in his recent

book on Italian terrorism, *Libro bianco sull' ultima generazione: tra candore e terrore* (Garzanti, Milan, 1978): in Italy there is and always has been a difficult rapport between population, space and resources. See Chapter 1, 'Il Pensiero Magico (Introduzione alla Crisi)'. The French historian, Jacques Le Goff, also has commented on the burden of Italy's past: 'It seems to me that the exceptional gravity of the weight of history in the Italian collective consciousness derives from the explosive combination of three elements: the consciousness of being a very old people, the sentiment of decline between the glory of [their] origins and present state, and the inquietude of existing [as a nation] for only a short time. Fascism, pouring its poison into this unstable compound, provoked a neurotic crisis that renders this peculiar burden more fatiguing.' See his 'Il peso del passato nella coscienza collettiva degli italiani' in Fabio Luca Cavazza and Stephen R. Graubard (eds.), *Il caso italiano*, (Garzanti, Milan, 1974), p. 536.

5. Richard Hofstadter, *The American Political Tradition* (Vintage, New York, 1948). See the introduction.

6. Maurice Merleau-Ponty, *Humanism and Terror: an Essay on the Communist Problem* (trans. by John O'Neill) (Beacon, Boston, 1969 edn), p. xiii.

7. Braudel, *Mediterranean* p. 21.

8. Of the 597 terrorist groups that have claimed credit for violent acts, 484 of them belong to the left and 113 to the right. However, most of the violence is the work of 15 major groups, above all of the Red Brigades, Prima Linea, Nuclei armati proletari and Proletari comunisti organizzati on the left and Ordine nuovo, Ordino nero, the Nuclei armati rivoluzionari and the Squadre azione 'Mussolini' on the right. Galleni, *Rapporto sul terrorismo*, p. 176.

9. After the Red Brigades the NAP (Nuclei armati proletari) has been the most active leftist terrorist organisation in Italy. Unlike the *brigatisti rossi*, with their northern and urban student-worker orientation, the *napisti* have been connected with the prisoner movement and the southern sub-proletariat, especially in Naples. Alessandro Silj, *Never Again Without a Rifle: the Origins of Italian Terrorism* (trans. by Salvator Attanasio) (Karz Publishers, New York, 1979), Part II, 'The Armed Proletarian Nuclei'.

10. Cited by Soccorso Rosso, *Brigate rosse* (Feltrinelli, Milan, 1976), pp. 70-1. Apparently, the Red Brigades were conceived as the shock troops of the Metropolitan Collective of Milan which, incidentally, changed its name to Sinistra proletaria in February 1971. The *Foglio di lotta di sinistra proletaria* was the bulletin of the Collective; in July 1970 the more theoretical *Sinistra proletaria* appeared. After April 1971 *Nuova resistenza* began to publish communiqués of both the Red Brigades and the Gruppi d'azione partigiana (GAP), as well as announcements from other terrorist formations. In addition, the Red Brigades periodically published their own theoretical pamphlets; see those published by Soccorso Rosso.

11. Ibid. In succeeding communiqués the Red Brigades continued to define themselves as 'the first formations of armed propaganda whose fundamental task is that of propagandizing with their existence and their action the contents of organizing . . . [the] strategy of class war', See Communiqué No. 7 (April 1971), ibid., p. 83.

12. Vincenzo Tessandori, *BR Imputazione: banda armata (cronaca e documenti delle Brigate rosse* (Garzanti, Milan, 1977). See Chapter 1.

13. Feltrinelli's story has been traced in lurid detail by Claire Sterling in *The Terror Network: the Secret War of International Terrorism* (Holt, Rinehart & Winston, New York, 1981). See 'Feltrinelli the Patron'.

14. See the following articles by Enrico Berlinguer in *Rinascita:* 'Imperialismo e consistenza alla luce dei fatti cileni', 28 September 1973; 'Riflessioni sull' Italia dopo i fatti di Cile: Via democratica o violenza reazionaria', 5 October 1973;

'Riflessioni sull'Italia dopo i fatti di Cile: Alleanze sociali e schieramenti politici', 12 October 1973. See Peter Lange's 'Crisis and Consent, Change and Compromise: Dilemmas of Italian Communism in the 1970s' in Peter Lange and Sidney Tarrow (eds.), *Italy in Transition* (Frank Cass, London, 1980), for an analysis of the PCI's 'historic compromise' strategy.

15. Soccorso Rosso, *Brigate rosse*, p. 147.

16. Alberto Ronchey, *Accade in Italia: 1968-1977* (Garzanti, Milan, 1977). See Chapter 3, 'Italinflazione'.

17. Alberto Ronchey, *Atlante ideologico: programmi e utopie degli anni Settanta alla prova dei fatti* (Garzanti, Milan, 1973). Chapter 18, 'L'eclisse d'Europa'.

18. Sabino S. Acquaviva argues that the social base of Italian terrorism is the student world in particular and the world of the *lumpenproletariat* in general, in *Guerriglia e guerra rivoluzionaria in Italia: ideologie, fatti, prospettive* (Rizzoli, Milan, 1979), p. 19. For more on the collapse of Italy's university system, see Alberto Ronchey, 'Guns and Grey Matter: Terrorism in Italy', *Foreign Affairs* (Spring 1979).

19. Ronchey *Libro bianco* Chapter 2, 'S'avanza uno strano studente (Il parco antropologico)'.

20. Rosario Romeo and George Urban, 'Troubled Italy', *The New York Times*, 2 January 1978.

21. Sabino S. Acquaviva and M. Santuccio, *Social Structure in Italy* (Robertson, London, 1976), p. 157.

22. Giorgio Manzini, *Indagine su un brigatista rosso: la storia di Walter Alasia* (Einaudi, Turin, 1978). p. 55.

23. Ronchey, *Libro bianco*. See 'S'avanza uno stranto studente (Il parco antropologico)'. For more on how Italian universities have been compromised since 1968, see the testimony of Angelo Ventura in Giampaolo Pansa, *Storie italiane di violenza e terrorismo* (Laterza, Roma-Bari, 1980). 'Insegnare a Padova'.

24. Michele Salvati, 'Muddling Through: Economics and Politics in Italy 1969-1979' in Lange and Tarrow (eds.), *Italy in Transition*, pp. 31-48. See also C. Crouch and A. Pizzorno (eds.), *The Resurgence of Class Conflict in Europe* (Macmillan, London, 1978) and L. Graziano and S. Tarrow (eds.), *La crisi italiana*, 2 vols. (Einaudi, Turin, 1979).

25. See Michael A. Ledeen, *Italy in Crisis* (Sage, Beverly Hills/London, 1977), especially 'The Political Economy'. See also Sidney Tarrow, 'Italy: Crisis, Crises or Transition?' in Lange and Tarrow (eds.), *Italy in Transition*, who writes that 'Italy is going through the second industrial revolution without having fully completed the first'. (p. 176).

26. Morris West, 'Terror as an Historical Inheritance', *Esquire*, 25 April 1978.

27. Galleni, *Rapporto sul terrorismo*, p. 49.

28. Nevertheless, Ugo Pecchioli speculates that Italian terrorists of the left have suffered a severe crisis since 1979, with the capture of numerous leaders and veteran personnel. The rise in the number of people killed, he concludes, is a consequence of the terrorists' efforts 'to cover the crisis'. Ibid. See his Preface, p. 32.

29. Ronchey, 'Guns and Grey Matter'. The movement has many more 'part-time' members (3,000-8,000) and 'active sympathisers (200,000-350,000). See Silj, *Never Again Without a Rifle*, p. xix.

30. Bocca, *Il terrorismo italiano*, Chapter V, 'L'Attacco alla Magistratura'.

31. Ibid., p. 63. The Sossi episode in 1974 is a good example of the restraint shown by the Red Brigades prior to 1975. Sossi was freed on 23 May 1974 after more than a month in a 'people's jail'. On 8 June 1976 the Red Brigades did not bother to abduct Francesco Coco, Genoa's hard-line anti-terrorist public prosecutor who had refused to honour the agreement he had made with them to gain

Sossi's release; they simply shot him and his two bodyguards as he was about to enter his house. See Tessandori, *BR Imputazione*, Chapter 1, 'L'esecuzione Coco'.

32. Indro Montanelli, 'Italians Have Lost All Faith in Democracy', *The New York Times*, 21 April 1978.

33. Bocca, *Il terrorismo italiano*. See 'Il punto di svolta'.

34. For a detailed description of this escape, see Piero Agostini, *Mara Cagol: una donna nelle prime brigate rosse* (Marsilio, Venice, 1980), 'Da Pinerolo a Casale Monferrato'.

35. One of the party's best known spokesmen of the 1970s, Giorgio Amendola, admitted that the major fault of the PCI leaders on the question of terrorism lay in their failure to 'combat it actively enough and with the necessary energy'. The party's reaction was regrettably 'insufficient'. Fabio Mussi (ed.), 'Chi è responsabile della violenza politica: intervista a Giorgio Amendola', *Rinascita*, 7 April 1978.

36. Pansa, *Storie italiane di violenze e terrorismo*, p. 107.

37. Suffering an even worse fate than Castellano, however, was Guido Rossa, a worker and PCI member whom the Red Brigades killed on 24 January 1979. His offence was to have reported a fellow factory worker for distributing Red Brigade leaflets in a Genoa factory. Ibid. See 'L'operaio Genova' and 'Cesare il postino'.

38. Fabio Mussi, 'Sulle teorie del partito armato', *Rinascita*, 20 January 1978.

39. Bocca, *Il terrorismo italiano*. See 'Il movimento'. For more on Italy's labour unions in the 1970s, see Marino Regini, 'Labour Unions, Industrial Action, and Politics' in Lange and Tarrow (eds.), *Italy in Transition*.

40. Cited by Ronchey in *Accade in Italia*. Chapter 16, 'La questione socialista'.

41. Since then the PCI has taken an unmistakably conservative law and order position on all political violence, e.g. see Luciano Lama's article, 'La sfida del terrorismo' in *Rinascita* (15 February 1980), calling for a strengthening of the Italian police and utterly rejecting a typically intellectualistic left response to the problem of terrorism, 'né con le Br né con lo Stato'.

42. Bocca, *Il terrorismo italiano*. See 'Il punto di svolta'.

43. Between 1975 and 1980 the Red Brigades were responsible for approximately 68 kneecappings; their closest competitors in this category was Prima Linea with 23. Galleni, *Rapporti sul terrorismo*, pp. 97-8.

44. His son had been a member of the extraparliamentary Lotta continua, and in a heart-rending *mea culpa* accepted the responsibility for helping to create 'the ideological and human climate in which terrorism emerged and was sustained. Our failure left a void that was then filled by him who took seriously what was for us only courtyard slogans, and he translated them into bloody deeds.' Pansa, *Storie italiane di violenza e terrorismo*, 'Mio padre, Casalegno'.

45. Cited by Leonardo Sciascia, *L'affaire Moro* (Sellerio, Palermo, 1978), p. 12.

46. Bocca, *Il terrorismo italiano*. See 'Le nuove B.R.'.

47. Ronchey, 'Guns and Grey Matter'.

48. Sciascia, *L'affaire Moro*, p. 12.

49. For more on the comparison between the Fascists and the Red Brigades see Ventura, 'Il problema storico del terrorismo italiano'.

50. Bocca, *Il terrorismo italiano*. See 'Il caso Moro'.

51. For the connections between Giangiacomo Feltrinelli and Negri see the testimony of Carlo Fioroni, the so-called 'supertestimone' (superwitness) in the Negri hearing. Pansa, *Storie italiane di violenza e terrorismo*, 'Il mito dell'insurrezione: una vita qualunque'. Fioroni, long associated with the violent left in Italy, apparently decided to turn state's evidence as a result of guilt that he felt

following the kidnapping and accidental death of his friend, Carlo Saronio, on 14 April 1975. Pansa's account of this complicated episode is very detailed. For a rebuttal of Pansa on the Fioroni question, see Giorgio Bocca, *Il caso 7 aprile* (Feltrinelli, Milan, 1980). Also see Franco Ferrarotti's discussion of Pansa and Bocca in 'Riflessioni e dati su dodici anni di terrorismo in Italia (1969-1981)' in Galleni (ed.), *Rapporto sul terrorismo*. Negri's formal trial is scheduled to begin in Rome on 14 June 1982.

52. For example, see the introduction to *Autonomia operaia* edited by the Comitati autonomi operai di Roma) (Savelli, Rome, 1976) in which the authors express their desire to organise the masses 'autonomously from the necessity of capital'. This is the essence of Negri's thinking, and it permeates the ambiance of the extraparliamentary left in Italy.

53. Antonio Negri, *Il dominio e il sabotaggio: sul metodo marxista della trasformazione sociale* (Feltrinelli, Milan, 1978), p. 12.

54. Negri, a former Catholic, often employs religious imagery in his writing, e.g. 'The revolutionary working movement is always reborn of a virgin mother'. Ibid., p. 18.

55. Ibid., p. 17.

56. Ibid., p. 36.

57. Negri's hatred of the socialist tradition moves him to quote Shakespeare, albeit a little shakily: 'We are all bastards/And that most venerable man wich [sic] I/Did call my father, was [?] know not where/When I was stamp'd.' See 'Non abbiamo più nulla a che fare'. Ibid.

58. Antonio Negri, *Proletari e stato: per una discussione su autonomia operaia e compromesso storico* (Feltrinelli, Milan, 1976), p. 41.

59. This phrase appears in Negri's *Dall'operaio massa all' operaio sociale: intervista sull'operaismo* (ed. by Paolo Pozzi and Roberta Tommasini) (Multhipia, Milan, 1979), p. 67.

60. Negri, *Proletari e stato*. See Proposition 4, 'L'ipotesi del compromesso storico'.

61. Negri, *Il dominio e il sabotaggio*, p. 42.

62. Cited by Bocca in *Il terrorismo italiano*. See 'Il Movimento'. Elsewhere Negri has expressed his scorn for the 'zio Tom' mentality of Italian workers. See proposition 6, 'In generale: la ristrutturazione e i suoi effetti' in *Proletari e stato.*

63. Fyodor Dostoyevsky, *The Possessed*, p. 415.

64. Negri, *Il dominio e il sabotaggio*, p. 43.

65. Ibid., p. 45.

66. As for the early history of Autonomia, Negri attributes much importance to the work of Raniero Panzieri, the director of *Mondo operaio* in the late 1950s and the founder of *Quaderni rossi* in 1961. Panzieri, according to Negri, undertook 'an analytical deepening of Italian politics and, above all, of the new situation of capitalist development' from a Marxist perspective (*Dall'operaio massa all operaio sociale*, p. 36). Furthermore, Negri asserted, Panzieri 'proposed a series of hypotheses for research' to the young Communist staff members on the *Quaderni rossi*. This journal affronted PCI sensibilities to such an extent that *l'Unità* attacked the *Quaderni rossi* writers – and Negri was one of them – as members of 'gruppi fascisti', a typical party response to the problem raised by the extraparliamentary left until quite recently. Ibid. See 'Alle origini dell'operaismo: i Quaderni rossi'.

67. Mikhail Bakunin, 'Revolution, Terrorism, Banditry' in Walter Laqueur (ed.), *The Terrorism Reader: A Historical Anthology* (Meridian, New York, 1978), p 65.

68. Mikhail Bakunin, *Ritratto dell'Italia borghese (1866-1871)* in Pier Carlo

Masini (ed.), *Scritti editi e inediti di Michele Bakunin*, vol. 2 (Novecento Grafico, Bergamo, 1961), p. 48.

69. Negri also acknowledged and denounced the atrocities perpetrated by Communist regimes in Cambodia and Vietnam, adding that Mao was never more wrong than when he designated the Third World as the most likely place for Communist revolution. What the Third World produces instead are dictatorships of a kind so savage and primitive that sophisticated Western intellectuals find it difficult to take them in. On this note we hear echoes of the 'hard' Marxism of Marx himself who had very little patience with anyone harbouring sentimental notions regarding 'backward people', a phrase he had no compunction about using in its most pejorative sense. For example, dreadful as the British occupation of India was, he wrote in 1853, the one good thing to come out of it would be 'the annihilation of old Asiatic society'. See 'The Future Results of British Rule in India' in David McClellan (ed.), *Karl Marx: Selected Writings* (Oxford University Press, Oxford, 1977), pp. 332-7.

70. Negri, *Dall'operaio massa all'operaio sociale*, p. 131. Indeed, Negri's Autonomia operaia has been defined as 'a communist movement which is led by the masses'. Manzini, *Indagine su un brigatista rossa: la storia di Walter Alasia*. See Part VI.

71. See D. Riazanov (ed.), 'From the Unpublished Manuscripts of Karl Marx and Friedrich Engels: Bakunin: *Statism and Anarchy*', in the Widener Library at Harvard. Marx dismissed Bakunin's ideas as 'Asinine!' 'Democratic Rubbish!' and 'Political Verbiage!' These were his marginal notes in his copy of *Statism and Anarchy*.

72. Negri, *Proletari e stato*. See Proposition 11, 'Ora subito: appunti sul programma'.

73. See the testimony of Carlo Fioroni in Pansa, *Storie italiane di violenza e terrorismo*, 'Il mito dell'insurrezione: una vita qualunque'. See also Pansa's account of the short life of Matteo Caggegi, a Sicilian youth who grew up in the underworld of Turin and moved easily into the clandestine groups of the terrorist left. Ibid., 'Al bar dell'Angelo'.

74. Bakunin's programme for revolutionary terror is analysed by Paul Thomas in *Karl Marx and the Anarchists* (Routledge & Kegan Paul, London, 1980), pp. 290.

75. In Pansa, *Storie italiane di violenza e terrorismo*, p. 191.

76. Ibid., 'Il tam-tam di Autonomia'.

77. Karl Mannheim, *Ideology and Utopia: an Introduction to the Sociology of Knowledge* (Harcourt, Brace and World, New York, 1936), p. 159. Curcio never saw the inside of a factory either and entertained a simlarly abstract and romanticised concept of the proletariat. See Silj, *Never Again Without a Rifle*, p. 79.

78. Negri, *Dall'operaio massa all'operaio sociale*. See 'La fine dei gruppi: la conflittualità diffusa e la nascita dell'autonomia'.

79. Potere operaio was torn apart by the rivalry of Negri and Franco Piperno. For the background of these ideological struggles, see Pansa, *Storie italiane di violenza e terrorismo*, pp. 38ff.

80. Negri, *Dall'operaio massa all'operaio sociale*, 'Dall'eclisse dell'operaio massa alla centralità dell'operaio sociale'. Prior to the Moro affair, however, Autonomia operaia pronouncements on the Red Brigades were more ambivalent, e.g. in 1976 the terrorists were criticised for lacking a co-ordinating revolutionary strategy which, presumably, only the leadership of Autonomia operaia could provide; but at the same time this accolade was betstowed on them: 'to these comrades goes, however, the merit of having created a concrete exigency, an integrating part of the revolutionary movement.' *Autonomia operaia*, p. 370. Angelo Ventura makes

the telling point that Autonomia's April 1978 rejection of the Red Brigades ('every last residual rapport has fallen') 'at the same time confirms a rapport that had existed until then'. See his 'Il problema storico del terrorismo italiano'.

81. Hannah Arendt, *The Origins of Totalitarianism* (Harcourt, Brace and Company, New York, 1951), p. 183.

82. See the testimony of Carlo Fioroni in Pansa, *Storie italiane di violenza e terrorismo*, pp. 36ff.

83. Thomas Sheehan, 'Italy Behind the Ski Mask' *The New York Review of Books*, 16 August 1979.

84. Negri, *Il dominio e il sabotaggio*. See 'Una quarta parentesi (sul partito)'.

85. Negri, *Dall'operaio massa all'operaio sociale*, p. 38.

86. Ibid., p. 131.

87. Karl Mannheim's *Essays on the Sociology of Culture* (Routledge, London, 1956) is an invaluable work for anyone interested in how a country's historic traditions exert a powerful and continuing force on contemporary politics and culture. Stated this baldly the connection sounds almost trite, but in view of how immediate most political analysis is, how lacking in historical perspective, the obvious bears repeating.

88. Antonio Gramsci, *The Modern Prince and Other Writings* (International Publishers, New York, 1957), p. 143.

89, Denis Mack Smith, *Victor Emanuel, Cavour, and the Risorgimento* (Oxford, London, 1971), See his Preface.

90. Regarding the failure of the Socialist Party, Angelo Tasca wrote, '. . . it shirked its task. It lurked in the background all through the postwar crisis. This desertion is the sole explanation of the Fascist success.' *The Rise of Italian Fascism* (Fertig, New York, 1966), p. 325.

91. The Communist opposition in particular badly misplayed its hand against Mussolini, with Amadeo Bordiga dismissing the March on Rome as a 'picturesque episode' and with Umberto Terracini calling it 'a slightly agitated ministerial crisis'. In 1978 Terracini remembered: 'We were all mistaken in our judgments and forecasts . . . Who then thought of a regime? Perhaps not even Mussolini.' See his *Intervista sul comunismo difficile* (ed. by Arturo Gismondi) (Laterza, Bari, 1978), p. 39. The PCI leadership was virtually eliminated by the Fascist dragnet, and Terracini asks, 'Was this not a final proof of our incomprehension of the totalitarian character of fascism, of its real reactionary nature?' (p. 63).

92. I think that this historical fact is the best answer to A. James Gregor's overly ambitious claims for Fascist ideology in his stimulating book, *The Ideology of Fascism: the Rationale of Totalitarianism* (Free Press, New York, 1969).

93. Rodolfo Brancoli, *Spettatori interessati: gli Stati Uniti e la crisi italiana, 1975-1980* (Garzanti, Milan, 1980). See Chapter 9. See also Gianfranco Pasquino, 'Italian Christian Democracy: a Party for all Seasons?' in Lange and Tarrow (eds.), *Italy in Transition*, for a cogent analysis of DC strengths and weaknesses.

94. Brancoli, citing Joseph La Palombara, attributes America's low opinion of the DC to the anti-Catholic and anti-Latin prejudices of the Wasp establishment, but this analysis fails to explain why so many Italian commentators — journalists, historians and sociologists — happen to share that opinion. Certainly, it is not for the same motives attributed to the Americans. *Spettatori interessati*, p. 327.

95. Ibid., p. 99.

96. Umberto Terracini, the veteran Communist activist and contemporary of Gramsci, recently explained: 'even if we had been able to foresee the fascist victory, with all its disastrous consequences, we still would have created our party.' This remark suggests something of the fanatical nature of Italian politics on the eve of Fascism. See his *Intervista sul comunismo difficile*, p. 28. Terracini

is also very good on the PCI in-fighting between 'i bordighiani' and 'gli ordinovisti'. See Part II,'La fondazione del Partito Comunista'.

97. See Terracini's illuminating distinction between Gramsci and Togliatti, ibid., p. 52. Although both fought against party members to the left led by Bordiga, and to the right, led by Angelo Tasca, Gramsci, who clearly had an intuition about the political degeneration of the Soviet Party under Stalin, looked to the International as the leading institution of world revolution, whereas Togliatti looked to the Soviet Communist Party. If Gramsci had reservations about the Soviet Party in 1926, what would he have thought in another dozen years?

98. Sciascia sees the Red Brigadists as 'the grandchildren or great-grandchildren of Stalinist communism'. *L'affaire Moro*, p. 17.

99. For a penetrating discussion of how the opposition parties influence the 'currents' within the DC, see Giorgio Galli and Paolo Facchi, *La sinistra democristiana: storia e ideologia* (Feltrinelli, Milan, 1962).

100. In *Social Structure in Italy* Acquaviva and Santuccio place great stress on the vital importance of the American model for Italians since the end of World War II. See Part I, 'Vertical and Horizontal Structure'. This somewhat abstractly stated point comes vividly alive in Giorgio Manzini's *Indagine su un brigatista rossa* when the author depicts the teenaged Alasia passing hours in his bedroom listening to records while lying in bed. His favourites were by Jimi Hendrix, Vanilla Fudge, Jethro Tull and by others who dominated the Top Forty record charts of the early 1970s in America (p. 70). In a very real cultural sense national boundaries have ceased to exist for the young in the West.

101. Pier Paolo Pasolini, 'Gli italiani non sono più quelli', *Il corriere della sera*, 10 June 1974.

102. Alberto Moravia, 'Quel moralismo armato che non esita a uccidere', *Il corriere della sera*, 6 November 1977. In his novel, *La vita interiore* (1978), Moravia presents an artistic vision of what he means by contemporary terrorism representing 'the dream of a heroic community'. See Angus Davidson's translation of this novel, rendered in English with a much more appropriate title, *Time of Desecration* (Farrar, Strauss, Giroux, New York, 1980).

103. Alberto Minucci, 'Non fanatici terroristi', *Rinascita*, 11 November 1977. See Moravia's rejoinder to this piece, 'Un terrorismo vecchio di secoli', *Il corriere della sera*, 13 November 1977.

104. Silj points out that Curcio's Catholic experience was atypical, in 'What Catholic Matrix?', *Never Again Without a Rifle*. However, see his biographical portrait of Alberto Franceschini for another example of a dissident Catholic who joined the Communist Party before turning to the extraparliamentary left and terrorism. Ibid., p. 37.

105. For Cagol's Catholic background, see Agostini, *Mara Cagol*, 'San Romedio: Margherita Cagol'.

106. Ronchey, 'Guns and Grey Matter'. Giorgio Bocca describes this ideology as 'cattocomunismo', in *Il terrorismo italiano*, p. 7. In *Social Structure in Italy* Acquaviva and Santuccio assert, 'It is well known that it is in Catholic countries that the more extreme forms of Marxism flourish (p. 177). In the same passage they add, 'The socialism of the countries of northern Europe is modeled on Protestant pluralism (e.g in England and Scandinavia), but Catholic countries (.eg. France, Spain, and Italy) think of their socialism as rather like a highly centralized Catholicism, a monolithic influence in society that dominates both the national culture and the individual conscience.' Ignazio Silone also addresses the consonance between the Catholic social vision with that of the Marxists, at least on the psychological level, in *Bread and Wine* (Harper, New York, 1937): 'Revolutionary action had always seemed to be demanded of him [Pietro Spina]

by the collective good. The ideal of the collective good had been inculcated into him from his earliest years by his Christian education. His subsequent intellectual development had modified the premises on which his original adherence to Socialism had been based, but he had not been able to modify the internal structure of his mind' (p. 129).

107. The Soccorso Rosso dossier on the Red Brigades advances the following thesis: 'To understand the genesis of the Red Brigades it is indispensable to turn to the sociology faculty in Trento.' *Brigate rosse*, p. 24. For background material on this department and on its founder, Bruno Kessler, see Agostini, *Mara Cagol*, 'L'esperienza trentina – sociologia'.

108. Curcio's articles for Walter Peruzzi's *Lavoro politico* (October 1967-January 1969) are also of interest for the student leader's views during this period. The entire staff of *Lavoro politico* belonged to the PC d'I (Partito Comunista d'Italia), a revolutionary party opposed to the reformism of the PCI.

109. Jane Kramer, *Unsettling Europe* (Random House, New York, 1980). See 'The San Vincenzo Cell (1979)'.

110. In *Il seme religioso della rivolta* (Rusconi, Milan, 1979) Acquaviva claims that 'the movements of the 'new' extraparliamentary left' are evangelical in nature, reacting against what their members view as the fall from revolutionary grace of the PCI. See no.40. Even the moderate Communist, Umberto Terracini, scolds his party for withdrawing too hastily and too far from a traditional Marxist position: 'In short, for me the class struggle is not a particular of secondary importance.' *Intervista sul comunismo difficile*, p. 182.

111. In a 15 June 1976 interview with Giampaolo Pansa of the *Corriere della sera*, Enrico Berlinguer reflected that 'the Italian way to socialism' is possible only *because* of NATO. Berlinguer is supervising a political experiment which is completely dependent upon a climate of freedom, and without such a climate his hopes for the PCI no doubt would have been blasted by the chilling example of Czechoslovakia in 1968, an event the Italian Communist leader had in mind when he made these remarks to Pansa. For a full analysis of this interview, see Ronchey, *Accade in italia: 1968-1977*, 'La questione dell'Est'.

112. Cited by Brancoli, *Spettatori interessati*, p. 316.

113. John F. Burns, 'Soviet Publishes Scathing Attack on Italian Party', *The New York Times*, 25 January 1982.

114. For an analysis of Turati's enduring legacy on the left, see Spencer di Scala, *Dilemmas of Italian Socialism: the Politics of Filippo Turati* (The University of Massachusetts Press, Amherst, 1980).

115. See Peter Lange's analysis of this point, 'Crisis and Consent, Change and Compromise: Dilemmas of Italian Communism in the 1970s', in Lange and Tarrow (eds.), *Italy in Transition*.

116. *Autonomia operaia*, p. 367.

117. Manzini, *Indagine su un brigatista rossa: la storia di Walter Alasia*, p. 70.

118. Ronchey, *Accade in Italia: 1968-1977*. See Chapter 9, 'Bande nere, brigate rosse'.

119. Gianfranco Pasquino, 'Italian Christian Democracy: a Party for all Seasons?' in Lange and Tarrow (eds.), *Italy in Transition*, p. 108.

120. Acquaviva describes Italian intellectual life as 'culturally closed in a kind of orthodox Marxist ghetto'. *Il seme religioso della rivolta*, no. 23. He also notes that the radicalisation of Italy's intellectuals has prepared the way for the possibility of revolution just as the radicalisation of intellectuals in France prepared the psychological climate for the French Revolution, although the role of the intellectuals is immeasurably greater today because of the impact of the media. See *Guerriglia e guerra rivoluzionaria in Italia*, p. 35.

121. According to Alberto Martinelli, the decline of the Italian bourgeoisie's

power 'can be traced both to the growing power of the labor unions and to the growing State intervention and to party management of the economy'. See his 'Organized Business and Italian Politics: Confindustria and the Christian Democrats in the Postwar Period' in Lange and Tarrow (eds.), *Italy in Transition*.

122. Ronchey, *Accade in Italia*, p. 219. See Angelo Ventura's analysis of the same problem in 'Il problema storico del terrorismo italiano'. He writes that the one thing the Catholic left has in common with the Marxist left is a 'visceral hatred of modern industrial society'.

123. Acquaviva and Santuccio, *Social Structure in Italy*, p. 57.

124. See Ermanno Gorrieri's devastating analysis of how the Italian government diverts the wealth produced by a minority of productive workers towards the maintenance of a constantly expanding 'intellectualistic-bureaucratic apparatus' in *La giungla retributiva* (Il Mulino, Bologna, 1972), pp. 15ff. Representative of this problem is the story of Gino Sferza, president of Standa, who had to spend more than a thousand million lire just to obtain marketing licences. Cited by Ronchey in *Accade in Italia: 1968-1977*, p. 108.

125. J. Bowyer Bell, *A Time of Terror: How Democratic Societies Respond to Revolutionary Violence* (Basic Books, New York, 1978), p. 259. Cesare Lombroso, *Gli anarchici* (Napoleone, Rome, 1972 edn), p. 35.

126. On pp. 288-9 she writes, 'No governing class has done more than Italy's to preserve the illusion that it alone is to blame for the terrorist torments inflicted upon it.' An international terrorist conspiracy cannot be ruled out, although Sterling rarely offers anything as firm as proof to support such claims, as she herself admits on p. 247: 'Few of the terrorist bands mentioned in this book can be shown to have had direct links with the Soviet Union.'

127. Mannheim, *Ideology and Utopia*, p. 159.

128. Silone, *Bread and Wine*, p. 157. The biography of the Red Brigadist, Roberto Ognibene, provides an apt illustration of this psychological process. According to one of his teachers, 'Robert was, and still is, a young man who aims at the absolute. He is alien to half measures.' Cited by Silj, *Never Again Without a Rifle*, p. 8.

129. Quoted by Walter Laqueur in *Terrorism: a Study of National and International Political Violence* (Little, Brown and Company, Boston, 1977), p. 5.

130. Juan Linz, 'Some Notes Toward a Comparative Study of Fascism in Sociological Historical Perspective' in Walter Laqueur (ed.), *Fascism A Reader's Guide*, (The University of California Press, Berkeley/Los Angeles, 1976).

131. Acquaviva and Santuccio, *Social Structure in Italy*, p. 178. Acquaviva makes this same point in *Guerriglia e guerra rivoluzionaria in Italia*. 'Italy is a country in which the passage from illegality to violence, to guerrilla warfare, has an ancient historical tradition' (p. 24).

132. Sciascia, *L'affaire Moro*, p. 128.

133. This statement was attributed to Negri by Carlo Fioroni, *Il corriere della sera*, 27 December 1979. Cited by Angelo Ventura, 'Il problema storico del terrorismo italiano'.

134. For a comparative analysis of homicides and assaults, see Michael Tonry and Norval Morris (eds.), *Crime and Justice: An Annual Review of Research*, vol. 3 (The University of Chicago Press, Chicago, 1981). See also Hugh Davis Graham and Ted Robert Gurr (eds.), *Violence in America* (Sage, Beverly Hills, 1979).

135. In 1978, Rosario Romeo claimed that: 'Since the 1968 upheavals in France and Italy, our country has never returned to normality. We are suffering from what could be described as a permanent general strike.' Rosario Romeo and George Urban, 'Troubled Italy'.

136. See Acquaviva, *Guerriglia e guerra rivoluzionaria in Italia*, for an analysis

of the six stages of guerrilla warfare: (1) sporadic terrorism; (2) diffuse terrorism; (3) emergence of a network of terrorist groups; (4) unity of action between these groups; (5) creating partisan areas of intensive action; and (6) controlling those areas (p. 145). Italy has witnessed, in varying degrees, all six of these phenomena, except perhaps the last, but even on this point it is worth noting that on 11 December 1979 Prima linea was able to attack the Istituto di amministrazione aziendale dell'università di Torino without interference, hold the entire school captive for 45 minutes, kneecap five professors and five students, and then escape without trace. Pansa, *Storie italiane di violenza e terrorismo*, 'Attacco a una scuola'.

6 SPAIN'S INTERNAL SECURITY: THE BASQUE AUTONOMOUS POLICE FORCE*

Jose A. Trevino

Introduction: The Current Predicament

Ultimate success or failure of Spain's Basque autonomy project[1] depends, to a large extent, on the government's ability to control the internal security problem. The future of Basque home rule is tied to the workability and acceptability of the plan dealing with the autonomous Basque police force and the issue of the continued presence and the intervention of national, as opposed to regional, police resources in given situations in the Basque provinces. To date, the almost exclusive use of the central security forces[2] there is one of the most sensitive issues which affects the attitudes of many Basques towards the central government. Two 'states of exception' (estados de excepcion)[3] or states of emergency declared by the Spanish government since 1968 and the rigorous police controls imposed after the Spanish Civil War (1936-9) have left bitter memories among the Basques. It is no wonder that police control is presently one of the most emotional issues in the Basque conflict. In fact one of the most persistent demands made by ETA,[4] the Basque separatist terrorist organisation and its radical political supporters, has been the immediate withdrawal of the police forces from Euzkadi. Through repeated and systematic acts of violence against the police and armed forces, ETA has made it clear it will not settle for less. Trained and organised as a clandestine armed organisation, ETA appears prepared to continue the armed struggle. ETA has in fact declared that it is waging a 'revolutionary war' against the state. This scenario creates a very hostile environment for the central police and armed forces in Euzkadi.

Consequently, the central police forces and to a certain degree also the military elements assigned to Euzkadi are in a very vulnerable position. For the most part, the Basque population is cold and indifferent towards the members of the state security. Not only is their presence resented and their isolation from the local population almost complete, but members of the security forces have been bearing the brunt of continued terrorist attacks since 1968. In 1979, of the 79

terrorist victims in Euzkadi, 32 were police officers.[5] ETA also assassinated seven high ranking military officers in 1979, including three general
officers. Only one of these general officers was killed in Euzkadi
however; he was the military governor for the Basque province of
Guipuzcoa who was killed in September 1979. He was shot from
behind as he went for a stroll with his wife one Sunday evening.

By far the typical ETA assassination however involves rank and file
policemen. Most killings occur in broad daylight in the streets.[6] On
other occasions the terrorists calmly walk into a bar or cafeteria serving
policemen on breaks from their duties. Often without even bothering
to conceal their identities, the terrorists single out their targets and
'execute' them in front of scores of onlookers. Yet, when police investigators try to ascertain the facts, witnesses are almost impossible to find.

The reluctance of Basque citizens to co-operate with the investigators comes mostly from fear or apathy, although there are those who
are truly sympathetic to ETA's cause. The fear of associating or collaborating with the police is well founded. There is little doubt that ETA
has an effective intelligence network which pervades almost every segment of Basque society. Further, ETA has repeatedly demonstrated its
ruthlessness against informants and 'collaborators'. Besides, the
ordinary citizen is generally noncommital. He wants to live in peace in
his homeland. The policemen are almost all outsiders, recruited from
other regions of Spain. They are largely unfamiliar with the local
culture and customs and within a year they are normally reassigned out
of the Basque region.

Consequently, in Euzkadi, a vicious circle sets in. The inability of
the police to cope with terrorism undermines the already shattered
confidence in the police. The public's reluctance to co-operate further
undermines the police forces' ability to fight terrorism effectively.

Understandably, these conditions lead to low morale and frustration
among the police forces as they become aware they are getting the
worst part of a deal in an apparently hopeless situation. Their visibility
makes them inviting targets for the terrorists. ETA labels them visible
tools of 'repression' and government officials concede there is no effective defence against these terrorist attacks. Unfortuntely for the police
officers, these attacks are becoming not only more numerous but
also more and more systematic. On some occasions, the tension, fear
and frustration resulting from this hostile situation has been reflected
in several incidents involving the breakdown of discipline and morale
of the police forces in Euzkadi. In October 1978, following a series of
repeated fatal ambushes by ETA against police units, almost an entire

National Police garrison in Bassauri, Bilbao mutinied. Most of the men at this garrison, 400 strong, refused to go on duty and engaged in acts of insubordination.The government quickly flew in reinforcements from the south and relieved the entire garrison. Formal charges were filed against 25 of the policemen.

In July 1978, a series of alleged excesses committed by the police forces discredited, in the eyes of the Basque population, the already tarnished image of the police and exposed a potential weakness in the current system. While quelling political demonstrations in Renteria, Guipuzcoa, police fired their weapons and a young demonstrator received a fatal bullet wound. Every policeman in the detail was placed under investigation and his weapon confiscated for ballistic tests. Soon, barricades went up and more Basque demonstrations erupted protesting at the death. Shortly thereafter, a police contingent patrolling a commercial zone in the city which was closed for business because of the tense situation, went on a rampage, destroying windows and other property. More internal inquiries followed.

It is obvious from the first episode that ETA achieved a psychological victory against the establishment. It demonstrated it could challenge the police authority in the streets and make them give it up. It is also apparent from the other episodes that the working conditions for the policemen in Euzkadi have had an impact on their mission of winning over the populace. In 1979, recognising the seriousness of the threat to the security forces, the government began to curtail a policeman's tour of duty to Euzkadi to one year, without dependents. Although the government has acted quickly and strongly every time to restore potentially grave situations back to normal, little can be done to reverse the damage to the public's confidence and police morale. Similarly, not much can be done to deny ETA the psychological gains it has made at the expense of the police and the establishment. In spite of sporadic attempts by the government to take the offensive against terrorism in Euzkadi,[7] the role of the security forces there is largely reactive and defensive. During every renewed offensive against the terrorists, police make numerous arrests of suspected ETA members and seize large quantities of explosives and guns, but the terrorist killings and bombings continue unabated afterwards. The main caches of explosives and weapons are seldom found however.[8] Most of those arrested belong to peripheral cells in the support apparatus of ETA. The triggermen are seldom identified let alone brought to trial. Most major terrorist crimes remain unresolved and even if the persons responsible were brought to trial it would be difficult to convict them. The difficulties of the Spanish government or of any civilised society faced with a similar problem regarding its internal security becomes very evident.

The Alternative: A Plan for the Future

The alternative to maintaining a highly visible security force in the Basque region is of course to allow the Basques to form their own local police organisation.[9] The central government and the political group representing the Basques, the Nationalist Basque Party (PNV), apparently agree in principle with the idea; who better qualified to deal with Basque security than the Basque themselves? The plan is even more appealing and logical when one considers that it is drawing most of the fire from the terrorists. The government in Madrid, however, holds certain reservations and to date this issue has become one of the major stumbling blocks and the plan still remains to be fully implemented.

In practical terms, the basic problem in establishing a Basque police force boils down to the selection process of the members who will comprise it and the legal mechanisms whereby the central security forces will intervene in Euzkadi. As to the membership of the new Basque police force, the questions of recruitment, training, leadership and functions of the new police force are of obvious importance. Both sides (moderate Basques and the central government) basically agree that the leadership cadre in the Basque police organisation, from the grades of lieutenant or captain and higher, should have a professional military background, i.e. they must be graduates of one of the Spanish military academies. It is feared that the difficult phase will be the recruitment of rank and file policemen.

One fear is that, at first at least, there may be a lack of Basque volunteers to join the police force. This lack of response may be due to a basic reluctance on the part of many young Basques to identify with a police system, especially one which is still subordinated to the central state. It is said that this reluctance to join will perhaps stem from the tarnished image police agencies have received over the years. In some cases, this image is not totally undeserved.[10] In addition, it is among Basque youth that the ideas of radical nationalism, separatism and anti-Spanish attitudes are evidently more firmly ingrained.[11] It is also from among the young that ETA gets most of its converts. The most serious concern, however, is that those who do decide to join the police may be sympathetic to ETA or its radical cause and may do so only to infiltrate the new police organisation. This infiltration will obviously downgrade

its integrity and effectiveness. In several instances members or sympathisers of ETA have already been discovered serving in the Spanish
military. Similarly, in May 1980 in Bilbao, police investigations led to
two municipal policemen of Basque extraction who were active
members of the ETA organisation.[12] One of them was arrested but the
other fled and apparently went underground.

Another issue with regard to the creation of the Basque police organisation is the question of personnel strength. Initially, it was said that
the PNV, the Basque incumbent political party, considered asking for a
total of 20,000 new policemen for the new police force. But the central
government reportedly dismissed the idea. This figure was considered
too inflated and some felt that a police force of this number would
practically constitute a 'People's Army of Euzkadi'. The formula
used in Spain to determine the ideal number of policemen required to
service a society is one policeman for every 700 to 800 inhabitants.
Because of the increased political tension in Euzkadi in recent years,
however, the present ratio there is about one policeman for every 600
inhabitants, for a total of approximately 5,000 members. This figure is
a combined total for the three police bodies; the Civil Guard, the
National Police and the Superior Police Corps. Since the central government obviously does not intend to withdraw its security forces from
Euzkadi in the immediate future, the number of quotas for Basque
policemen would be offset by the already existing national forces.

The numbers and functions of this new Basque police force have
been arrived at more or less firmly and the result appears to be a
relatively limited and innocuous Basque force. The total number of
Basque policemen was set at approximately 800 policemen, or about
one Basque policeman for every 2,500 inhabitants. The Basque policemen will only be armed with small sidearms however. Their duties will
be limited to patrolling the cities. The closest that Basque policemen
will ever come to handling internal subversion will be in the handling of
local demonstrations and low level agitation. The Basque police force
will also be responsible for policing the local secondary highways but
the Civil Guard will continue to monitor the national highway system.

Initially, the plan envisions for each of the three Basque provinces
to have its own provincial police force. In two to three years from their
creation, however, these provincial police units can merge and form a
consolidated regional police organisation under the new president of
the Basque regional government. The Basque president could, under the
statute, have a police inspector or similar official as chief of police
operations and adviser on security matters (or comparable positions)

on his staff. The positions of responsibility within the chain of command of this incipient Basque police force will be filled with military officers or graduates of the central police academy. Whereas the autonomous Basque government can select and recruit the policemen, the central government will maintain a review mechanism in order to try to detect infiltrations by subversive elements. Also, according to the plan, the central security forces will intervene only in extreme cases, when the limits of public order get out of control or appear to be of a grave nature. When this intervention will actually take place and who will determine that the situation is indeed out of control are questions which are still unsettled. There is no time-tested legal mechanism to achieve this complicated interface.

The Legal Mechanisms: What Kind of Security?

The legal basis for the autonomous police force in Euzkadi lies in the Spanish constitution and the 1979 Basque Home Rule Statute. Questions arise, however, as to how these provisions should be implemented in a way that will satisfy both sides. The Spanish government's incumbent political party UCD (Centre Democratic Union) tried to reconcile two principles which appear to be mutually exclusive. One principle which holds that as part of the overall settlement Basques are entitled to their own security force, may clash with the principle that Spain's central government should retain ultimate control over public order and security matters throughout the country. After the Basque police have taken over, the central forces will try to lower their visibility in Euzkadi or withdraw altogether according to a specific timetable. Basque radicals and ETA demand the latter programme of total withdrawal. The government, however, appears to be more inclined towards the former alternative.

Undoubtedly the question of who exercises ultimate control over the security forces is crucial to the success of the autonomy programme. The Spanish constitution in Art. 154 envisions a government-appointed delegate (Marcelino Creja, former Foreign Minister in the Suarez administration was appointed to that position on 10 October 1980) who would direct the central state's administration and act as a liaison point between the autonomous region and the central government. He is called Governor General of Euzkadi. The Basque Home Rule Statute (Art. 17) in turn envisions a Joint Commission for Security which is supposed to co-ordinate Basque security with the central government. Membership in this Commission is to to be divided equally between representatives from the central state administration and the Basque autonomous region. Although the Basque Home Rule Statute officially went into effect on 11 January 1980, necessary legislation which will elaborate on the provision of Art. 17 of the statute regarding Basque autonomous police forces is still pending. When completed, this legislation will specifically define the role of the central security forces in the Basque provinces under the new legal configuration.

Theoretically, the mechanism for the transfer of police powers and their subsequent interface with the central government appears to be sound and workable, under ideal conditions. The reality and actual application of this mechanism, however, are much more complicated. In May 1980 the central government apparently tried to strengthen its hand within the Basque security scheme. In the draft legislation which the government was required to submit to Parliament concerning the specific provisions for the Basque police force, the government proposed that the delegate appointed by Madrid, the Governor General of Euzkadi, also preside over the Joint Security Commission. It is obvious this arrangement would give the central government undisputed superiority on security matters. There was strong opposition to this proposal, however, both in Parliament and among the public in the Basque provinces. The government withdrew the draft legislation from Parliament rather than risk facing the rising opposition.

There is little doubt that not only internal security but the entire autonomy issue turns on the intended or actual future role of the central security forces in the Basque region. The mechanism which will bring them into play is still untested and fraught with uncertainty. The government apparently intends to maintain a substantial police presence in Euzkadi, albeit a less visible and active one. The Civil Guard and the National Police, the two uniformed national police bodies, will spend more time in their respective garrisons and curtail their patrolling duties. The functions of the Superior Police Corps, comprised of plainclothes investigators, will remain relatively unchanged however. Under the central direction, they will continue to carry out investigations of major crimes, including terrorist matters, in Euzkadi. No one seems to know with certainty, however, what will be the result if the internal security situation in Euzkadi deteriorates to such an extent that the central government regards it as intolerable.[13] What will happen for instance when terrorism slides into guerrilla operations to include take-overs of government installations?

What will be the result when the number of terrorist killings increases alarmingly in that region or when barricades set up by agitators become virtual battle lines? How will the central government react when confronted with deteriorating law and order in the northern provinces?[14] The question is, how *can* it react under the autonomous relationship created by the constitution and the Home Rule Statute for the Basques. In that regard, the text of the Home Rule Statute provides that the maintenance of public order in Euzkadi is the exclusive responsibility of Basque institutions. It further provides that if the central security forces must intervene in Euzkadi because of an acute internal security problem which exceeds the public order domain, they may do so, but only when requested by the Basque regional government.

The Basque Home Rule Statute also contains what appears to be a possible shortcut to this intervention process. It provides that the central security forces can intervene on the central government's initiative, if in that government's estimation the general interests of the state are seriously jeopardised by events in Euzkadi. This provision is qualified, however. The Statute requires this self-initiated intervention to hinge on the approval of the Joint Security Commission, the organisation created by the Statute and which the central government presumably still wants to be presided over by its Governor General for the Basque provinces.

In essence then, the so-called self-initiated response to intervene in Euzkadi when the general interests of Spain are at stake is not a decision to intervene, but a decision to request approval to do so. When this request to intervene is considered by the Joint Commission, a body comprised of an equal number of representatives from the central state and the autonomous region, a deadlocked or delayed response can easily result. The members of the Commission will most likely fail to agree that a serious alteration of public order in Euzkadi actually jeopardises the general interests of Spain.

Theoretically, the central security forces including the armed forces, can still intervene on their own initiative under a different and more serious scenario than the two described above. They can intervene to handle a situation of 'extreme urgency' to discharge the duties assigned to them by the constituion. The constitution charges the armed forces with 'protecting the rights and liberties of citizens and guaranteeing the public security'. This mission, however, is also assigned to the autonomous security organisations within their respective territories. This constitutional provision presumably gives the armed forces justification for intervening in the governing process by claiming that the unity of

Spain is in jeopardy. Legally, however, the decision to intervene under this scenario is not left entirely to the armed forces' leadership, the central government must again play a role by notifying the central Parliament of the desire to intervene. In a country experiencing a political transition, this process of checks and balances holds great uncertainty.

The Future: Internal Security in Perspective

Without granting full independence to the Basques the Spanish government negotiated the Home Rule Statute with the PNV, the major political force in Euzkadi and head of the new regional government there since the March 1980 local elections. The PNV, however, is under growing pressure from the left. Two leftist groups, Euzkadio Ezkerra (EE) and Herri Batasuna (NB)[15] which together drew a substantial portion of the Basque popular vote in the local elections of March 1980, vehemently oppose the Home Rule Statute, they want full independence. When the Statute went into effect the Basques themselves were apparently still politically divided on this issue. The rate of voting absenteeism was high during the referendum held in the Basque provinces to ratify the Home Rule. Nevertheless, some believed one of the most difficult hurdles in the autonomy project had been cleared when the referendum showed that all who voted did so in the affirmative. Under a great deal of political tension, the Home Rule Statute for Euzkadi was negotiated, debated and finally approved by Parliament. Ratified by Spanish Parliament in October 1979, the Statute was to take effect on 11 January 1980.

Still to speak definitely on the subject, however, was ETA. When it came, ETA's message was timely and symbolic. On 10 January 1980, in a very selective operation, ETA terrorists gunned down army Major Jesus Velazco, the commander of the provincial police force for the Basque province of Alava. As Major Velazco stopped his car at a traffic light, two gunmen with automatic weapons stepped in front of his car and opened fire.

The assassination had special political significance because of the victim's position and the organisation he represented. Unlike its sister provinces of Guipuzcoa and Vizcaya, Alava did not lose its privilege of maintaining its own police force after the civil war. Therefore, the Alavese police force, comprised of approximately 100 men, was considered the prototype for the future Basque police organisation. The victim was almost certain to receive confirmation in his post, thus making Alava a showcase for the government's plan. With a provincial police force already in existence in Alava the transition in that province would have been smooth; it simply required the formality of transferring the line of authority to the Basque regional government. ETA was to show its determination again, however, to insure its message and the significance of this action against the provincial police chief was not lost. In a flagrant act of defiance and ruthlessness, ETA decided to eliminate Captain Eugenio Lazaro, the deputy to Major Velazco who had automatically become the new chief of the Alavese police force. So, on a Sunday morning, as Lazaro departed church services, ETA gunmen shot him at point blank range. His death occurred on 13 April 1980, only three months after Major Velazco was killed. No one could doubt where ETA stood on the issue of a separate police force for Euzkadi or that ETA's actions spoke louder than words.

Under the plan for a Basque police force, the key positions in the new organisation would be filled with army officers or career policemen loyal to the central government. The two other Basque provinces who did not already have their own police force would form local police bodies commanded by individuals like Major Velazco and Captain Lazaro. Evidently, this arrangement is inconsistent with ETA's vision of national independence. The state, however, is not willing and cannot afford to relinquish full control of such a critical area as internal security. Presumably, fewer rank and file policemen will be killed under the new plan, since most of the rank and file policemen will be ethnic Basques and the central police bodies will maintain a low profile. The key positions, however, those filled with people ETA considers as outsiders, will become more lucrative targets in the future. Other government targets, representative of the central state, will also remain in place in Euzkadi. Military installations there, for example, may become increasingly vulnerable. The creation of a Basque police force is not likely to solve the problem of internal security posed by Basque terrorism in Spain. With the shootings of Major Velazco and Captain Lazaro in Alava, the history of violence against Spanish security forces in Euzkadi comes full circle. It has been repeating itself ever since August 1968 when ETA terrorists assassinated the first Spanish policemen in Euzkadi in cold blood. That year, ETA made a deliberate decision to cross an important threshold in its tactical programme. It was a new tactical phase in its revolutionary strategy. Ten years later, in July 1978, ETA began targeting military officers also. By frontally attacking the security apparatus, ETA has assumed a status of being permanently at war against the Spanish state and ETA's leadership has expressly declared as much.

Postscript

This article is not intended to raise doubts about the capabilities and professionalism of the Spanish Security Forces in dealing with Basque terrorism. On the contrary, the Spanish Security Forces have proven to be among the best in Europe. The article simply alludes to some of the seemingly insurmountable problems they initially had to face with respect to Basque terrorism. In recent months the Spanish Security Forces have demonstrated this professional and overall ability to cope with the internal terrorist problem without straining or putting in jeopardy the legal framework of the young Spanish democracy. Working within the law, they have scored a series of unqualified successes against ETA and noticeably weakened its organisational structure. More importantly, however, these successes have deprived ETA of one of its most crucial weapons: public perception. The Spanish Security Forces have thus earned a large measure of public respect and admiration. They crowned a long series of successes against ETA in January 1982 with the impressive rescue of Julio Ingesias Sr while he was being held hostage in an ETA hideout. This rescue was quickly followed by a recovery of a massive terrorist arsenal. The Spanish Security Forces have indeed made a quantum leap after overcoming a series of historical handicaps. They have insured that the infant Spanish democracy was not smothered in the cradle.

Notes

*This article expresses the perceptions, views and analysis of the writer which are not necessarily those of AFOSI, the United States Air Force or the US Department of Defense.

1. Under its new constitution, Spain adopted a federalist approach in its internal state organisation. This formula allows the regional communities with distinct cultural and linguistic differences to form autonomous governments. The two most important regions are Cataluna, comprised of four provinces in the east, and Euzkadi comprised of three Basque provinces in the north. These two communities have already achieved some degree of autonomy, but some Basques desire full independence.

2. In Spain, the central police force is divided into three major organisations. The Superior Police Corps, which is comparable to the FBI, conducts most substantive investigations and operations. This is the senior police body in Spain and

it is under the Directorate General of the Police (DGP). Also under the DGP is the National Police (NP) which is made up of uniformed policemen. They are used to quell disturbances and patrol the large cities. The third police body is the paramilitary Civil Guard (CG) which maintains public order in rural areas and small communities with populations under 20,000. CG members wear an olive drab uniform with a unique black patent leather tricorn hat. Both the CG and the NP have special weapons attack teams.

3. A 'state of exception' amounts to a state of siege imposed by government decree which curtails or suspends civil liberties within certain designated regions. These decrees suspend habaeas corpus, abrogate citizens' rights against search and seizure and give the police forces more latitude and discretion in their operations. Generally, these decrees are imposed following serious breakdowns in public order and when it is felt police are being hampered by legal requirements. In August 1968, such a state of exception was declared. First it was applied only to the province of Guipuzcoa which is regarded as the bedrock of Basque separatism. Later it was extended to the entire country. It was finally lifted in March 1969. In August 1975, just prior to the death of General Franco, another 'state of exception' was imposed for the Basque provinces. It was lifted shortly after Franco's death by the new regime. So far the new regime has not resorted to this measure.

4. The acronym ETA stands for Euzkadi Ta Askatasuna, which translated from Basque means Basque Fatherland and Liberty. ETA's goal is full independence of the four northern Spanish provinces which ETA calls Euzkadi South. The government only recognises three of these provinces as essentially Basque, however. ETA patterns itself somewhat after the Irish Republican Army (IRA) and some observers have even described ETA's short-range goal as one of trying to 'Ulsterise' the Basque region, i.e. provoke a military intervention to pacifythe area. ETA expects that such an intervention would irretrievably alienate the Basque population and rally further support for ETA against the central authority.

5. A total of 55 policemen died at the hands of terrorists throughout Spain in 1979. Although ETA has targeted police officers consistently since 1968, it only began to target military officers systematically since 1978. The shift in ETA's tactics became very clear in July of that year when ETA commandos struck in the capital of Spain killing a general officer and a lieutenant colonel. Curiously enough, however, ETA has not been known to assassinate policemen outside of Euzkadi. Military targets, however, apparently are not subject to that restriction. A possible explanation could be that ETA regards the withdrawal of the central police forces as simply one stage towards full independence. ETA's real enemy is the military arm of the state and by engaging the military ETA intends to force the government's hand and make it declare that the internal security problem in Euzkadi transcends the public order realm and exceeds the powers of the police to cope with it. Similarly, ETA wants to provoke the military into a unilateral move to intervene in the governing process.

6. There have been instances, however, of indiscriminate firing at off-duty policemen while inside their garrison or while frequenting local eating or drinking establishments.

7. Large-scale crackdowns against ETA normally precede significant political events such as referendums, elections or parliamentary debates related to the home rule issue in Euzkadi. They are also normally undertaken following serious attacks by ETA.

8. It should be noted that even in such a small geographical area as Euzkadi, with a low ratio of policemen *per capita* (one to 600) ETA can still manage to steal and hide several tons of explosives. These are logistical feats of great proportions

but ETA has managed to carry them out several times in the last two or three years. The quantities of explosives normally recovered by the police in their operations are those issued by the organisation to each ETA cell, normally a ten-pound package. Failures by the police to locate the large caches may be due to ETA's extremely tight internal security and the use of well concealed safe houses, possibly in southern France.

9. The Basque provinces had their own police force until this privilege was abrogated along with other autonomous rights which were taken away after the civil war. Only one of the Basque provinces, Alava, retained its police force. Alava sided with Franco during the civil war while Guipuzcoa and Vizcaya were on the losing side.

10. It has been said that ETA's best recruiting aids are the police tactics and the resentment they create among the Basques.

11. It has been stated that the bilingual schools in Euzkadi, which began operating semi-clandestinely in the 1960s, serve more as 'centres of subversion' than of learning. Some maintain that the Ikastolas instil in the young a strong Basque nationalist pride, frequently at the expense of loyalty to the central Spanish state. Most of the young Basque generation of today has been touched by the teachings at these centres.

12. The municipal police is strictly a local organisation which employs large numbers of Basques. This body however has no direct responsibility for law enforcement or security. It is mainly involved in routine administrative duties and traffic control within the cities. They do, however, interface with the other police bodies. In connection with the arrest of the municipal policeman to whom the police applied the anti-terrorist law, the town mayor and the members of the municipal council protested the action and demanded the release of the suspect.

13. A scenario involving continued deterioration of public order such as an unacceptable rise in violence is not far-fetched. One potential source of growing violence in Eujzkadi, in addition to continued acts of terrorism from ETA, is the intra-group fighting between ultra-right elements and separatists This intra-fighting is already going on and it simply compounds the government's problem. This fighting could easily slide into a small civil war.

14. Under the present security arrangement, the government has shown it can and will react strongly to a breakdown in public order. In February 1980 an ETA guerrilla-style ambush on a weapons convoy resulted in the deaths of six Civil Guards and one terrorist. Shortly thereafter, ultra-right terrorists retaliated by bombing an establishment frequented by Basque separatists. The government ordered police reinforcements sent to the Basque provinces and named an army general as commanding officer for all police operations in the area. This enhanced security posture in Euzkadi was terminated in the summer of 1980. Following another serious breakdown in law and order in March 1981 and yielding to military pressures to take a firm stance against terrorists, the government assigned the armed forces to perform duties in combatting terrorism. These duties were limited, however, to augmentation of the police forces.

15. Basque Left and People United respectively. Basque Left (EE) is believed to be but a political front for the political-miltary wing of ETA while People United (HB) is considered ETA-Military's political arm.The objectives of thse two groups are apparently in harmony with the goals pursued by ETA, i.e. total independence with no compromise.

7 GERMANY: FROM PROTEST TO TERRORISM

Schura Cook

Introduction

This paper (originally sponsored by the Psychopolitics and Conflict Research Certificate Program at the University of Southern California) is an attempt to answer some of the more puzzling questions concerning political terrorism in West Germany. Why did the youth and student protest movement of the 1960s and 1970s develop into brutal and senseless terrorism in Germany, Italy and Japan and not in other nations? Equally perplexing is why these terrorists, often from affluent and privileged backgrounds, changed from sensitive and idealistic young people to extremely brutal and violent social outcasts? This dramatic change, from peaceful protest to hard-core fanatic terrorism, can be attributed, I think, to a complex interaction of socio-cultural and psychological factors.

The first part of the paper deals with the socio-cultural background of the youth and student movement in Germany. It shows how the 'export of American counterculture resulted in some young Germans in an 'over-identification' with 'imported' counterculture and political and social issues. The second part shows why this 'over-identification' with imported culture and issues was particularly strong in Germany. The need to 'over-identify' is seen as a result of an 'under-identification' with the present German system because of Germany's Fascist past. The inability of the German terrorists to see the difference between the past Fascist Germany and the present democratic Germany represents a 'reality loss'. The third part of the paper explains how 'reality loss' in the isolated terroristic groups was a key factor in the change from sensitivity to hyposensitivity. Examining the concept of sensitivity I attempted to show that there was a regressive development in the social and psychological sensitivity of the terrorists. Their sensitivity and their awareness of the political and social injustices in their society developed into hypersensitivity. Hypersensitivity is a subjective magnification of these injustices. Finally, sensitivity and hypersensitivity changed to hyposensitivity, that is the complete negation of sensitivity. The terrorists' brutality demonstrated that their sensitivity and hypersensitivity

154

had regressed to hyposensitivity.

This paper was inspired to a great extent by Michael Baumann's book, *Terror or Love, Bommi Baumann's Own Story of His Life as a West German Urban Guerrilla* (Grove Press Inc., New York, 1978), a translation of Baumann's *Wie Alles Anfing (How It All Began)* published in West Germany in 1977. This book served as a rich source of information and helped me to understand the socio-cultural background of the German youth and student movement which eventually deteriorated into terrorism. Baumann, an early communard and later a terrorist, names social, cultural and psychological forces which drove him and others into extreme radicalism and violence. His description of his life in the German counterculture and in the terroristic organisation, 'June 2nd Movement', facilitated my decision to choose a socio-psychological approach to the explanation of this phenomenon. I have made some attempts to conceptualise my evaluations and theories derived from the reading. Although my concepts and theories are not empirically tested and are mainly speculative, I hope that they will contribute to a better understanding of the development of political terrorism in West Germany.

From Socio-cultural Protest to Political Terrorism

American Countercuture: Export to the Western World

The US youth and student protest movement of the 1960s and 1970s was an extremely vital and dynamic mass movement with a distinct and almost revolutionary socio-cultural content. It had its antecedents in the black civil rights movement as well as in the labour movement of the Thirties. When rock-'n'-roll music merged with the tradition of American folk and black music, it gained political significance and inspired a whole new generation of musicians such as the Beatles and Rolling Stones in England. Concerts like Woodstock, with a crowd of 500,000, seemed to symbolise for an historical moment that the youth of America was in the vanguard of a socio-cultural revolutionary movement. Yet, the main emphasis of this movement, promptly exported to the rest of the Western world, was anti-authoritarian in nature and had its roots in American history, politics and changed economic conditions. This movement was soon praised by many scholars as either an 'increase in sensitive livestyles',[1] a 'reaction to capitalist society with its performance principle'[2] or a 'new narcissism in which consumption of life styles was replacing the consumption of goods'.[3] Kenneth Keniston points out that the change of socio-cultural values — from the industrial ethic to the post-industrial ethic — was an important factor explaining the specific character of the youth movement. He writes:

A growing number of the young are brought up in the family environment where abundance, relative economic security, political freedom, and affluence are simple facts of life, not goals to be striven for. To such people, the psychological imperatives, social institutions and cultural values of the industrial ethic seem largely outdated and irrelevant to their lives.[4]

The export of elements of the American counterculture to the rest of the Western world owed a large part of its success to the new technology of mass communication, which made it possible for the new music and pop culture to reach not only the masses of American youth through radio, television, films and records, but youth all over the world. This resulted not only in the adoption of the American counterculture by the youth of most of the world, but also in an increased identification with American social and political problems, such as racism, the Vietnam war, etc. This supplied the student and youth movement in Germany, France, Austria, Scandinavia, Italy and Japan with political issues and an enemy to hate, resulting in the seemingly paradoxical situation of American problems becoming the problems of the international youth, who used them to legitimise protests against their own systems. The youth of Germany, Italy and Japan, the former Axis countries, especially appeared to 'over-identify' with the imported issues since they could not or did not want to identify with their own democratic system. Their history of Fascism may explain why political terrorism developed in these countries and not in others.

Juergen Habermas, a German philosopher and social scientist, analysed the German student movement in this context and points out that:

Culture transmitted through electronic gadgetry never quite loses its game character and superficiality and has the inherent danger to portray the pseudo world of entertainment as reality. This results in an incapacity to see the difference between symbols and reality and corresponds on the psychopathological level to a state of paranoia.[5]

Frederick Hacker thinks that the euphoric feeling of the counterculture with its passion to revolutionise society owes a large part of its success to the mass media. He states:

> Events become socially effective and important through their mass-reproduced image. Often they take place only for the sake of the image; they are produced in order to be reproduced. The image is no longer only the reflection of reality; the image is reality, most likely the only one accessible to us.[6]

Counterculture in Germany: From 'Funny' Communards to 'Serious' Terrorist

Michael Baumann started his 'career' as a terrorist (he claimed to love only the funny and spontaneous aspect of terrorist protest, in the anarchist and nihilist tradition) as an early communard. He describes the communes as attempts to translate one's ideas about equality, justice and humanism into practice, where one had to share everything with everybody, and as a link from the youth movement to politics. In the communes the members actively and collectively engaged in political analysis and discussed sociological, cultural, political and psychological issues, problems, literature and theories. They considered themselves part subculture and part political underground. They read a lot, mainly leftist and revolutionary writers such as Reich, Marcuse, Marx, Fanon, Lenin, Che Guervara, Mao, Bakunin and Debray.

Communal activities, according to Baumann, comprised psychological self-finding processes using psycho-drama, discussions and readings of selected psychological theories. There were also attempts to decrease sexual restraints as well as a growing belief in activism, which they praised as creative living. The cultural significance of protest was emphasised by stressing spontaneity and fun. Eventually drugs became important, both to 'flip out' on or to raise consciousness. Political work meant to politicise delinquent youth. It also meant participating in demonstrations, sit-ins and destruction of property, while being careful not to injure people. The communards cherished funny terroristic acts which required 'chutzpah', courage and boldness. They had a slogan, 'terror without limit is limitless fun'.[7] Later on, the RAF (Red Army Faction) composed of the Baader-Meinhof Group, criticised the the methods of the communards as not being serious enough. Terrorism, the RAF believed, should not be enjoyable, but a hard job.

In the beginning, all the anti-authoritarian protest (street demonstrations, arranging of fake funerals, taunting of the police by debating with them works of famous German philosophers) seemed like good, if not entirely clean, fun. But the German authorities and the population did not share their sense of humour. They responded to the jokes and ridicule with bitter earnestness and German thoroughness. Soon the amusing and witty symbolic actions, questioning and undermining legitimacy, were punished severely. The jokesters soon had heavy prison terms waiting for them and had to go underground if they did not want to go to jail for years. The fun was soon over since the authorities did not want to play. The pranksters became marginal social figures: fugitives. The dull and weary existence in illegitimacy posed new problems. In the fugitive underground groups, the internal pressure often became unbearable. Contacts with the outside and within the groups were limited to the strictly necessary. Was it then surprising, that Baumann soon himself felt 'like the machine' he was 'trying to fight against in the beginning'?[8]

But even before the groups and communards had to go underground, there was a tendency to be unconcerned and insensitive to the needs and feelings of some members who could not or did not want to identify completely with the group. Baumann also points out that women in the early communes had an inferior position. They were considered sex objects, but had to perform equally with the men in actions like bombings and bank robberies. In these actions, in spite of the fact that they were considered inferior, they often outdid the men in courage and boldness.

The different positions, one a playful protest movement and the other the beginning of a 'serious' terroristic movement, can be exemplified by Ulrike Meinhof's criticism of the communards, and Dieter Kunzelmann of Commune I's announcement to reporters at a news conference that 'I do not study, I do not work, I have trouble with my orgasm, and I wish the public to be informed of this.'[9]

Ulrike Meinhof, at the time chief staff writer of a leftist magazine called *Konkret*, wrote in her column:

> They used their sudden publicity only for private exhibitionism; they snubbed not only interviewing journalists, but also their viewers and readers, and gave away the chance to mediate between their better knowledge of what was going on in Vietnam and a badly informed public.[10]

Thus, even at this early stage, Meinhof demonstrated her intolerance for socio-cultural protest. Later she became a deadly earnest modern terrorist outraged by compromise and appalled by hypocrisy.

As a terrorist she did not tolerate subtleties, laughter or jokes. She considered her bluntly military deeds more eloquent than any words and more forthright than any deliberations and discussions. Blinded by her self-produced identity and sense of importance, she gave up her revolutionary mission, the realisation of which depends on winning the heart and minds of the people one proposes to liberate.

The Politics of the Socialist Student Union (SDS): Imported Issues

Communards like Fritz Teufel, Rudi Dutschke and Rainer Langhans found they could attract a lot of followers, imitators and attention among the students of the University of Berlin. The students particularly adored Fritz Teufel and his satirical 'happenings' which ridiculed authorities. His stories became famous, especially the one about breaking into the university rector's room and seizing his cigars and the seal of his office. After leaving (wearing the rector's cap, gown and chain, and pedalling a small-wheeled bicycle), he rode along the paths and roads among the university institutes, honking his horn to attract attention.

Some of the early communards became actively involved in student politics. When Rudi Dutschke was active in the SDS (Sozialistischer Deutscher Studentenbund) and later founded the Extraparliamentary Opposition (APO), student politics were not only concerned with agitation for university reform, but also with 'imported' issues. In 1959, an SDS congress declared itself against the rearmament of Germany and against the use of nuclear weapons, while a few years later, demonstrations against the Vietnam war, the Shah of Iran, the junta in Greece, etc. seemed to arouse greater participation and enthusiasm among the students than political work for university reform or specific German domestic problems.

Germany, in 1966, had several important developments in domestic politics. The two biggest political parties, the Social Democrats (SPD) and the Christian Democrats (CDU) formed a Coalition which resulted in the exodus of many ardent leftists from the SPD. They felt betrayed by the conservative politics of the Social Democrats, the party they had hoped would change or even revolutionise German society. At this time of political crisis within the leftist camp, charismatic student leaders, like Fritz Teufel and Rudi Dutschke, exerted great influence, because they had the functions of opinion leaders and trendsetters. Rudi Dutschke called for the formation of an Extraparliamentary Opposition (APO) since there was no party to voice the radical viewpoint in the Bonn Parliament itself.[11]

Some of the prominent student leaders were convinced that the anti-authoritarian, socio-cultural youth and student movement of the 1960s and 1970s was the beginning of a political revolution that would change society radically. Rudi Dutschke, a student leader of the SDS in Berlin, interpreted the social significance and the political implications of the youth and student movement. He defined the cultural revolution as a transitional or pre-revolutionary phase of an authentic social revolution. He believed that the new culture would create in the next century a 'new man'[12] who would be the precursor of a new society. He saw this new man as the result of a long and painful fight throughout history. Dutschke also felt that, while the pre-revolutionary phase of the cultural revolution at that time still showed many signs of illusions, abstract theories and utopian projects eventually turn into a real revolution. The lawyer Horst Mahler, later one of the theoreticians and activists of the Red Army Faction sees the aim of the revolutionary intellectual vanguard as recognising, developing and organising each beginning sign of a socio-cultural or political-economic movement which could eventually lead to or be modified into a collective resistance movement.

It appears that Rudi Dutschke and Horst Mahler wanted to give the cultural 'explosion' a political significance by labeling it a pre-revolutionary phase. They therefore mistook wishful thinking or fantasies for reality. Habermas thinks that this false consciousness of revolution existed because of the weaknesses of intellectuals who are only successful in times of intellectual, political and social unrest and uncertainty. 'They are grossly overestimating their positions of power, sometimes to the limit of fantasies of omnipotence.'[13] In this situation, the agitator has lost his contact with reality and only thrives on short-lived, narcissistic actions for self-recognition. Understanding only the effects of mass reactions, he is, as a terrorist, still able to incite, polarise or radicalise mass movements.

Many students, once actively and enthusiastically involved with the student politics of the SDS, eventually realised that the SDS politically exploited an idealistic and anti-authoritarian movement. Inga Buhmann, a student during the political upheavals in the 1960s and 1970s, analyses in her book her experiences and impressions of the anti-authoritarianism of her time. She comes to the conclusion that the student movement was politicised by a few student leaders who cared only for their own positions of power. The SDS attempted in the summer of 1968 to control and centralise all anti-authoritarian initiatives, intending them to be building blocks for an anti-authoritarian countersociety, which they hoped would contribute to the breakdown of the old 'rotten' system. The wide array of initiatives proposed by the communes included initiatives against militarism, established authority, the ruling system, the justice system, the police; initiatives for a change in life styles, for women's liberation and for university reform. Buhmann believes that the bureaucratisation and the attempts to control these initiatives destroyed the fighting spirit and spontaneity of the youth. The SDS tried to put the traditional workers' movement like a new hat over the anti-authoritarian initiatives. Whatever did not fit under the 'new-old' hat was insulted, threatened and ridiculed as counter-revolutionary and counterproductive. Eventually when the SDS could not succeed in controlling these initiatives politically and pulling them together into collectives, a great number of the leaders left student politics and founded in 1970 the Communist Party in Germany (KPD).

Escalation of Violence: Violence and Counterviolence

The transition from an anti-authoritarian youth protest movement to a political movement that eventually deteriorated into a hard core group of fanatically determined terrorists was brought about as much by the role of the press and police actions as by any intrinsic characteristics of the movement itself. In the course of political polarisation and violent escalation, determined terrorists, criminals and crazies succeeded in infiltrating the anti-authoritarian youth movement and used its moral prestige for terroristic violence. At this point, indiscriminate activism for the sake of action was eventually transformed into strategic terror. Hacker states:

> The establishment was not prepared to meet the world-wide protest of moralizing sensitivity against their aggressive competitiveness and reacted with fear and violence to the provocations of the youth movement.[14]

In 1961 students were infuriated by police actions when they demonstrated against the Berlin Wall and the West Berlin police moved in with tear gas and rubber truncheons. Unjustified arrests of prominent student leaders incited the hostility even more. For example, the police arrested Rudi Dutschke and Rainer Langhans in 1967 for demonstrating at a Vietnam demonstration, when in fact they had not participated. Afterwards, they confiscated the membership files of the SDS. For many students, this was proof that Germany still adhered to

Fascistic police methods. Because of this incident, the Socialist Student Union decided that the policy of isolated protest actions was insufficiently effective and should be changed to one of 'permanent university revolt'[15] (the membership files were eventually returned to the SDS with their seals unbroken on a judge's order).

Another tremendous impact that furthered the radicalisation of the student movement was the shooting to death of Benno Ohnesorg by a policeman at a demonstration against the visit of the Shah of Iran to West Berlin on 2 June 1968. Most of the German terrorists used this incident to legitimise their own violence as the 'June 2nd Movement', a terroristic organisation, indicates. Baumann, a member of this group, known for his bombings, described how he lost his mental restraints about using violence, not only against property but also against human enemies at the funeral of Benno Ohnesorg. He writes:

> When the coffin went by it made click . . . something went off . . . this bullet was also meant against you . . . who shot did not matter a shit . . . it became clear to me, now is the time to act, don't show any mercy . . . at this point, I understood the meaning of terrorism . . . this insight gave me a real strength, a real high.[16]

The role of the press in escalating violence in Germany must be stressed in this context. The scandal sheets of Axel Springer (*Bild Zeitung*) influenced to a great extent the opinion-making process in the German population. These papers had always had a strong bias against the youth and student movement. Youths with long hair were either called dirty apes or Communist terrorists. Hacker sees the majority reacting 'to the commotion of their world view with resentment, rage and the mobilization of latent and manifest aggression against the young'.[17] The clearly false depiction of the killing of Benno Ohnesorg on 2 June is just another example of the aggressiveness of the press against the youth movement. *Bild Zeitung* described the shooting like this:

> First they were kicking, then they pulled out their knives . . . They pushed him [the Kripo officer] into a yard, surrounded him, and kicked him down. When they pulled out their knives the Kripo officer pulled out his police gun . . . Teufel functioned as the leader of a group which threw stones at policemen, in which actions two officers were wounded.[18]

Benno Ohnesorg was shot in the back of his head while running away with several other students from the pursuing police. The aftermath of the shooting proved to be even worse. The police officer, Karl-Heinz Kurras (whose hobby was collecting firearms), was acquitted of charges of 'careless manslaughter' while Fritz Teufel was held in custody for throwing a stone at a policeman on 2 June. Hundreds of students went on a hunger strike to protest Teufel's being held in custody. There was great intensification of demonstrations after the shooting of Benno Ohnesorg. The Extraparliamentary Opposition (APO) had attracted all shades of left-wingers and staged large demonstrations. It was common at these demonstrations to sing songs praising Ho Chi Minh as well as the International. The press exaggerated the importance of the student demonstrations in their headlines. Headlines like 'Stop the Terror of the Young Reds Now' or 'Young Reds want to Communise German Property' mobilised great fear and anger among the general population towards the student revolt and especially against the SDS. Therefore, when the leader of the SDS, Rudi Dutschke, was shot three times in the head, chest and throat by Erwin Bachmann, a deranged individual from Munich, on 11 April 1968, the students blamed the press for inciting this attempted murder. Thousands of enraged students demonstrated in front of the Axel Springer building on the evening of Rudi Dutschke's shooting (he survived the surgery). Although hindered by armed security guards of the Springer company, police cordons and water cannons, the demonstrators smashed the glass front of the entrance hall, and damaged and set fire to cars parked on the premises. During the following Easter weekend, there were bloody demonstrations all over the country and anti-Springer, pro-Dutschke enthusiasm spread to many major capitals of the world.

The escalation of violence started then and was later used by terrorists as a justification for their guerrilla warfare against the German state. It did not make any difference to them that a major aim of the student revolt was reached in 1969, when they were granted a new constitution. Under this constitution students were represented directly on the governing bodies of the university, in some cases to the extent of composing a third of the council, the other two-thirds being composed equally of the senior and junior teachers.[19]

The killing of Benno Ohnesorg signalled to the traumatised students that politics was not just a funny game but could be hard and bitter reality. They awakened from their dream that they could change the world instantly to the harsh fact of life, that there was a limit to their freedom to do what they felt and thought right. They found out that their protest could bring about only limited changes without seriously coming into conflict with the authorities. It was soon after this incident that the left split and the student movement dissolved itself. Only a small group of people were so hypersensitised and traumatised that in their paranoid state of mind, they felt, that there was nothing which could change the 'Fascist' German system except recourse to political terrorism.

Terrorism in Germany: A Result of Conflicting Identification Processes

German Terrorists: Identification Conflicts due to the Past of Fascism

The question remains as to why terrorism developed out of the anti-authoritarian youth and student movement in Germany and not in most other countries. All Western countries were affected by the same movement, which was met by the establishment of most countries with repressions. Antagonism and contradictions are found today in all the Western democracies but not all of them were plagued by extreme forms of terrorism. It is assumed here that it was not a coincidence that Germany, Italy and Japan produced the most extreme cases of political violence and terrorism. The fact that the radicalisation and political-isation of a world-wide rebellion took its most distinct and violent forms in the former Axis countries is not to assign all responsibility to the scapegoat of Fascism, but to demonstrate the long-range psychological effects or violence proneness of sociological structures on character formation.

All active terrorists of today were born and raised after the end of World War II. They had no personal experience at all with the Fascistic authoritarian systems that shaped the thinking and the actions of their fathers and grandfathers. Yet, Fascism − the temptation of Fascism and the fear of Fascism − continued to dominate their lives in their crucial developmental phases. Conflicting identification processes are seen as the root causes for political terrorism in these countries. On the one hand there is an 'over-identification' with 'imported' culture, political issues and revolutionary models, and on the other hand there is an 'under-identification' with their own democratic system. As Ellbogen and Parker pointed out:

> It is one thing to note that the radical forms and gestures which America exported to Europe during these tumultuous years were eagerly taken up and utilized by the European revolutionaries; it is

another to realize that these forms and gestures acquired, gradually, a new content in the concrete circumstances of the European situation and eventually spawned a mode of revolutionary expression which remained at a fairly rudimentary stage in the North American context.[20]

The need of many young Germans to be totally different from their parents' generation resulted in identification problems. How could they identify with their parents' generation which exterminated millions in concentration camps and fought brutal and aggressive wars? Therefore, the German youth was characterised by a hypersensitivity towards all authoritarian structures in society. Anxiety and tension were the result of this identification conflict. Collective guilt feelings for the horrible deeds of the parents' generation predestined them for the anti-authoritarian role of the youth movement. In Germany this resulted in a generation conflict manifested in a particular 'hypersensitive' atmosphere.

The unrelieved gap between the subconscious need to identify with the German system and the conscious hate against this system created a large section of estranged hypersensitive German youth. They felt they had become chronic injustice collectors, constantly aware of the insincerity, hypocrisy and greed of their environment, which they had learned to hate with unmitigated passion. Providing a remedy for injustices is the basic motivation for terrorism and the hypersensitive Germans saw evidence of this injustice everywhere and reacted accordingly. It was not by coincidence that they chose the top German industrialist, Dr Hans-Martin Schleyer, as one of their prominent kidnapping victims. Schleyer (who, after his callous murder by the terrorists, was given a state funeral and celebrated as a hero and martyr) had held high positions in the Nazi hierarchy. It was only by a fluke that he escaped being killed together with his immediate boss Heydrich, when partisan Czechs blew up Heydrich's car during World War II.

Gillian Becker argues in her book, *Hitler's Children*, that Schleyer was kidnapped, tormented and killed by the young terrorists not because he had been a Nazi, but because he had been a Democrat for more than a quarter of a century, and worked for freedom and the prosperity of his country. She claims that what his murderers did was to practice Nazism not oppose it. His kidnappers believed that Schleyer was not only a highly placed Nazi, but that he had never recanted. He appeared to them an unregenerated Nazi, who as such fitted very well into the present German structure. He had been able, using the same attitudes and capabilities that made him successful in today's Germany, to make a spectacular career in the old Germany. Didn't that seem like a signal example that not very much had changed? Or so it appeared to the terroristic youth, who at the funeral of the terrorists, Baader, Ensslin and Raspe, mockingly greeted the police (that had appeared in force) with shouts of 'Sieg Heil'.

This example (and many similar ones) express the conflict between stated and actualised values experienced by German youth. They were told over and over again that everything had changed with the triumph of democratic forces over the despised Nazi regime. But they saw the situation as similar to what had happened after World War I (the Emperor went, the generals stayed): nothing fundamentally had changed. Many of the old structures and the same personages continued their existence and functioning without a major break or change. This reasoning gave rise to the undoubtedly mistaken belief that nothing or nothing essential had changed. The fact that these regime critics could not recognise any fundamental differences between the present democratic and the past Nazi regime represents a 'reality loss' (resulting from a chronic and habituated hypersensitivity). Therefore, it was not deprivation or oppression as such, but the perception and experience of injustice, and the belief that such injustice is not natural or inevitable but arbitrary, unnecessary and remediable that caused terrorism.

German Terrorists: Their Need for an Enemy to Hate

German youth had acquired a very superficial national identity which was given up by some when they 'over-identified' with the causes of the international youth and student rebellion. This movement was liberal, individualistic, and in its local and parochial context almost anti-social. It seemed to me that since democratic character traits were not strongly developed and encouraged in many German youth, they repressed their need for system identification and projected it as hate against the system. Germany (itself a former terroristic state) made it easy for the young to find it legitimate to use the state as an enemy to hate. While student rebellion in other countries resulted partly also from systemic identity problems, in Germany, Italy and Japan hate and enemy figures and symbols (projection screens) were readily provided by the recent tradition of past totalitarianism or remnants of it in the present.

'Society with its dusty laws serves as the scapegoat for their over-sensitivity', wrote Guenther.[21] The need for scapegoats and enemies is not the result of a critical analysis of history but corresponds to a personality requirement. This requirement developed in the process of cliché formation, a psychoanalytic concept first introduced by Freud. There all negative experiences are repressed in order to avoid anxiety. The child forms clichés when it represses punishment experiences. Punishment is carried out according to the prevailing norms of society. These norms become (through the child's internalised conscience and negative identifications) part of the child's personality. The repressed content becomes a cliché, which can find an outlet in behaviour, for example prejudice. Prejudice results from repressing thoughts, feelings or wishes from consciousness (because those thoughts are connected to the experience of anxiety) and from the projection of such repressed thoughts and wishes onto other people or objects. Those people or objects then become bearers of unwished and unwanted feelings or thoughts. The repressed wishes, projected onto another person or object, are hated, rejected and despised in this person or object. Using this psychological concept, it is hypothesised that because of conflicting identification processes the need for system identification resulted in exactly the opposite in the German terrorists: their total hate and resentment of the present German system.

Discrepancies in the identification processes make for either diffuse and uncertain identifications or for regressed, primitive ones. This results in an irresistible need to belong to a legitimate community. The ever present enemy is quickly recognised and unmasked. For the German terrorists, the enemy was Fascism in all its various overt and hidden, past and present manifestations and concealments. Anti-Fascists (armed with Fascist slogans from their immediate historic past) became the vanguard of a regressive trend in which violence is not just a means to accomplish a goal, but is itself the very end goal.

German Terrorists: Identity Through Violence

Identity search and the pathology of identity diffusion is characteristic of the adolescent who acquires feelings of inner solidarity by new identifications and by the voluntary choice of societal role assignations. Identity instructs the individual who he really is in reference to an 'in group'. Identity imposes a group code of behaviour but also confers a security-giving feeling that is experienced as more than just rational evidence and certainty. Individual narcissism is transcended in favour of the collective narcissism of group identity which demands personal sacrifices. Identity, particularly in its modern form of national identity, is used as the foremost justification of violence. In group solidarity members experience not only a feeling of increased genuineness, meaning, loyalty and security, but also a guilt-free expression of aggression. Identity feeling, which colours reality testing, is also frequently experienced as liberation, awakening, emancipation and expansion of consciousness. Yet, identity has a built-in conformist bias and is frequently imagined and manufactured in order to obtain the characteristic benefits of unquestioned security and togetherness.

When terroristic groups use violence for the sake of violence, it demonstrates their need for a strong group identity. Aggressive and violent releases against the outside enhance group solidarity. In all societies, institutions in power have an aggression monopoly. This means that the aggression and violence taboo can only be broken by the 'legal' authorities. Terroristic groups have basically two motivations for their use of violence against the state: first, to reach a particular goal and secondly, as an end in itself. Terroristic acts committed by the PLO (Palestine Liberation Organisation) are examples of goal-directed terrorism. The goal, the founding of their own state, is clearly stated. The goals of the German terrorists were not clearly defined. Their ideologies and theories were a diffuse mixture of leftist and revolutionary literature without a clear direction. The emphasis lies on the use of violence and not on accomplishing a particular goal.

When Michael Baumann robbed a bank for the first time, he remembered, 'that it was a new thing, a new experience'.[22] In terroristic actions, Baumann felt, 'you develop a whole new set of instincts',[23] and the use of weapons and pistols 'had its own dynamics'.[24] In Baumann's descriptions, it becomes obvious how important the 'kicks' and the 'excitement' of terroristic action were. He tells about an incident when they passed a police barricade with a stolen car:

It was brightly painted and on the back, in big letters was written: Careful Dynamite Transporter! And there were really bombs in it and the police just looked at it and said, Dynamite Transporter! – Idiot just go on.[25]

While the 'June 2nd Movement' was still somewhat unco-ordinated, the RAF (Red Army Faction) proved to be less inhibited in its use of violence. The concept and strategy of the RAF was mainly copied from the South American revolutionary, Marighela. He recommended terror against the political machine, and all suitable actions against 'all institutions of the class enemy, police stations and administrations, against the head offices of big companies, but also against all executives of these institutions, against high placed bureaucrats, judges, presidents of companies and politicians'.

On 11 May 1973, the RAF bombed the US army headquarters in Frankfurt, injuring 13 and killing Lieutenant Colonel Paul Abel Bloomquist. On 12 May, police headquarters in Augsburg was bombed, wounding five policeman; on 15 May, the wife of the Federal Judge Wolfgang Buddenberg, who had signed most of the warrants for the arrest of Baader-Meinhof members was severely crippled when her car blew up. On 24 May, at the US Army Supreme Headquarters in Heidelberg, two men were blown to pieces when a 50 pound bomb exploded in a car. For all these bombings, the RAF or related terrorist organisations claimed responsibility. Then the president of the West Berlin High Court, Guenther von Drenkmann, was shot while he celebrated his 64th birthday. After this cold-blooded murder, the chairman of the West Berlin CDU, Peter Lorenz, was kidnapped, and eventually released in exchange for the release of five imprisoned terrorists who were flown to Aden with DM 20,000 each in cash. Other terroristic acts included the assassination of the Chief Federal Prosecutor Siegfried Buback and Juergen Ponto. Ponto was one of the most important people in finance and industry in the German Federal Republic. He was Chief Executive of the Dresdner Bank and a member of the board of numerous big West German companies. Ponto's killing was similar to that of von Drenkman. He was shot in his house on 20 July 1977, when his own goddaughter, Susanne Albrecht, visited him with two friends who killed him with a gun they had hidden in a bunch of red roses. The most spectacular terroristic act was the kidnapping on 5 September 1977 of Dr Hans-Martin Schleyer, president of the West German Federation of Industries and of the Employers' Federation. Three policemen who guarded his car and the driver of Dr Schleyer's car were shot to death while Schleyer was abducted and dragged to a waiting car.

The RAF's killings alienated even their 'so-called sympathizers'.[26] In the first stages of terrorism in Germany, a relatively large group of mostly young Germans aided the terroristic groups with money, cars, medication and places to hide. The RAF was criticised for their lack of 'political dialogue'.[27] Baumann wrote in his book:

The RAF threw bombs suddenly, not against a specific target, but against God and the world, police, Americans, judges, Springer. In the process, of course, they made large mistakes, and blew up workers at Springer. And that's when the real turnabout happened, a total falling away, people really started to withhold their support.[28]

The only goal the RAF seemed to have was to get as many headlines as possible. They believed that a revolution could be incited through repeated press coverage of their guerrilla fight against the German state. Baumann stated:

This overestimation of the press, that's where it completely falls apart. Not only do they have to imitate the machine completely, and fall into the trap of only getting into it politically with the police, but their only justification comes through the media. They establish themselves only by these means.[29]

By now, the German terrorists did not care anymore about the possible short- and long-range effects of their actions.They had become action addicts, interested only in living out their fantasies. In their self-imposed isolation in the underground these fantasies had become realities for them, the only realities they knew. Hacker expresses it this way:

Taking the high of their family feelings for the reality of an established community of the people, they confused their own revolutionary desires and their passion for revolution with the revolution. They died in the belief that to feel and talk revolution is to achieve revolution.[30]

The Terroristic Mind: A Mixture of Hypersensitive and Hyposensitive Elements

Socio-cultural Determinants of Sensitivity

When it began in the late 1950s and early 1960s, the search for a new sensitivity was characteristic of the social and political goals of a movement seeking primarily socio-cultural changes. 'Sensitivity' was the psychological state of mind of the youth movement. Religious (Buddhism, Hinduism, Transcendental Meditation), philosophies (Existentialism), psychologies (Gestalt, sensitivity training, psychodrama, humanistic psychologies), politics (pacifism) and literature (New Mutants) were embraced to indicate the change from the old insensitivity into the new, expanded sensitivity. The new 'sensitive' generation wanted to lead a life compatible with sensitivity – an easy life style, lots of free time for contemplation, artisitic work, meditation, consciousness raising drugs, free unrestricted sexuality, etc. They looked with contempt at the old 'insensitive', 'one-dimensional' generation which worked hard, and was irritable and impatient with the young and their 'new' ideas. The relative economic security of the young gave them some room and time to prolong their adolescent phase during which they were independent of economic demands and pressures of society.

Keniston was convinced that affluence had freed the young from concerns of money and power. He implied that the new type of radical showed signs of a new, liberated man with potential for self-actualisation and humanity. Bruno Bettelheim emphasised the age-old Oedipal rebellion as an explanation for the youth protest movement. Alexander Mitscherlich believed that the youth were rebelling against a fatherless society and the lack of authority. Some academic liberals idealised the New Left. They felt that the young generation was more sensitive than the old one and that they would be less likely to perform violent acts. Edward Shils described student radicals as romantics. For this romantic generation it seemed important to experience new sensations and gratifications and to realise new sensibilities. At the time of the youth movement in the 1950s and 1960s many publications showed that there was a distinct shift from the belief in the vigour of capitalism to the prediction that capitalism had come to an end because of ecological problems and a limit in resources. Theodor Roszak urged that scientific objectivity should be de-emphasised for the sake of new life styles which involve oneness with nature, a religious consciousness and increased sensitivity. This position was criticised by David Gutman who saw in the youth movement a new narcissism in which the consumption of life styles was replacing the consumption of goods. Daniel Bell pointed to some inherent contradictions in the capitalist system concerning individualism. He showed that the economic institutions are still dependent on the ideology of self-discipline while the cultural system of the post-industrial society valued personal liberation.

Psychological Determinants of Sensitivity

Sensitivity is the capacity of the organism and the psyche to respond to external stimuli. Sensitivity is developed in the process of socialisation and acculturation. In these processes sensitivity is adapted to the societal conditions. Adaptation means the habituation of patterns of behaviour to anticipated stimuli, their selection, anchorage, channelling, etc. The existing societal conditions are stimulus filters, stimuli reinforcements of stimuli reducers. The societal environment sensitises (sensitivation for weak, forgotten or repressed stimuli) but provides also an institutional stimuli protection for repression, denial, etc. Socially undesirable defences (repression, denial, etc.) can elicit fear and other psychopathological conditions. The protection against stimulus flooding is bought at the expense of defensive manoeuvres which are again repressed or denied. Anxiety becomes manifest when stimulus protection is insufficient or exaggerated. Psychologcal mechanisms are then developed like repression, sublimation, projection, etc. This is done to protect the organism and the psyche from internal or external stimulus demands. While these protectional functions are essential to the survival of the individual, the selection of the anxiety and repression content depends on the moral, religious, socio-cultural, psychological degree of awareness. Therefore, it is the societal environment which defines (a) the intensity of the stimulus readiness; and (b) the type and degree of stimulus response. According to the intensity of the stimulus readiness and the type and degree of stimulus response, rough distinctions can be made between (1) average sensitivity (under normally expected conditions); (2) hypersensitivity; and (3) hyposensitivity. These somewhat stereotyped personality attributes result from the combination of drive derivatives and psychological defences which in turn correspond to the socially instituted and habituated stimulus protection mechanism which has been internalised. Sustained mistrust in societal institutions leads to weak or absent internalisations of stimuli protection.

The Transition from Hypersensitivity to Hyposensitivity

The youth protest movement had a strong individualistic bias. Many youngsters searched for a new identity. They felt they had to change the world in the process of finding themselves. This self-finding process included social experiments and political protest. They were open (only too open) to problems and stimuli, ever ready to change (protean personalities), to expand awareness and consciousness and to respond in original, unpredictable ways. But gradually a definite change in the opposite direction towards hyposensitivity took place. This changeover was accounted for by increasing isolation from society, reality loss, due to an institutionalised outsider position and increased internal group pressure. Increasing social isolation produced in the counterculture an elitism of the persecuted. They had the certainty that because they were persecuted, they must be better and nobler than their persecutors. Pushed into a position of total antagonism against the establishment, the ostracised outcasts and fugitives could not help rigidifying their own perspective into a primitive world view. This resulted in a concomitant loss of reality. Overly strong group commitment blurred their sensitivity towards the outside and rendered them hypersensitive to their comrades' actions. In order to reflect a 'new sensitivity', the counterculture strove for an unprecedented style of living. Eventually their style of living approached the organisational pattern of total institution which, according to Hacker, 'selects and manipulates rewards and punishment, stimuli and response possibilities'.[31]

Life in 'conventional' society seemed to Baumann senseless, vacuous, empty and inhuman. Therefore, he broke away from the establishment 'in order to experience feelings of joy, of tenderness, of community'.[32] He felt that society denied him this experience. Another quote from Baumann:

> The expectation of living a whole life under existing circumstances, and to have to work, seems so horrifying, that we turn away, reach for poison, and just drone along without caring about anything anymore.[33]

Communes were for Baumann a place where 'all sorts of characters showed up and a kind of institution'.[34] He also pointed out that communes were soon isolated which increased the pressure from the outside. When some communes went underground, a distinct change took place. Baumann writes:

> All their sensitivity, things which were experienced, in the commune and were to result in a new sensitivity didn't come through anymore among this troop of bombers. It was eliminated, and then destroyed in favor of rigid actionism.[35]

The escalation of violence and counterviolence soon had their first victims. Baumann wrote about the death of his friend George von Rauch:

> That was the first time I thought about the whole thing taking on forms that have nothing to do with its origins: neither with the commune business, nor with our dropouts in the 60's, nor with our Blues and Hash Rebels, nor with our drug experiences, nor with our sexual experiences, nothing about our new sensibility and tenderness and understanding, getting into another person, it has nothing to do with all that anymore. It just got crazier, it got more and more like a hall

in a Siemens factory.[36]

About the increasing group pressure in terroristic organisations, due to outside pressure, Baumann writes:

> Consequently, the group becomes increasingly closed. The greater the pressure from the outside, the more you stick together, the more mistakes you make, the more pressure is turned inward . . . This crazy concentration, all day long, those are all the things that come together horribly at the end, when there's no more sensibility in the group: only rigid continuation, total pressure to achieve, and it keeps going, always gets worse.[37]

Characteristics of Hypersensitivity and Hyposensitivity

Hypersensitivity	Hyposensitivity
— open to problems and stimuli (influenceable and changeable)	— premature closure (open and shut)
— over-reactive, low stimulus barrier	— minimum or non-reactive, high stimulus barrier
— multiple (abundant) associations and 'Gestalt' responses	— few (fewer) associations and concrete responses
— original, seeking, reaching, vulnerable	— conventional, stereotyped, simplistic, 'safe'
— unpredictable, because of rich repertoire of possibilities	— predictable because of restrictive repertoire of same responses
— readiness to experiment and take chances	— insistence on (emotional) safety
— fast reacting	— slow reacting
— unstable, unreliable	— relatively stable and reliable
— avoidance of authority and hierarchies	— need for authority, structures and hierarchies
— symbolic interaction	— incapacity for symbolic interaction
— decreased usage of clichés	— cliché formation
— changing justifications	— total justification (hypersensitivity justifies hyposensitivity)
— increased capacity to communicate	— decreased capacity to communicate
— self-finding process	— loss of 'self' total identification as in childhood

— increased conflict awareness and conflict perception	— loss of conflict perception
— multi-dimensional problem solving	— one-dimensional problem solving
— expansion of consciousness, awareness and sensitivity	— loss of consciousness, awareness, sensitivity, restriction
— complex solutions	— simplistic solutions
— abundance of feeling of guilt and shame	— relative absence of feelings of guilt and shame

Hypersensitivity and hyposensitivity do not exclude each other but co-exist, frequently in the same individual and in the same group. This combination of psychological dynamics resulted in an explosive mixture in some German youth. Over-stimulation by moral issues and their over-reaction to any kind of injustice, imagined or real, made them hyper-sensitive. The terrorists were sensitised to the environment like a seismograph that becomes useless because it registers even the slightest, perfectly normal commotion as if it were a major earthquake. They viewed themselves as constantly surrounded by a determined coalition of implacable enemies. They felt that they were definitely on the defensive and fighting for self-preservation. Therefore, they thought that even extremes of violence are justified in their self-defence. Because of their total preoccupation with instant and radical solutions, they became impatient with other forms of conflict solutions. In their self-imposed isolation they over-reacted to personal stress. Action for action's sake blinded them to the existence of alternatives for themselves or for the problems they claimed to be concerned with.

The basic attitude of hyposensitivity is characterised by a loss of reality. This makes the terrorists unable to respond, except in a most simplistic fashion. Their communication is confined to the giving or following of orders. Human contacts are restricted to the group with no contact or interest outside the group. Due to action orientation and intense pressure from the outside, life is reduced to the guarantee of survival; moral issues do not appear as problems anymore, but only in the form of justifications or prefabricated solutions. All interpersonal relationships are reduced to purpose-oriented, goal-directed communi-cations deprived of any emotional humanistic overtones. Having made the (group reinforced) decision to dedicate and sacrifice their own lives, they are ready and eager to sacrifice other lives on the altar of a sacred cause. The morally disguised and rationalised (hence honestly experi-enced) hypersensitivity serves to excuse and deny the hyposensitive (ruthless, inhuman) behaviour. Stereotypically escalated oversensitivity disguises lack of sensitivity for human life and welfare. Hence, the combination of hypersensitivity and hyposensitivity made the action addicts, who set out to right Fascism in all its forms, into dehumanised mechanical instruments who resemble the opponent they claim to fight.

Conclusions

Political terrorism in Germany started as a socio-cultural protest movement that was gradually transformed from the nonviolent propaganda of a different life style to a violently destructive terroristic activity pattern. The memory and tradition of Fascist systems in the recent past were seen as determining factors in the personality formation and 'action addiction' of present terrorists. This accounts for the fact that the radicalisation and politicisation of a world-wide youth rebellion took its most distinct and violent forms in Germany, Italy and Japan, the former Axis countries.

Conflicting identification processes are seen as aiding the development of political terrorism in these countries. The identification conflict in German youth manifests itself on the one hand in an 'over-identification' with 'imported' culture, political issues and revolutionary models, and on the other hand in an 'under-identification' with their own democratic system. The terrorists' fight against the German state is seen as 'displaced aggression'; because what they really hated was Fascism in the past and not the present democratic German state.

Youth and student protest movements in other countries have their antecedents partly also in systemic identity problems, but in Germany, Italy and Japan enemy figures and symbols were readily provided by the Fascist past and remnants of it in the present. The identification conflict in Germany resulted in a hypersensitivity for all authoritarian structures in society. Using the largely commonsense concept of sensitivity, with some support from contemporary psychological theory, an attempt is made to show, that the inner-psychological state of the terroristic ruthlessness, the violent terroristic mind, presents a curious yet definitely definable mixture of hypersensitive and hyposensitive contrasting socialisation processes and patterns of identity formation. The change-over from the 'sensitive' youth culture to the paranoid, hypersensitive and hyposensitive terrorists came gradually and must be attributed to environmental and psychological factors. I believe that isolation, reality loss and group pressure are the three most important variables explaining the change from sensitivity to hypersensitivity to hyposensitivity representing the gradual loss of inhibitions to use violence as a means of political protest. The dialectic opposites of hypersensitivity and hyposensitivity represent different stages of an historical process that eventually regressed from Adorno's theories to the use of Molotov cocktails and to the most emphatic and anti-intellectual terroristic activism in the name of seemingly highly intellectualised, philosophical and moralistic values.

Notes

1. Edward Shils, 'Plenitude and Scarcity', *Encounter*, vol. 32 (May 1969), pp. 37-58.
2. Ibid.
3. David Gutmann, 'The Subjective Politics of Power: the Dilemma of Post Superego Man', *Social Research*, vol. 40 (Winter 1973), pp. 570-616.
4. Kenneth Keniston, *Youth and Dissent* (Harcourt Brace Jovanovich, New York, 1971), p. 311.
5. Juergen Havermas, *Protestbewegung und Hochschulreform* (Shurkamp, Frankfurt am Main, 1969), p. 189.
6. Frederick J. Hacker, *Crusaders, Criminals, Crazies* (Bantam Books, New York, 1978), p. 178.
7. Michael Baumnn, *Wie alles anfing* (Trikont Verlag, Muenchen, 1975).
8. Ibid.
9. Gillian Becker, *Hitler's Children* (Panther Books, London, 1978), p. 42.
10. Ibid., p. 41.
11. Ibid., p. 34.
12. Rudi Dutschke, *Rebellion der Studenten* (Rowohlt, Reinbeck bei Hamburg, 1968), p. 91.
13. Habermas, *Protestbewegung und Hochschulreform*, p. 200.
14. Frederick J. Hacker, *Aggression* (Molden Verlag, Wien, 1971), p. 334.
15. Becker, *Hitler's Children*, p. 38.
16. Baumann, *Wie alles anfing*.
17. Hacker, *Aggression*, p. 334.
18. Becker, *Hitler's Children*, p. 47.
19. Ibid., p. 63.
20. Michael Baumann, *Terror or Love*, (Grove Press, New York, 1979), p. 8.
21. Klaus Guenther, *Protest der Jungen* (Paul List Verlag, Muenchen, 1961), p. 87.
22. Baumann, *Terror or Love*, p. 90.
23. Ibid.
24. Ibid.
25. Ibid., p. 92.
26. Baumann, *Terror or Love*, p. 109.
27. Ibid., p. 109.
28. Ibid., p. 110.
29. Ibid., p. 110.
30. Hacker, *Crusaders, Criminals, Crazies*, p. 180.

31. Ibid.
32. Baumann, *Terror or Love*, p. 82.
33. Ibid., p. 82.
34. Ibid., p. 26.
35. Ibid., p. 75.
36. Ibid., p. 89.
37. Ibid., pp. 108, 109.

8 THE ABROGATION OF DOMESTIC HUMAN RIGHTS: NORTHERN IRELAND AND THE RULE OF BRITISH LAW

Matthew Lippman

But law has its origin in the pathology of social relations and functions only when there are frequent disturbances of the social equilibrium. Law arises in the breach of a prior customary order and increases in force with the conflicts that divide political societies internally and among themselves. Law *and* order is the historical illusion; law versus order is the historical reality.

> Stanley Diamond, 'The Rule of Law Versus The Order of Custom' in Robert Paul Wolff (ed.), *The Rule of Law* (TouchstoneBooks, New York, 1971), pp. 140.

When times are normal and fear is not stalking the land, English law sturdily protects the freedom of the individuals and respects human personality. But when times are abnormally alive with fear and prejudice, the common law is at a disadvantage. It cannot resist the will, however frightened and prejudiced it may be, of Parliament . . . It is the helplessness of the Law in face of the legislative sovereignty of Parliament which makes it difficult for the legal system to accommodate the concept of fundamental and inviolable human rights.

> Sir Leslie Scarman, *English law – the New Dimension* (Stevens, London, 1974), p. 15.

In the Anglo-American legal tradition the rule of law is considered the major safeguard against governmental abuse of individual 'rights'.[1] However, over the last decade 'terrorist' activity in Northern Ireland has led the British government to enact several 'anti-terrorist' Acts which have abrogated some of the traditional legal protections afforded to individuals.[2] The Acts provide for such measures as arrest and detention of 'suspected terrorists', a 'reverse onus of proof' for defendants charged with particular criminal offences and denial, under certain cir-

179

cumstances, of trial by jury. This paper presents a partial summary of the debates in the British House of Commons (between the years 1972 and 1977) during consideration of these anti-terrorist acts.[3]

Great Britain is a relatively stable political system whose 'legal culture' embodies a strong commitment to 'civil liberties'.[4] Analysing the process by which the abrogation of 'civil liberties' has occurred and has been accepted in Great Britain may provide insight into the process by which the violation of civil liberties has occurred in other, less stable, political and legal systems.

A theoretical discussion of the dilemma confronting regimes, particularly democratic regimes, facing the threat of collective violence is followed by an historical sketch of the Northern Ireland situation and of the legal measures adopted by the British Parliament to combat terrorism in Northern Ireland. Then, a partial summary of the British House of Commons debates on the *Northern Ireland (Emergency Provisions) Act* and the *Prevention of Terrorism (Temporary Provisions) Act* is presented. In conclusion, a number of summary remarks are offered on the significance of this case study for the protection of universal human rights.

The Dilemma of Order with Law[5]

Collective political violence or unrest may confront regimes, particularly democratic regimes which afford intricate procedural protections to criminal defendants, with a dilemma. The combating of unrest and preservation of order may be perceived by governmental officials as requiring abrogation of the very legal and philosophical principles and values upon which the legitimacy of the regime is, in part, based.

The 'due process' model of criminal law and procedure entails a slow and involved process which interferes with the ability of a regime to prosecute efficiently a large number of aggressive, politically dissident defendants.[6] As a result, according to Cooper, regimes which perceived themselves as being threatened by political unrest have utilised various devices for circumventing the legal procedures and protections required by the 'due process' model:

(1)   the creation or invoking of special emergency laws that facilitate certain practical responses by the authorities that otherwise would be unconstitutional, illegal or inhibited by some existing state of affairs;

(2)   the enactment of special substantive laws making new offences clarifying certain aspects of conduct already incriminated, or punishing more severely certain acts that already are classified as crimes under the ordinary laws of the state;

(3)   the revision or enactment of certain procedural laws that permit a more effective or less restricted response on the part of the authorities. These measures might be direct, such as those relating to powers of arrest, search and detention; or indirect, such as those relating to various forms of intelligence gathering.[7]

A fourth response by regimes towards political dissidents has been the resort to administrative (rather than to judicial) processes and procedures[8] — to intern individuals 'suspected' of 'anti-governmental activity'.[9] Kirchheimer comments that:

Purely administrative procedures become almost mandatory where, for examples, huge numbers of people are involved and the operation must occur with great speed.[10]

Cooper adds that 'the intensity of terrorist activity directed against any particular state generally has determined the extent to which recourse to one or all of the normative modifications indicated has been felt necessary'.[11]

The modification of legal procedures and processes to control political dissent or unrest appears to be most easily accomplished in a legal system which has no entrenched 'Bill of Rights' or institutional or parliamentary check on parliamentary sovereignty[12] For instance, the United Kingdom 'has an omnipresent Parliament with power to enact any law and change any previous law; the courts in England and Wales have not, since the Seventeenth Century, recognised even in theory any higher legal order by reference to which Acts of Parliament could be held void'.[13] The abrogation of legal protection often also is facilitated, in some legal systems, both by the citizenry's respect for and faith in the integrity of the legal process[14] and by regimes effectively portraying their political foes as 'common criminals'.[15]

Cooper observes that the emergency measures 'tend to last a long time and sometimes become institutionalized',[16] and 'not infrequently leads to excesses due to the absence of regular controls and can be a prelude to a veritable reign of terror'.[17] These excesses are 'exempt from all inquiry unless massive international opinion can be mobilized so as to bring them under scrutiny'.[18]

The British government in the late 1960s and early 1970s faced a 'perceived terrorist' threat in Northern Ireland which gradually spread to Great Britain. In order to combat this 'terrorist threat', the British government enacted various measures, the most significant of which are the *Detention of Terrorists Order 1972, Northern Ireland (Emergency Provisions) Act 1973 (and 1975 and 1978)* and the *Prevention of Terrorism (Temporary Provisions) Act 1974 (and 1976)*. These Acts, like the emergency measures enacted by other regimes to circumvent 'due process' procedures and protections, create new substantive criminal offences, modify the procedural protections normally accorded to defendants and utilise the administrative process to detain individuals 'suspected of terrorist activity'.

The Situation in Northern Ireland — An Overview[19]

The Government of Ireland Act 1920 forms the constitutional basis for the Northern Ireland government.[20] The Act establishes a devolutionary system of government in the North. Under the Act Northern Ireland legally remains part of the United Kingdom but is granted limited powers of self-rule which can be revoked by an Act of the Westminster Parliament.[21] At partition, the population of the island of Ireland was approximately 4,390,219, of which 1,250,531 resided in Northern Ireland. Two-thirds of the Northern Ireland population were Protestants.[22]

The religious conflict between Protestants, who by and large support continued union with Great Britain, and Catholics, who by and large favour either an independent, republican Northern Ireland government or union with The Irish Free Republic, has been the major theme in the history of Northern Ireland. However, the 1920 Act established a non-sectarian state in which the government may not 'give preference, privilege or advantage, or impose a disability or disadvantage on any person on account of religious belief' and the government also is 'prohibited' from 'the making of laws interfering with religious equality'. Despite this formal prohibition against discrimination, the Protestant majority has dominated and continues to dominate the social, political and economic life of Northern Ireland. For instance, throughout the period between 1921 and 1972 the Protestant, Ulster Unionist Party has secured a majority in Stormont and so 'predictable was the vote that the proportion of uncontested seats was invariably large, from 38.5 to

63.5per cent'.[23] Where the Protestants, at the local level, lacked a majority' [t]hrough the use of gerrymandering, the Protestants assured their control'.[24]

The Protestant social and political control of Northern Ireland has been bolstered by the 'use of the legal system to secure themselves both against peaceful political challenge and against internal and external terrorist attacks'.[25]

> Protestant control was reinforced by the introduction of a special auxiliary and police force . . . The normal powers of the police were supplemented by the Special Powers Act passed as emergency legislation at the state's inception, the Special Powers Act . . . denies almost every civil right. These repressive measures were taken because the Catholic minority which comprised 38 per cent of the population, was regarded as dangerously disloyal.[26]

Richard Rose argues that the position of Catholics in Northern Ireland is analogous to that of American blacks in the southern United States in the 1950s and 1960s.[27] According to Rose's analysis both the Catholics in Northern Ireland and southern blacks in the United States constitute a numerical minority in a geographical area which is physically, culturally and socially isolated from the 'larger society'. As a result, in both regions, the majority Protestant population was able to freely manipulate the political and legal processes in order to perpetuate their control over the socio-economic structure of society.[28]

Rose argues that southern blacks were, to some extent, able to overcome their lack of resources by utilising the United States 'Bill of Rights' and various 'civil rights acts' to gain access to and combat discrimination in the federal courts. According to Rose, the intense violence in Northern Ireland is a result of the fact that Northern Irish Catholics possessed no such legal tools with which to advance their cause and were forced to look exclusively to the Protestant-controlled political process and ultimately to violence to advance their position.[29]

The Upsurge of Violence in Northern Ireland – An Overview

In the early 1960s violence in Northern Ireland was limited to sporadic vandalism by Catholics and Protestants of schools, businesses and dwellings.[30] The formation of the Northern Ireland Civil Rights Association in February 1967 resulted in unprecedented mass protest marches by Catholics. Attempts by the government of Northern Ireland to halt such demonstrations led, particularly in Londonderry in late 1968 and early 1969, to mass street violence by Catholics throughout Northern Ireland.

In 1969 violence by both Catholics and Protestants escalated to include the use of bombs and explosives against government offices and utility installations. Large-scale rioting again broke out in Londonderry during a Protestant parade which sparked rioting throughout Northern Ireland. The rioting was quelled only by the intervention of British troops. In 1970 the first large-scale attacks on security forces, most of which were conducted by the IRA, occurred. This period also witnessed widespread intimidation and 'punishment shootings' designed to discourage individuals from testifying in court, from serving as jurors or in order to force families to evacuate their homes.

The inability of the security forces and normal criminal processes to control this violence resulted in the Northern Ireland government introducing internment in August 1971. The introduction of internment, which was almost exclusively directed against the Catholic community, was greeted by the intiation of organised IRA guerrilla warfare directed against the security forces.

The continuing deterioration of the situation in Northern Ireland led to the prorogation of Stormont in March 1972 and to the imposition of direct rule from Westminster. The imposition of direct rule led to mass demonstrations and attacks on Catholics by Protestants who felt betrayed by the action of the British government. The Catholic community, which initially supported the imposition of direct rule, was disappointed by the failure of the British government to implement sweeping reforms and, after a brief ceasefire, the IRA resumed large-scale attacks on the security forces in Northern Ireland.

Since 1 February 1973, Northern Ireland has been continuously torn by inter-communal violence, guerrilla warfare, street demonstrations and random explosions, 'punishment shootings' and intimidation of 'innocent' individuals.

The Cameron Commission, which was formed to investigate the causes of violence which broke out in 1968, summarised the cause of violence in Northern Ireland as:[31]

(1)   A rising sense of 'continuing injustice and grievance' among a large section of the Catholic population of Northern Ireland,

in particular in Londonderry and in Dungannon in respect of:
(i) the insufficient and inadequate housing provided by local authorities; (ii) the allocation of the available houses to Protestants in preference to Catholics; (iii) the hiring by local authorities of Protestants in preference to Catholics.

(2) Manipulation of local governmental electoral boundaries and limitations on electoral franchise in order to maintain Unionist political control.

(3) The failure of the Protestant government authorities to investigate complaints.

(4) Resentment among Catholics concerning the existence of the Ulster Special Constabulary (B Specials) as a partisan and para-military force recruited exclusively from the Protestant community; and resentment over the continuance of the Special Powers Act Regulations.

(5) The inflammatory rhetoric of various Protestant extremist groups such as the Ulster Protestant Volunteers and Ulster Constitutional Defence Committee which contributed to the polarisation between the Catholic and Protestant communities.

(6) The resentment by Catholics towards governmental policies such as the banning of street marches in Londonderry in October 1968 and the security forces' ill-co-ordinated and inept conduct and uncontrolled use of violence at demonstrations and the small number of police available to protect demonstrators from attack by counter-demonstrators.

The Response from Westminster: A Sketch of British Anti-terrorist Legislation

In response to pressure from the British government,[32] a number of reforms were implemented by the Northern Ireland government. The reform programme was continued by the Westminster government following the imposition of direct rule.[33] However, the major response by the British government to violence in Northern Ireland has been the promulgation of various 'special powers acts'. These measures provide the security and police forces an intricate set of laws with which to apprehend, detain and limit the activities of 'suspected terrorists' in Northern Ireland and in Great Britain.

The British Parliament in recent years has enacted two major anti-terrorist acts, *The Northern Ireland (Emergency Provisions) Act 1973 as amended* (consolidated in *Northern Ireland (Emergency Provisions) Act 1978)* and the *Prevention of Terrorism (Temporary Provisions Act 1974 (and 1976).*[34] The Acts, in combination, limit the activities in Great Britain of organisations connected with terrorism; expand the substantive criminal law in Great Britain and in Northern Ireland to encompass activities which may be supportive of terrorist activity; curtail the procedural, 'due process' protections afforded to defendants in Northern Ireland charged with 'scheduled' (certain felonious) offences; authorise, under certain conditions, warrantless searches, seizures and arrests by the police and security forces in Northern Ireland; permit the Secretary of State to exclude 'suspected terrorists' from Great Britain, Northern Ireland and the United Kingdom; and empower the Secretary of State for Northern Ireland to issue detention orders of unlimited duration for 'suspected terrorists'.

Proscription of Organisations

The Acts 'proscribe' in Great Britain and in Northern Ireland organisations 'connected with terrorism' and prohibit membership in such organisations.[35] The Acts also prohibit such activities as the soliciting, receiving or giving of financial contributions to 'proscribed organisations';[36] the recruiting of individuals into 'proscribed organisations';[37] the carrying out of any task on behalf of a 'proscribed organisation';[38] the arranging for an individual to address an assembly of three or more persons on behalf of a 'proscribed organisation' or the giving of such an address.[39] It also is a criminal offence for an individual to dress or display any article n public so as to 'arouse reasonable apprehension' that they are a member of a proscribed organisation.[40]

Expansion of Substantive Criminal Law

The Acts expand the range of substantive offences punishable under the criminal law in Great Britain and in Northern Ireland. For example, it is a criminal offence in Northern Ireland to wear a hood or mask 'concealing the identity' in a public place without 'reasonable excuse'.[41] It also is a criminal offence in Northern Ireland to collect, record, publish, communicate, possess or attempt to elicit information concerning the police, security forces, judicial officials and prison officers 'likely to be useful to terrorists'.[42]

In Great Britain it is a criminal offence for an individual to withhold information concerning terrorism which is 'connected with Northern Irish affairs' which 'he knows or believes' might be of 'material assistance' in preventing acts of terrorism or in securing the 'apprehension, prosecution or conviction of those involved in terrorism'.[43]

Limitation on Procedural Protections

The Acts limit the procedural protections afforded to individuals charged with scheduled or certain felonious offences in Northern Ireland. The limitations on procedural protections include limiting the availability of bail,[44] the abolition of jury trials[45] permitting the admissibility of statements by the accused 'unless the accused was subjected to torture or to inhumane or degrading treatment in order to induce him to make a statement'[46] and establishing a 'reverse onus of proof' for the crimes of possessioon of firearms, munitions and explosives.[47]

Expansion of the Powers of Warrantless Search, Seizure, Arrest and Detention

Warrantless searches are authorised in Northern Ireland in order to search for 'unlawful munitions';[48] for 'transmitters';[49] for individuals suspected of having committed offences involving the use or possession of firearms or explosions[50] or suspected of having committed any serious felony or offence under the act;[51] in order to ascertain whether an individual is being 'unlawfully detained in such circumstances that his life is in danger';[52] and for the 'preservation of the peace or the maintenance of order'.[53] Constables and members of Her Majesty's forces also may stop and search individuals for 'unlawful munitions' and 'transmitters'[54] and may stop and question individuals as to their knowledge of 'terrorist incidents'.[55]

Warrantless arrests by constables in Northern Ireland are permitted of 'suspected terrorists' who may be detained for up to 72 hours before being brought before a magistrate.[56] A member of Her Majesty's forces in Northern Ireland may arrest, without warrant, and detain, for not more than four hours, a person who is suspected of 'committing, having committed or being about to commit any offence'.[57] In Great Britain, a constable may arrest without warrant individuals suspected of having committed various offences under the *Prevention of Terrorism Act* or who are 'suspected of being concerned in the commission, preparation or instigation of acts of terrorism'. Individuals so arrested may be detained for up to 48 hours before being brought before a magistrate and, by order of the Secretary of State, this 48-hour period may be extended 'for a further period of 5 days'.[58]

The police and security forces in Northern Ireland also have wide powers under the Acts to 'interfere' with 'any public right or with any private rights of property'.[59]

Detention

The Secretary of State for Northern Ireland may issue interim custody orders authorising the detention of persons in Northern Ireland 'concerned in the commission or attempted commission of any act of terrorism, or in directing, organising or training persons for the purpose of terrorism'. The case must be referred to an adviser for a report and if the Secretary of State is then 'satisfied' that the person has been 'concerned' in such activities and that the person's 'detention is necessary for the protection of the public', the Secretary of State 'may make a detention order for the detention of that person' for an unlimited duration.[60]

Exclusion

The *Prevention of Terrorism (Temporary Provisons) Act 1974 (and 1976)* authorises the Secretary of State to exclude individuals from Great Britain,[61] Northern Ireland[62] and from the United Kingdom[63] if the Secretary of State is 'satisifed' that the 'person' is or has been concerned (whether in Northern Ireland or elsewhere) in the 'commission, preparation or instigation of acts of terrorism, or the person is attempting or may attempt to enter Great Britain or Northern Ireland with a view to being concerned in the commission, preparation or instigation of acts of terrorism'.[64] The police may detain an individual, on their own authority, for up to seven days in order to determine whether to recommend to the Secretary of State that an exclusion order be issued against an individual.[65]

The House of Commons Debates

The major arguments which were used by the proponents and by the opponents of the *Northern Ireland (Emergency Provisions) Act* and the *Prevention of Terrorism (Temporary Provisions) Act* are, in part, summarised below.

Arguments of the Proponents of the Acts: Summary or Arguments

The Terrorists are Common Criminals

The violence in Northern Ireland is not 'politically motivated'. The Northern Irish terrorists are 'common criminals' with no 'altruistic motives', 'the terrorists have no realistic political cause' and they are an 'unyielding band of subversives led by "godfathers" '.[66] They are ' . . . bloody murderers . . . the fixed look of malevolence on their faces, . . . '[67] who engaged in 'horrifying assassinations . . . senseless sectarian violence, . . . provocative marches . . . crimes for personal gain'.[68]

In short, the terrorists are 'dishonourable enemies of democracy, of liberty, of Christian religion'[69] who would 'do well to keep the word humane out of their mouths'[70] and they are 'Fascist hoodlums'[71] who must be considered as 'criminals of the lowest type'.[72]

The horror and cruelty of these terrorists is apparent to anyone who has to visit 'the home of the little girl who was blown to pieces, and to anyone who has to visit the home of a young man of 25 who was slaughtered and in some way, try to find words of comfort for a widow of 25 left with two children'.[73]

In another incident 'a council workman – a Protestant who volunteered to assist in the repair of bomb-damaged homes in the Catholic Lower Falls was beaten to death by a Provisional IRA gang'.[74]

The Terrorist Threat is so Great that if it is not Halted in Northern Ireland it will Spread to Great Britain

Government speakers offered statistical summaries of the 'terrorist threat':

> In only the past three months, 178 bombs were exploded by terrorists and there were 909 shooting incidents, 581 involving the security forces, six soldiers, 21 policemen and 458 civilians were injured and treated in the hospital . . .

> In the last month, there have been 12 punishment shootings . . . nearly all by knee-capping . . . '[75]

If the violence in Northern Ireland is not halted, it may 'create a "Congo" in Ireland which would spill over into Britain . . . '[76] Thus, the Acts provide a framework to combat a 'continuing threat' which may 'escalate tomorrow' in Great Britain.[77]

The Powers Contained in the Acts are Temporary Measures Which will Remain in Force Only so Long as they are Required by the Police

The powers contained in the Acts are those powers that the police 'need to protect freedom and democracy against the killers and the wreakers and the enemies of humanity and freedom . . . '[78] The police are 'highly intelligent, level-headed men' and they 'have no wish to be given powers that they do not believe to be essential'.[79] The police are the 'great instruments for the defeat of terrorism'[80] and many of the attacks on the police are part of 'a concrete compaign to discredit the police and the operation of the rule of law'.[81]

These admittedly 'exceptional powers' shall 'not remain in force a moment longer than is necessary'.[82] But, the situation demands action since 'the first duty of government is defence of citizens from external and internal threat . . . everything else is secondary'.[83] The primary threat to a free society comes from 'a collapse of authority and an inability to enforce law and order, not from the handing out of a few additional powers to the security forces'.[84] 'For most people in the country, life itself comes before a reasonable infringement of liberties'[85] and 'in times of stress and strain our people have been prepared without hesitation to surrender a great deal of their liberties and to have measures imposed upon them'.[86]

The Right of Innocent Individuals to be Secure and Safe must take Precedence over other Civil Liberties the Provision of Which may Inhibit the Law Enforcement Process

The surrender of liberties is 'for the greater welfare of the whole community . . . '[87] and 'whenever there is a terrorist situation in any country, the rights of the individual in the community have to be surrendered to a degree'.[88] Critics of the Acts discuss the 'rights' of terrorists. But, '[w]hat right has the man who is taken out and knee-capped? . . . What right has the person who is stopped on the road . . . ' The protection of human life 'is the fundamental civil liberty that it is the Government's duty to protect'.[89]

The English Parliament must set an example for the Northern Irish people by 'sacrificing many of the jealously guarded rights of British citizens to enable us . . . to meet this terrorist threat'.[90]

Legal procedures and protections only inhibit the effort to combat terrorism. 'The ordinary systems of law in this country are not sufficient to match the . . . subversive elements at work in Ulster.'[91] For instance, one 'difficulty of operating within the rules is converting intelligence into evidence which will stand up in court'[92] and lead to the conviction of terrorists who at present 'hide behind the ordinary rules of evidence'.[93] The terrorists 'would be delighted if we introduced measures of such an elaborate character that the effect of them would be to tie up much of the life of the country and direct the resources of the security agencies into needless paperwork'.[94]

The Legal Measures Provided Under the Acts to Combat Terrorism are not Strong Enough

The legal measures provided to combat terrorism are too lenient. 'It is incredible that this is all that the Government can suggest for the conduct of the anti-terrorist campaign . . . '[95]

The 'British people' are 'impatient with a Parliament which refuses to reintroduce capital punishment for violence of this kind . . . '[96] If 'Soviet Troops' were in Northern Ireland and there were 'one single-shot sniper in a block of flats, the flats would be razed to the ground — as in Budapest.'[97] 'The campaign of terror can and will last for another seven years unless sterner measures are taken to defeat terrorism'.[98]

Those who caution restraint 'fall into two categories — the subversive and the confused'.[99] They talk in 'theoretical language without understanding the real dangers and practical difficulties encountered by ordinary citizens of Northern Ireland'.[100] They provide terrorists 'encouragement by talking of our withdrawal' and should 'realize their responsibility for the murders which are being committed'.[101]

Critics of the Acts do not appreciate that Great Britain faces a 'war' and that 'the present position is just as serious as if the Nazis were preparing to invade'[102] and the Acts are required to put Great Britain on a 'war footing'.[103] As for withdrawal from Northern Ireland: 'I wonder what the Hon. Members would think if the Germans parachuted into West Lothian and we decided to pull out and leave it to the Germans.'[104]

Great Britain Faces a Threat Comparable to the German Invasion of Great Britain During World War II and Extraordinary Measures are Required

This 'war' presents an 'internal threat' to the government. 'Some people, like me, were in Germany in 1933 when Hitler came to power and saw the Nazis in action. Those who have seen that will realize the importance of this legislation'[105] and will appreciate that the IRA is similar to the Brownshirts'.[106]

The 'terrorists should be liqudated' and 'deserve to be dealt with swiftly and executed'.[107] There 'was no argument that was used at the time of the execution of the war criminals at the end of the war which . . . could not be applied to the execution for crimes such as have recently been committed in Birmingham and elsewhere in Britain'.[108] 'I would have court martial and execution of the sentence within hours' and where people are 'obstructing the troops there should be collective punishment'.[109]

Unfortunately, various legal procedures are, of necessity, included in the Acts which are 'incompatible with the ordinary rules of justice as we have known it in this country for generations'.[110] Thus, jury trials are abolished for some offences in Northern Ireland on the grounds that '[O]ur duty is to restore law and order' and the 'common law favours the accused'.[111] This is because the jury system is unworkable so long 'as there are sectarian barriers coupled with the present state of bitterness, violence and disorder, there will be perverse verdicts, and they will arise mostly in important and notorious cases'.[112]

The detention and internment of 'suspected terrorists' is required so that we can 'try to deal with them before they have committed acts of terrorism'.[113] 'It is wrong . . . that the police should have grounds for suspecting that a person is involved in terrorist activities but be unable to detain him . . . because they do not have evidence of a specific offence.'[114] 'Due process' and 'natural justice' are not applicable since detention and internment involve 'prevention' rather than 'punishment' which 'is dealt with under the ordinary law'.[115]

'In present circumstances an extra-judicial process is necessary' for 'law and order'.[116] The terrorists 'are every bit as vicious as the Nazis' and they are the kind of people 'whom it must be possible to intern'.[117]

Arguments of the Opponents of the Acts: Summary of Arguments

The Acts were Passed During Periods of Crisis and have not been Adequately Debated

Critics of the Acts observed that they were passed during a period of 'hysterical clamour'.[118] But, thereafter, the debates were marked by a 'decided disinterest' and the Northern Ireland problem was 'considered to be peripheral' by those Westminster Members 'representing United Kingdom constituencies'.[119] The Acts were renewed by 'order instead of by Bill' and these are 'too fundamental a matter for Parliament to be able to say that it has not got time'.[120] It was pointed out that 'one and a half hours . . . is precious little time in which to debate such major issues as civil liberty and terrorism itself'.[121]

The Acts are an Attempt to Re-enact the Special Powers Act

The Acts are, in effect, re-institutionalising the 'Special Powers Act' and '[W]hat we now have is an addition to the repressive measures of that Act.'[122] They are an attempt 'to legalize every act of every policeman, every soldier, everyone remotely connected with the security forces. There will be no redress for an aggrieved or innocent individual.'[123]

At the same time the government is unable 'to justify' these Acts 'in terms of results, in terms of positive, constructive benefit to the British people'[124] and the government cannot 'prove a correlation' between the Acts 'and the decrease in acts of terrorism and the arrests said to have been made'.[125] The 'onus' should be on 'the Home Secretary to show how the Act has contributed to the lessening of terrorism'.[126]

It is hypocrisy to support these Acts. 'The pains felt by victims referred to in *Gulag Archipelago* are imposed by the Bill(s) upon some of your citizens.'[127] If 'this kind of thing happens in the Soviet Union, in Czechoslovakia, in Chile or in South Africa, my hon. Friends are the first people to stand up, along with us, and shout about the loss of freedom in those countries.'[128]

The Acts Violate the 'Minimum Derogation Principle' and Provide a Greater Limitation on Civil Liberties than is Required to Combat Terrorism

Legally, the powers in the Act go too far and violate ' "the minimum derogation principle"; the principle that when it is necessary to derogate from constitutional safeguards the derogation should be to the minimum extent necessitated by the exigencies of the situation'.[129] It is clear that the Acts victimise 'innocent' people. 'The number of charges brought works out to 100 detentions per charge within the terms of the Act. That is a pretty extravagant way of bringing charges against people.'[130]

As a result of these measures 'the traditions of justice that we cherish in this country are filthied and sullied'.[131] 'It has taken a thousand years to build up the British judicial system, which in many respects is the envy of the world: this legislation has taken much less time to abolish that system.'[132]

These measures are 'law and order in British interests, conceived in British interests and not in the interests of the people who live in

Ireland'.[133] The British are implementing measures in Northern Ireland
'which they would not accept for one instant in their own constituencies in Great Britain'.[134] It is, as a result, not surprising that in
Northern Ireland there 'is an erosion of values and standards' and a
breakdown of all law 'the repudiation of debts and the evasion of payment for services' and 'protection rackets' and 'a high level of crime
committed by juveniles'.[135]

The Acts are Repressive and Discriminatory and may be the First Step in the Erosion of Political and Civil Liberties in the United Kingdom

Legal repression had been institutionalised in Northern Ireland and in
Great Britain. 'The first proposal seemed . . . to innoculate us against
similar scruples later, so that we become more ready to swallow an
increasing number of inroads upon what are normally considered essential constitutional safeguards.'[136] The acts are 'one more dangerous . . .
step down a slope which is very slippery . . . that is simply following
the delusion that, being ever more repressive, we might one day be
successful.'[137] In addition, 'seldom in history has the erosion of civil
liberties been static' and one day a minister may 'rise and say "Because
of the increase in terrorism we will do away with the General Elections" '.[138] We are 'familiarising' people with 'the concepts and pre-
cepts of the police state by process of gradualism' and 'with the idea
that it is right to arrest someone without charge and to hold him incom-
municado without charge and that it is right for the police to make a
political judgement about a human being'.[139]

The Acts also label a certain group of people as suspect 'because
they are Irish, because they have Irish associations or Irish friends, or
because they drink in a pub or a club that is known to be a place where
Irishmen congregate . . . '[140]

The 'Ulster Problem' Requires a Political Solution and Cannot be Solved by Restricting Civil Liberties

The situation in Northern Ireland cannot be solved by passing repressive legislation. It is clear that 'no Act that we pass here can guarantee
the safety of the citizen . . . repressive measures of this sort do not solve
the problem. They simply lead to more violence . . . and . . . assist the
terrorists to achieve their aims.'[141] In Cyprus 'there was the extension
of capital punishment to . . . the new offence of consorting with
terrorists' and in Kenya 'there was a massive attempt to control movements . . . None of that legislation was to any avail, it led only to one
thing — withdrawal.'[142] Similarly, in Northern Ireland, the law has not

limited terrorist activities. 'We have had far more of these illegal collections taking place . . . The dressing up continues. It has not been stopped by proscribing the IRA . . . I have not been convinced that by detaining people for long periods we have ended up getting a great deal of extra information . . . (it) has probably ensured less sympathy for the Government amongst the Irish community in this country.'[143]

The violence 'in all its forms is politically motivated . . . behind the most bestial, even the most apparently insane, acts of violence . . . there is a political motive'.[144] The situation in Northern Irelnd can only be approached in terms of 'a political solution'.[145]

Some Concluding Observations

When faced with internal unrest governmental regimes have resorted to various measures to circumvent the procedural and substantive requirements of the 'due process' legal model. These measures include enacting emergency power acts, expanding the scope of criminal statutes, restricting the procedural rights granted to defendants and resorting to administrative detention of 'suspected terrorists'. In Great Britain such measures have been implemented in order to provide the police with the legal powers they require to combat the 'perceived terrorist threat' in Northern Ireland. A number of observations concerning the protection of human rights can be drawn from this analysis of the British House of Commons debates on 'terrorism' in Northern Ireland.

First, the human rights movement has viewed the 'rule of law' as the vehicle for protecting human rights. However, 'the rule of law' can be used to limit as well as protect human rights. In Great Britain, the inflammatory political rhetoric in the House of Commons was translated into the neutral legal language of the *Northern Ireland (Emergency Procedures) Act and the Prevention of Terrorism (Temporary Provisons) Act*. The abrogation of civil liberties thus has been codified into statutes which are accorded the respect and authority of 'The Law'. As a result, 'political acts', such as demonstrating support for the IRA, have been labelled as 'criminal acts' for which an individual can be fined and jailed.

Secondly, the House of Commons' debates suggest that the international human rights instruments have a limited ability to guide or restrain regimes' conduct in combating an 'internal threat'.[146] In addition, all major international human rights instruments permit some derogation from the protection of human rights during 'public emergencies'.[147] This type of clause is particularly difficult to justify when such 'public emergencies' often result from protests against regimes' past failure to provide socio-economic and civil and political rights to its citizens.

Thirdly, the failure to place human rights on a firm philosophical foundation and to establish any ranking among human rights permits regimes to abrogate certain 'human rights' in the interests of 'national security' or in order to safeguard the 'essential liberties' of the citizenry.

Fourthly, during periods of stress, as in Great Britain, the campaign against terrorism has bipartisan support. The absence of an effective opposition during periods of crisis often results in the enactment of legislation which limits civil liberties to a greater extent than is necessary to control 'terrorist activity'. Once having obtained such powers regimes may be reluctant to risk returning to a less centralised governmental and legal structure.

Lastly, during periods of 'public emergency' it is the substantive and procedural criminal law which is most subject to manipulation and abuse. Despite scepticism concerning the value of international human rights instruments, it would appear that an instrument protecting the rights of 'political criminals' and of those 'detained during public emergencies' would be desirable.[148]

Notes

1. See Harry Street, *Freedom, The Individual and the Law*, (Penguin, Middlesex, 1972). Thomas I. Emerson, David Haber and Norman Dorsen, *Political and Civil Rights in the United States* (Little Brown, Boston, 1967).

The international human rights movement, which has been inspired by the Anglo-American legal tradition, has encouraged a number of governments to incorporate more fully the protection of human rights in their constitutions and to expand the coverage of human rights afforded under their municipal law. See *United Nations Actions in the Field of Human Rights* (United Nations, New York,1974).

2. It should be noted that many of the measures which in this paper are considered as 'violative of humn rights' have been determined to be in conformity with the requirements of the European Convention for the Protection of Human Rights and Fundamental Freedoms. Provision for derogation of certain rights is permitted under Article 15; 'In time of war or other public emergency threatening the life of the nation . . . to the extent strictly required by the exigencies of the situation . . . ' See 'Ireland v. The United Kingdom', *Year Book of the European Convention on Human Rights* (1976), p. 512 and European Court of Human Rights, *Case of Ireland v. The United Kingdom*, decision of 29 April 1976, series A, no. 25.

3. The sample includes the major debates which occurred following the imposition of direct rule in 1972. The 'cut-off' date of May 1978 is based on the necessity of keeping the sample to a 'manageable size' and by the difficulty of obtaining additional materials. The written discussion is based on the debates on the two major emergency measures – *Northern Ireland (Emergency Provisions) Act* and *Prevention of Terrorism (Temporary Provisions) Act*. However, all the following parliamentary debates were consulted:

Debate on Compton Report, 940 Parl. Deb., HC 1672-82 (9 December 1971); debate on Parker Report, 851 Parl. Deb., HC 743-52 (2 March 1972); debate on capital punishment for terrorist offences causing death, 902 Parl. Deb., HC 664-724 (11 December 1975); debate on *Detention of Terrorists Order 1972*, 848 Parl. Deb., HC 45-103 (11 December 1972); debate on *Northern Ireland (Temporary Provisions) Bill 1972*, 883 Parl. Deb., HC 1859-75 (24 March 1972), 834 Parl. Deb. HC 238-370 (28 March 1972) and 445-801 (29 March 1972); debate on *Northern Ireland (Emergency Provisions) Act 1973*, 855 Parl. Deb., HC 275-391 (17 April 1973), 859 Parl. Deb., HC 735-880 (5 July 1973), 856 Parl Deb., HC 1025-177 (14 May 1973); *Northern Ireland (Emergency Provisions) Act 1973 (Continuance Order 1974)*, 895 Parl. Deb., HC 1273-1316 (9 July 1974), 882 Parl. Deb., HC 2071-102 (5 December 1974); debate on *Northern Ireland (Emergency Provisions) Act 1973 (Continuance Order 1975)*, 894 Parl. Deb., HC 814-74 (26 June 1975), 902 Parl. Deb., HC 760-814 (11 December 1975); debate on *Northern Ireland (Emergency Provisions) (Amendment) Act 1975*, ibid., 886-980 (27 June 1975), 895 Parl. Deb., HC 1191-201 (2 July 1976), 922 Parl. Deb., HC 1933-2048 (17 December 1976); debate on *Northern Ireland (Emergency Provisions) Act 1973 (Continuance Order 1977)*, 934 Parl. Deb., HC 633-720 (30 June 1977), 940 Parl Deb., HC 1678-760 (8 December 1977); debate on *Northern Ireland (Emergency Provisions) Act 1973* (Amendment Order 1977), debate on *Prevention of Terrorism (Temporary Provisions) Act 1974*, 881 Parl.Deb., HC 1672-81 (22 November 1974), 882 Parl. Deb., HC 29-44 (25 November 1974), 882 Parl. Deb., HC 634-944 (28 November 1974); debate on *Prevention of Terrorism (Temporary Provisions) Act 1974 (Continuance Order 1975), 892 Parl. Deb., HC 1082-162 (9 May 1975), 901 Parl. Deb., HC* 875-1004 (26 November 1975); debate on *Prevention of Terrorism (Temporary Provisions) Act 1974, (Amendments and Continuance Order 1976)*, 924 Parl. Deb., HC 442-594 (28 January 1976), 908 Parl. Deb., HC 157-67 (22 March 1976), 910 Parl. Deb., HC 114-56 (26 April 1976); debate on *Prevention of Terrorism (Temporary Provisions) Act 1974, (Continuance Order 1977)*, 927 Parl. Deb., HC 1472-569 (9 March 1977); debate on *Prevention of Terrorism (Temporary Provisions) Bill 1974 (Continuance Order 1978)*, 946 Parl. Deb., HC 543-96 (15 March 1978).

The following Royal Commission reports also were consulted:

Report of the Enquiry into Allegations against the Security Forces of Physical Brutality in Northern Ireland Arising out of Events on the 9th August, 1971 (November 1971) (Cmnd. 4823) (Compton Committee); *Report of the Committee of Privy Counsellors Appointed to Consider Authorised Procedures for the Interrogation of Persons Suspected of Terrorism* (March 1972) (Cmnd. 4901) (Parker Committee); *Report of a Commission to Consider in the Context of Civil Liberties and Human Rights, Measures to Deal With Terrorism in Northern Ireland (January 1975)* (Cmnd. 5847) (Gardiner Commission); *Report of the Committee of Inquiry into Police Interrogation Procedures in Northern Ireland* (March 1979) (Cmnd. 7497) (Bennett Report); *Report of the Commission to Consider Legal Procedures to Deal with Terrorist Activities in Northern Ireland* (December 1972) (Cmnd. 5185) (Diplock Report); *Report by Mr. Roderick Bowen, Q.C., on Procedures for the Arrest, Interrogation and Detention of*

Suspected Terrorists in Aden (14 November 1966) (Cmnd. 3165) (Bowen Report); *Review of the Operation of the Prevention of Terrorism (Temporary Provisions) Acts 1974 and 1976 (August 1978)* (Cmnd. 7324) (Shackleton Report); Standing Advisory Commission on Human Rights, *The Protection of Human Rights by Law in Northern Ireland* (November 1977) (Cmnd. 7009); *Violence and Civil Disturbances in Northern Ireland in 1969* (April 1972) (Cmnd. 566) (Scarman Committee); *Report of the Advisory Committee on Police in Northern Ireland (Belfast,* 1969) (Cmnd. 535) (Hunt Committee); *Disturbances in Northern Ireland (September 1969)* (Cameron Commission); *The Handling of Complaints against the Police* (December 1975) (Cmnd. 6475) (Black Committee).

The House of Commons debates were analysed and a number of major, recurring arguments were identified. I then reconstructed these arguments by excerpting 'representative' quotations. This 'impressionistic approach' is justified since the paper's focus is on the 'reasoning process' used to justify the abrogation of 'civil liberties' rather than on 'the number of times' a particular idea was mentioned during the debates by party spokesmen. This mode of analysis of parliamentary debates fails to control for arguments which might be persuasive or significant but which are only articulated by a small number of speakers; and fails to control for the fact that the prestige or formal position of a speaker may give a particular argument, although not articulated by other speakers, particular importance. Focusing on the parliamentary debates also assumes, contrary to most modern psychology, that there is a close relationship between the verbal explanations offered by an individual to explain their behaviour and the 'actual motivations' behind the individual's behaviour. Unfortunately, most questions which arose during the debate were decided by 'voice vote' making an analysis of parliamentary voting behaviour of limited utility for the purposes of this paper.

The analysis makes no differentiation between the debates which took place concerning the *Northern Ireland (Emergency Provisions) Act* and the *Prevention of Terrorism (Temporary Provisions) Act* nor does the analysis distinguish between the party affiliation of the various speakers in the debates. Although this form of analysis may appear 'crude', this mode of analysis is based on the finding that the same arguments were used in the debates over the two Acts and that all political parties, with the exception of the predominantly Catholic, Northern Irish parties, supported the Acts.

4. A 'legal culture' is comprised of a set of 'ideas, attitudes, beliefs, expectations and opinions about law'. See Lawrence Friedman, *Law and Society*, (Prentice Hall, Englewood Cliffs, NJ, 1977). See also, Henry W. Ehrmann, *Comparative Legal Cultures* (Prentice Hall, Englewood Cliffs, NJ, 1976).

5. The discussion in this section of the paper is inspired by: Isaac D. Balbus, *The Dialectics of Legal Repression* (Russell Sage, New York, 1973); Stanley Diamond, 'The Rule of Law versus the Order of Custom' in Robert Paul Wolff (ed.), *The Rule of Law* (Touchstone Books, New York, 1971) p. 137; K.T. Erickson, *Wayward Puritans* (Wiley, New York, 1966); Edgar Z. Friedenberg, 'The Side Effects of the Legal Process' in Wolff (ed.), *The Rule of Law*, p. 37; Otto Kircheimer, *Political Justice* (Princeton University Press, Princeton, 1961); Stuart Hall *et al., Policing the Crisis* (Macmillan, London, 1978), Georg Lukacs, *History and Class Consciousness* (MIT Press, Boston, 1971); Douglas Hay *et al., Albion's Fatal Tree* (Allen Lane, London, 1975);Richard Quinney, *Criminal Justice in America: A Critical Understanding* (Little Brown, Boston, 1974); E.P. Thompson, *Whigs and Hunters* (Allen Lane, London, 1975); Max Weber, *The Theory of Social and Economic Organization* (ed. Talcott Parsons, The Free Press, New York, 1947) (trans. A.M. Henderson and Talcott Parsons); Max Weber, *On Law in Economy and Society* (ed. Max Rheinstein, Touchstone

Books, New York, 1954) (trans. Edward Sills and Max Rheinstein); Howard Zinn, 'The Conspiracy of Law' in Wolff (ed.), *The Rule of Law*, p. 15.

6. The tension between the 'due process' and 'crime control' models is discussed by Herbert L. Packer, *The Limits of the Criminal Sanction* (Stanford University Press, Stanford, 1968), pp. 149-246.

7. H.Y.A. Cooper 'The International Experience with Terrorism: An Overview' in National Advisory Committee on Criminal Justice Standards and Goals, *Disorders and Terrorism: Report of the Task Force on Disorders and Terrorism* (Government Printing Office, Washington, DC, 1976), pp. 419, 439.

8. See generally, *Korematsu v. United States*, 323 US 214, 65 S. Ct 193, 89 L. Ed. 194 (1942) *Ex Parte* Endo 323 US 283, 65 S. Ct 298, 89 L. Ed. 243 (1944). These cases are discussed in Jacobus ten Broek, Edward N. Barnhart and Floyd W. Matson, *Prejudice, War and the Constitution* (University of Chicago Press, Chicago, 1958). See also Robert S. Rankin and Winifred R. Dallmayer, *Freedom and Emergency Powers in the Cold War*, (Meredith, New York, 1964).

9. The bureaucratic model was epitomised by the process of 'Jewish extermination' in Nazi Germany; see Paul Hilberg, *The Destruction of the European Jews* (Harper and Row, New York, 1961). Hilberg remarks; 'It is the bureaucratic destruction process which, in its step-by-step manner, finally led to the annihilation of five million victims' (p. 11). The bureaucratic process also permits policies to be carried out by a division of labour between specialists which often conceals from bureaucrats the 'nature' of the activity they are engaged in. See generally, Hannah Arendt, *Eichmann in Jerusalem* (Viking, New York, 1964).

10. Kircheimer, *Political Justice*, pp. 96-7, note 5.

11. Cooper, 'The International Experience with Terrorism', note 7.

12. But see note 8 above.

13. Standing Advisory Commission on Human Rights, *The Protection of Human Rights by Law in Northern Ireland*, p. 19, para. 3.97 (a), note 3.

Questions of the validity of the enactments of the United Kingdom Parliament are not legal at all – they are political and historical. The central doctrine of the British Constitution is that Parliament is sovereign; neither the courts nor a previous Act of Parliament can set aside any executive action authorised by the government of the day. Since the government of the day has the power to pass retrospective legislation (even after a court has ruled that it has done something without statutory authorisation there is no effective limitation upon what a government can do and then claim authorisation for). B.J. Naran, *Public Law in Northern Ireland* (Shanway, Buckamore, County Antrim, 1975) p. 43 quoted in Richard Rose, 'On the Priorities of Citizenship in The Deep South and Northern Ireland' The Journal of Politics, vol. 38, (1976), pp. 247, 275-6.

S.A. de Smith, *Constitutional and Administrative Law*, 2nd edn (Penguin, Harmondsworth, 1973) observes that there are three principles underlying 'the traditional legal approach to civil liberties in Britain':

First, freedoms are not to be guaranteed by statements of general principle. Secondly, they are residual . . . to define the content of liberty one has merely to subtract from its totality the sum of the legal restraints to which it is subject. Thirdly, for every wrongful encroachment upon one's liberty there is a legal remedy awarded by an independent court of justice (p. 452).

See also, A.V. Dicey, *An Introduction to the Study of the Law of the Constitution*, 10th edn (Macmillan, London, 1959).

For discussion as to the 'effectiveness' of a bill of rights in protecting individual liberties see Albert S. Abel, 'The Bill of Rights in the United States: What has it Accomplished?', *Canadian Bar Review*, vol. 47 (1959), p. 147; Ian W. Duncanson, 'Balloonists, Bills of Rights and Dinosaurs', *Public Law* (1970), p. 39; Enid Campbell, 'Pros and Cons of Bills of Rights in Australia', *Justice* (June 1970), p. 1; W. Don Carroll, 'The Search for Justice in Northern Ireland', *NYU Journal of Int. L. & Politics*, vol. 6 (1973), p. 28; Gareth Evans, 'An Australian Bill of Rights', *Australian Quarterly*, vol. 45 (1973), p. 4; The Hon. Mr Justice M.D. Kirby, 'An Australian Bill of Rights?', *Modern L. Rev.*, vol. 39 (1976), p. 121; A.J. Milne, 'Should We Have a Bill of Rights?', *Modern L. Rev.*, vol. 40 (1977), p. 389; G.W.R.Palmer, 'A Bill of Rights for New Zealand' in K.J. Keith (ed.), *Essays on Human Rights* (Sweet & Maxwell, Wellington, 1968), p. 106; Sir Leslie Scarman, *English Law – the New Dimension* (Stevens, London, 1974); Stuart A. Scheingold, *The Politics of Right* (Yale University Press, New Haven, 1974).

14. Carol Ackroyd, Karen Margolis, Jonathan Rosenhead and Tim Shallice, *The Technology of Political Control* (Penguin, Harmondsworth, 1977) comment on law as a mechanism for social control:

> Firstly, it is extremely flexible. If the introduction or re-interpretation of a law provokes mass protest it can always be repealed or softened, or simply not used. Secondly, if the law is used cleverly it is less likely to provoke an adverse reaction than the use of more overt repression by the security forces. The ideology of respect for law is very deeply rooted in British society. People are extremely reluctant to break the law, even if they consider that it threatens their freedom of political expression . . . Finally, the law is a highly complex and technical subject. Most people probably do not even know their rights if they are stopped in the street or arrested by the police. They certainly do not recognize the full significance of new legislation passed by Parliament, or understand the implication of particular rulings by judges. The widespread ignorance lays the basis for the subtle application of legal means to suppress movements which threaten social passivity (pp. 78-9).

The Anglo-American legal tradition's faith in the rule of law has been extended to the international human rights movement which, until recently, has concentrated on the drafting and ratification of international instruments which guarantee various'rights' and 'remedies' to individuals under international law. These instruments have served as a model and an incentive for a large number of municipal governments to entrench certain human rights protections in their constitutions and to expand the human rights protections afforded under their domestic law, See, *United Nations Actions in the Field of Human Rights*, pp. 17-19, note 1. One ironic result of this emphasis of the international human rights movement on the rule of law is that governments have come to rely upon domestic law and legal processes to facilitate, legitimate and obscure their violations of human rights. See generally, *Amnesty International Report 1979* (Amnesty International, London, 1980).

15. The 'labelling' of 'political dissidents' in Northern Ireland as 'common criminals' has been referred to as 'felon setting'. See Frank Burton, 'The Irish Republican Army and its Community: a Struggle for Legitimacy' in Pat Carlen (ed.), *The Sociology of Law* (Monograph 23, University of Keele, December 1976), p. 23.

16. Cooper, 'The International Experience with Terrorism', pp. 439-40, note 7.

17. Ibid., p. 440.

18. Ibid. The more insecure a regime the greater the number of social activities which are likely to be 'labelled' as criminal. Richard Rose, *Governing without Consensus* (Beacon, Boston, 1972) comments that:

As a regime moves towards totalitarianism, there is a great increase in the proportion of social activities defined as violations of basic political laws. Even drunkenness or abstract painting (or in the United States, the waving of red flags or the burning of red, white and blue flags) can be considered anti-regime activity (p. 29).

Thomas I. Emerson, *The System of Freedom of Expression* (Vintage, New York. 1970), pp. 3-20 distinguishes between harmful 'action' which may properly be regulated and 'expression' which results in no measurable social harm and should not be subject to legal regulation. The legal regulation of such 'harmless activity' has been viewed as 'political repression'.

19. A good summary account of Northern Ireland history is Claire Palley, 'The Evolution, Disintegration and Possible Reconstruction of the Northern Ireland Constitution', *Anglo-American L. Rev.* vol. 1 (1972), p. 368. The best histories of Northern Ireland are J.C. Beckett, *The Making of Modern Ireland 1603-1923* (Alfred A. Knopf, New York, 1966); Nicholas Mansergh, *The Irish Question: 1840-1921* (Allen and Unwin, London, 1965). A 'Marxist' approach is L. de Paor, *Divided Ulster* (Penguin, Harmondsworth, 1970).

20. 'Northern Ireland' refers to the six northern counties of Ireland presently 'under British rule' for which 'Ulster' is a common designation. Irish Republicans often use 'Northern Ireland to refer to nine northern counties, three of which currently are part of the Irish Free State. The 1920 Act created subordinate Parliaments both in 'Northern' and in 'Southern' Ireland under British rule. Insurrectionary violence in 'southern' Ireland resulted in the promulgation of the *Irish Free State (Agreement) Act 1922* which granted dominion status to the 26 southern counties. In 1937 an autonomous Irish constitution was adopted by plebiscite and the Irish Free State left the Commonwealth in 1949 and became known as the Irish Republic. Despite the Irish Free State's recognition of the border with Northern Ireland, the 1937 Republic of Ireland Constitution in Article II states that the national territory 'consists of the whole island of Ireland', but Article III recognises that this division exists 'pending the re-integration of the national territory'.

21. The independence of the Northern Ireland government is limited by the Crown's failure to transfer powers in such areas as fiscal powers, defence, international relations, prosecution of treason, alienage, naturalisation, external trade, marine and aerial navigation, merchant shipping, cable and wireless tele-graphy, coinage and trademarks, copyright and patents. In fact, there have been four diffdrent systems of government in Northern Ireland since 1921.

(i)   devolution of powers to the Parliament and government of Northern Ireland under the *Government of Ireland Act 1920*, up to March 1972;

(ii)   direct rule under the *Northern Ireland (Temporary Provisions) Act 1972*, with the government of Northern Ireland suspended and its Parliament prorogued, executive powers being exercised by a Secretary of State and laws made by Order in Council, from March 1972 to 1 January 1974;

(iii)   a new system of devolution of powers to an Assembly and Executive under the Northern Ireland Constitution Act 1973, from January to May 1974; and since that time,

(iv)   discharge of the constitutional functions of the Executive by Northern

Ireland Office Ministers' with the Assembly dissolved (which is effectively the same as direct role under (ii)).

22. C. Desmond Greaves, *The Irish Crisis*, (Seven Seas, Berlin, 1974), p. 18. At partition, Catholics

inhabited the two counties of Fermanagh and Tyrone, where, as in Derry City, they constituted the majority, as well as southwest Derry, South Down, South Armagh, about a quarter of Belfast and the Northwest corner of Antrim. (Ibid., p. 19)

Currently, Protestants comprise 70 per cent of Northern Ireland and 27 per cent of the 32 county population. See Richard Clutterbuck, 'Ireland's American Enemies', *The New Republic*, vol. 181 (15 December 1979), pp. 17-18.

23. Rose, 'On the Priorities of Citizenship, pp. 261-2, note 13.

24. Carroll, 'The Search for Justice in Northern Ireland', p. 31, note 13.

25. Kevin Boyle, Tom Hadden and Paddy Hillyard, *Law and State*, (Martin Robertson, Birmingham, 1975), p. 7.

26. Carroll, 'The Search for Justice in Northern Ireland', p. 30, note 13.

27. Rose, On the Priorities of Citizenship', pp. 258-60, note 13.

28. Boyle, *et al., Law and State*, p. 8, note 25, point out that the political goals of southern blacks in the USA in the 1950s and 1960s and of Irish Catholics in contemporary Northern Ireland are similar:

the right to participate in the election of central and local government through a scrupulously fair electoral system; the right to pursue legitimate political and social objectives without interference from government; the right to share equitably in the allocation of state resources; and the right to freedom from arbitrary arrest or detention. In the specific Northern Ireland context attention was focused primarily on allegations of the gerrymandering of electoral boundaries, of discrimination in public housing and unemployment and in the implementation of government schemes for social welfare and economic development and of the infringement of basic legal rights under the Special Powers Act.

29. Rose, 'On the Priorities of Citizenship', pp. 275-91, note 13. See also, Carroll, 'The Search for Justice in Northern Ireland', pp. 35-6, note 13.

30. A detailed account of the violence in Northern Ireland can be found in 'Ireland v. The United Kingdom', *Year Book of the European Convention on Human Rights*, note 3 and in European Court of Human Rights, *Case of Ireland v. The United Kingdom*, note 3. Clutterbuck, 'Ireland's American Enemies', p. 17, note 22 lists the fatal casualties in Northern Ireland 1969 and 1979 as:

Irish:	
Civilians	1433
Royal Ulster Constabulary (RUC)	132
Ulster Defence Regiment (UDR)	98
Total	1663
British:	
British soldiers	322
Combined Total	1985

31. *Disturbances in Northern Ireland* (Cameron Commission), pp. 55-72,

paras. 126-71, note 3, pp. 91-8, para. 229. See also Carroll, 'The Search for Justice in Northern Ireland',pp. 30-1, note 31 and Boyle *et al., Law and State*, pp. 27-36, note 25.

Carroll sees three developments as contributing to the upsurge of violence in Northern Ireland in the late 1960s. First, the rise of the Catholic civil rights movement which was organised to protest against discriminatory housing practices by the Northern Ireland Civil Rights Association in 1967, both of which contributed to the 'politicalisation' of the Catholic community in Northern Ireland. Secondly, the civil rights movement was identified by radical Unionists such as the Revd. Ian Paisley with the 'revolutionary aims' of the Irish Republican Army and any concessions to the civil rights movement were resisted by Protestants on the grounds that such reforms might lend credibility to the Irish Republican Army. This led to Catholics becoming disenchanted with the political process.

Boyle *et al*. argue that in addition to the sense of frustration in the Catholic community over social conditions and the failure of conventional political strategies to achieve reforms, the 'slide from peaceful protest into guerrilla warfare' is largely explained by the 'repressive response' of the Northern Ireland government towards attempts by Catholics to change government policies. The authors point to the government's banning of Republican Clubs in 1967, the banning of marches in Londonderry in October 1968, the often excessive reaction of the largely Protestant Royal Ulster Constabulary and inexperienced British troops towards Catholic street demonstrators and the internment of 'innocent' individuals and the use of harsh interrogation techniques in the early 1970s. See also, Amnesty International, *Report of an Amnesty International Mission to Northern Ireland* (28 November-6 December 1977) (Amnesty International, London, 1978); Ian Brownlie, 'Interrogation in Depth: The Compton and Parker Reports', *Modern L. Rev.* vol. 35 (September 1972) p. 501; David Lowry, 'Ill-treatment, Brutality and Torture: Some Thoughts Upon the "Treatment" of Irish Political Prisoners', *De Paul L. Rev.*, vol 22 (1973) p. 553; Michael O'Boyle, 'Torture and Emergency Powers Under the European Convention on Human Rights: Ireland v. The United Kingdom' *AJIL*, vol. 71 (1977) p. 674, 'Torture under the European Convention on Human rights', *AJIL* vol. 73 (1979), p. 267.

The extent of Catholic discontent in Northern Ireland should not be exaggerated. Clutterbuck, 'Ireland's American Enemies', p. 18, note 22 argues that surveys indicated that less than one-half of Northern Ireland Catholics desire union with 'the South'.

32. See *Text of a Communique and Declaration Issued after a Meeting held at 10 Downing Street on 19 August* (August 1969) (Cmnd. 4154); *Text of a Communique Issued Following Discussions Between the Secretary of State for the Home Department and the Northern Ireland Government in Belfast on 9th and 10th Otober 1969* (October 1969) (Cmnd. 4178); *Text of a Communique Issued on 29 August, 1969 at the Conclusion of the Visit of the Secretary of State for the Home Department to Northern Ireland* (September 1969) (Cmnd. 4158).

33. Palley, 'Evolution' Disintegration and Possible Reconstruction', pp. 43-4, note 19.

There were major changes in law, structure of government and most significantly, of power. The power changes comprised a shift of initiative and activity to the Government and Parliament at Westminster, a disbandment by the Govenment of Northern Ireland of its 'private army', the Ulster Special Constabulary, and the renunciation of para-military functions by the police force, the R.U.C., and full implementation of the democratic principle in Parliamentary and local governmental elections. Structurally the whole of local government was reorganised in order to remove possible controversial areas of power from local authorities which were more likely to reflect partisan prejudices, and so as to transfer the administration of these powers into the hands of the independent Civil Service of Northern Ireland. Special institutions were created to insure that there would in the future be no discrimination in any aspect of public administration or in any respect of any public appointment.

These reforms are set forth in *Standing Advisory Commission on Human Rights The Protection of Human Rights by Law in Northern Ireland*, pp. 11-15, para 2.18, note 3.

34. The Provisions of these Acts are based on the *Civil Authorities (Special Powers) Act* (Northern Ireland) 1922 (which in turn was based on the *Restoration of Order in Ireland Act* (1920) which was enacted by the Northern Ireland Parliament to provide the executive branch of government with the legal mechanism to respond effectively to domestic unrest. See generally, J.L. Edwards, 'Special Powers in Northern Ireland' *Crim. L. Rev.*, vol. 7 (1956); National Council for Civil Liberties, *The Special Powers Act of Northern Ireland* (National Council for Civil Liberties, London, 1936); European Court of Human Rights, *Case of Ireland v. The United Kingdom*, p. 35, para. 85, note 2. The 'Special Powers Act' was administered by the Secretary of State for Northern Ireland following the imposition of 'direct rule' on 30 March 1972 and on 7 November 1972 the British Parliament passed the *Detention of Terrorists Order 1972* which revoked Special Powers Regulations 11(2) and 12(1) and replaced them with an internment procedure providing for an independent review by advisers of interim custody orders issued by the Secretary of State. The *Detention of Terrorists Order 1972* was an interim measure pending the enactment by the British Parliament of a comprehensive 'anti-terrorist' Act.

35. *Northern Ireland (Emergency Provisions) Act 1978*, S 21(1) (a), Schedule II (proscribes in Northern Ireland, Cummann na m'Ban, Fianna na h'Eireann, IRA, The Red Hand Command, Saor Eire, Sinn Fein, Ulster Freedom Fighters, Ulster Volunteer Force); *Prevention of Terrorism (Temporary Provisions) Act 1976* S1 (a), Schedule I (proscribes in Great Britain, IRA).

36. *Northern Ireand Act 1978*, S 21(1) (a); *Prevention of Terrorism Act 1976*, S 1 (b).

37. *Northern Ireland Act 1978*, S 21 (b).

38. Ibid.

39. *Prevention of Terrorism Act 1976*, S 1(c).

40. Ibid., S 2; *Northern Ireland Act 1978*, S 25.

41. *Northern Ireland Act 1978*, S 26.

42. Ibid., S 22.

43. *Prevention of Terrorism Act*, S 11.

44. *Northern Ireland Act 1978*, S 2(2).

45. Ibid., S 7.

46. Ibid., S 8 (2).

47. Ibid., S 9.

48. Ibid., S 15 (1) (a).

49. Ibid., S 15 (1) (b).

50. Ibid., S 11 (2).

51. Ibid., S (13) (2), 14 (3).

52. Ibid., S 17.

53. Ibid., S 19.

54. Ibid., S 15 (3) (a) (b).

55. Ibid., S 18.

56. Ibid., S 11 (3).

57. Ibid., S 14 (1) (2).

58. *Prevention of Terrorism Act*, S 12 (1) (2).

59. *Northern Ireland Act 1978*, S 19 (2) (d). See also S 19 (a) (b) (c), S 24.

60. Ibid., Schedule I.

61. *Prevention of Terrorism Act*, S 4.

62. Ibid., S 5.

63. Ibid., S 6.

64. Ibid., SS 4(1) (a) (b), 5 (1) (a) (b), 6 (1) (a) (b).

65. *Prevention of Terrorism (Supplemental Temporary Provisions) Order 1976*, Art. 10.

66. Mr Airey Neave (Abingdon), *Northern Ireland (Emergency Provisions) Act 1973 (Continuance Order 1977)* (30 June 1977), p. 650.

67. Ibid., (8 December 1977), 1691.

68. Mr Merlyn Rees (Secretary of State for Northern Ireland), *Northern Ireland (Emergency Provisions) Act 1973 (Continuance Order 1976)* (11 June 1976), 88.

69. Mr Edward du Cann (Faunton), *Prevention of Terrorism (Temporary Provisions) Act 1974* (28 November 1974), 708.

70. Mr Ian Gilmour (Chesham and Amersham), *Prevention of Terrorism (Temporary Provisions) Act 1974 (Continuance Order 1975)* (26 November 1975), 893.

71. Mr Phillip Whitehead (Derby, North), *Prevention of Terrorism (Temporary Provisions) Act 1974 (Continuance Order 1977)* (9 March 1977), 732.

72. Mr R.C. Mitchell (Southampton, Itchen), *Prevention of Terrorism (Temporary Provisions) Act 1974 (Continuance Order 1977)* (26 November 1975), 903-4.

73. Mr William Bradford (Belfast, South), *Northern Ireland (Emergency Powers) (Amendment Act, 1975)* (27 June 1975), 942.

74. Mr Merlyn Rees (Secretary of State for Northern Ireland), *Northern Ireland (Emergency Provisions) Act 1973 (Conitinuance Order 1975)* (11 December 1975), 763, 764.

75. Mr Merlyn Rees (Secretary of State for Northern Ireland), *Northern Ireland (Emergency Provisions) Act 1973 (Continuance Order 1974)* (5 December 1974), 1274, 1275.

76. Mr John Biggs-Davison (Epping Forest), *Northern Ireland (Emergency Provisons) Act (Continuance Order 1975)* (11 December 1975), 810.

77. Mr Roger Moate (Faversham), *Prevention of Terrorism Act (Temporary Provisions) Act 1976 (Continuance Order 1978)* (15 March 1978), 578-9.

78. Mr Ian Gilmour (Opposition Leader-Conservative), *Prevention of Terrorism (Emergency Provisions) Act 1974 (Continuance Order 1975)* (26 November 1975), 895.

79. Ibid., 894.

80. Mr Hugh Fraser (Stafford and Stone), ibid., 967.

81. Mr Roy Mason (Secretary of State for Northern Ireland), *Northern Ireland (Emergency Provisions) Act 1974 (Continuance Order 1977)* (30 June 1977), 639.

82. Mr Roy Jenkins (Secretary of State for the Home Department), *Prevention of Terrorism (Temporary Provisions) Act 1974* (28 November 1974), 642.

83. Mr Percy Grieve (Solihull), ibid., 696, 697.

84. Mr Ian Gilmour, see note 78, 894.

85. Mr Ivan Lawrence (Burton), *Prevention of Terrorism (Temporary Provisions) Act 1974* (28 November 1974), 739.

86. Mr William Molloy (Ealing, North), ibid., 706.

87. Mr Philip Goodhart (Beckenham), *Northern Ireland (Emergency*

Provisions Act (Continuance Order 1977) (8 December 1977), 1706.

88. Ibid.

89. Ibid.

90. Mr James Molyneaux (Antrim, South), *Prevention of Terrorism (Temporary Provisions) Act 1974* (28 November 1974), 831.

91. Mr Stanley R. McMaster (Belfast, East), *Northern Ireland (Emergency Provisions) Act 1973* (17 April 1973), 307, 308.

92. Mr Philip Goodhart (Beckenham), *Northern Ireland (Emergency Provisions) Act 1973 (Continuance Order 1977)* (8 December 1977), 1709.

93. Mr Stanley R. McMaster (Belfast, East), see note 91.

94. Mr Roy Jenkins (The Secretary of State for the Home Department), *Prevention of Detention (Temporary Provisions) Act 1974 (Continuance Order 1975)* (26 November 1975), 891.

95. Mr James Kilfedder (Down, North), *Northern Ireland (Emergency Provisions) Act 1973 (Continuance Order 1976)* (17 December 1976), 2024.

96. Mr Ivan Lawrence (Burton), *Prevention of Terrorism (Temporary Provisions) Act 1974 (Continuance Order 1975)* (26 November 1975), 982.

97. Mr John Biggs-Davison (Epping Forest), *Northern Ireland (Emergency Provisions) Act 1974 (Continuance Order 1975)* (8 December 1977), 1749.

98. Mr James Kilfedder (Down, North), see note 90, 2026.

99. Mr John Biggs-Davison (Epping Forest), *Northern Ireland (Emergency Provisions) Act (Continuance Order 1975)* (11 December 1975), 810.

100. Mr Airey Neave (Abingdon), *Northern Ireland (Emergency Provisions (Amendment) Act 1975* (27 June 1975), 913.

101. Mr Airey Neave (Abingdon), *Northern Ireland (Emergency Provisions) (Continuance Order 1976)* (17 December 1976), 1945.

102. Mr William Molloy (Ealing, North), see note 86, 705.

103. Mr Ivan Lawrence (Burton), see note 85.

104. Mr Merlyn Rees (Secretary of State for Northern Ireland), Northern Ireland (Emergency Provisions) Act 1973 (Continuance Order 1974) (28 November 1974), 739.

105. Mr Airey Neave (Abingdon), see note 100.

106. Mr Michael Alison (Barston Ash), *Prevention of Terrorism (Temporary Provisions) Act 1976* (28 January 1976), 498.

197. Mr. W.R. Rees-Davies (Thanet, West), *Prevention of Terrorism (Temporary Provisions) Act 1974* (28 November 1974), 692, 693.

108. Mr Percy Grieve (Solihull), ibid., 697.

109. Mr R.T. Paget (Northampton), *Northern Ireland (Emergency Provisions) Act 1973* (5 July, 1973), 747, 748.

110. Mr S.C. Silkin (Dulwich), *Northern Ireland (Emergency Provisions) Act 1973* (5 July 1973), 737.

111. Mr Stanley R. McMaster (Belfast, East), ibid., 750.

112. Sir Peter Rawlinson (Attorney-General), ibid., 770.

113. Mr Roy Jenkins (Secretary of State for the Home Department), see note 82, 854.

114. Ibid., 641.

115. Mr Roy Jenkins (The Secretary of State for the Home Department), *Prevention of Terrorism Act 1973 (Continuance Order 1975)* (19 May 1975), 1090.

116. Mr W.R. van Straubenzee (The Minister of State for Northern Ireland), *Northern Ireland (Emergency Provisions) Act 1973* (5 July 1973), 848.

117. Mr Stanley R. McMaster (Belfast, East), ibid., 830.

118. Mr Frank Hooley (Sheffield, Heeley), *Prevention of Terrorism (Temporary Provisions) Act 1974* (28 November 1974), 636.

119. Mr James Molyneaux (Antrim, South), *Northern Ireland (Emergency Provisions) Act 1973 (Continuance Order 1977)* (30 June 1977), 662.

120. Mr George Cunningham (Islington, South and Finsbury), *Prevention of Terrorism (Temporary Provisions) Act (Continuance Order 1975)* (19 May1975), 1102.

121. Mr H.J. Beith (Berwick-upon-Tweed), *Prevention of Terrorism (Temporary Provisions) Act (Continuance Order 1977)* (9 March 1977), 1497.

122. Mr Gerard Fitt (Belfast, West), *Northern Ireland (Emergency Powers) Act 1973* (5 July 1973), 877.

123. Ibid.

124. Mr Tom Litterick (Birmingham, Selly Oak), *Prevention of Terrorism (Temporary Provisions) Act 1976 (Continuance Order 1978)* (15 March 1978), 583.

125. Mr Ron Thomas (Bristol, Northwest), ibid., 574.

126. Mr Ron Thomas (Bristol, Northwest), *Prevention of Terrorism (Temporary Provisions) Act 1976 (Continuance Order 1977)* (9 March 1977), 1543.

127. Mr Ian Mikardo (Bethnal Green and Bow, *Prevention of Terrorism (Temporary Provisions) Act 1976* and *(Continuance Order 1976)* (28 January 1976), 516.

128. Mr Ron Thomas (Bristol, Northwest), *Prevention of Terrorism (Temporary Provisions) Act 1966 (Continuance Order 1978)* (15 March 1976), 577.

129. Mr Peter Archer (Rowley Regis), *Northern Ireland (Emergency Provisions) Act 1973* (5 July 1973), 852.

130. Mr Tom Litterick (Birmingham Selly Oak), *Prevention of Terrorism (Temporary Provisions Act 1976 (Continuance Order 1977)* (9 March 1977), 1528.

132. Mr Gerard Kaufman (Manchester, Ardwick), *Northern Ireland (Emergency Provisions) Act 1973* (5 July 1973), 833.

132. Mr Gerard Fitt (Belfast, West), see note 127, 877.

133. Mr Tom Litterick (Birmingham, Selly Oak), *Prevention of Terrorism (Emergency Provisions Act 1973 (Continuance Order 1977)* (8 December 1977), 1711.

134. Mr Gerard Kaufman (Manchester, Ardwick), see note 136.

135. Mr Merlyn Rees (The Secretary of State for Northern Ireland), *Northern Ireland (Emergency Provisions) Act 1973 (Continuance Order 1976)* (2 July 1976), 881.

136. Mr Peter Archer (Rowley Regis), *Northern Ireland (Emergency Provisions Act 1973*, see note 134, 849.

137. Mr Tom Litterick (Birmingham, Selly Oak), *Prevention of Terrorism (Temporary Provisions) Act 1974 (Continuance Order 1975)* (26 November 1975), 968.

138. Mr Robin Corbett (Hemel Hempstead), ibid., 911.

139. Mr Tom Litterick (Birmingham, Selly Oak) see note 129, 585.

140. Mr Tom Litterick (Birmingham, Selly Oak), see note 135, 1529.

141. Mr Robin Corbett (Hemel Hempstead), see note 143,, 913, 914.

142. Mr Leo Abse (Pontypool), *Prevention of Terrorism (Temporary Provisions) Act 1974* (28 November 1974), 657.

143. Mr Kevin McNamara (Kingston upon Hull, Central), *Prevention of Terrorism (Temporary Provisions) Act 1974 (Continuance Order 1975)* at 1129.

144. Mr Enoch Powell (Down, South), *Northern Ireland (Emergency Provisions) Act 1973 (Continuance Order 1975)* (11 December 1975), 781.

145. Mr Gerard Kaufman (Manchester, Ardwick), see note 136, 831.

146. The European Convention on Human Rights rarely was mentioned during the debate. Ironically, it was pointed to by a few speakers as justifying the abrogation of human rights during periods of 'public emergency'. See Mr W.R. van Straubenzee, see note 117, 843.

147. See International Covenant on Civil and Political Rights, Article 4; The European Convention of Human Rights, Article 15; American Convention on Human Rights, Article 15.

148. Such individuals often are subject to physical abuse. See, Matthew Lippmann, 'The Protection of Universal Human Rights: The Problem of Torture', *Universal Human Rights*, vol. 1 (October-December 1979), p. 25.

NOTES ON CONTRIBUTORS

Yonah Alexander is Professor of International Studies and Director of the Institute for Studies in International Terrorism at the State University of New York. He is also Senior Staff Member at the Center for Strategic and International Studies, Georgetown University, and Fellow at both the Institute for Social and Behavioral Pathology, University of Chicago, and the Center for Strategic Studies, Tel-Aviv University. He is Editor-in-Chief of *Terrorism: an International Journal* and *Political Communication and Persuasion: an International Journal* and has written, edited and co-edited 15 books in international affairs and political violence.

Schura Cook is a Consultant to the Psychopolitics and Conflict Research Certificate Program at the University of Southern California, Los Angeles and the Institute for Conflict Research in Vienna.

Richard Drake is currently a lecturer in history at Princeton University and will become an Assistant Professor at the University of Montana in autumn 1982. He is the author of *Byzantium for Rome: the Politics of Nostalgia in Umbertian Italy (1878-1900)* (The University of North Carolina Press, Chapel Hill, 1980 and Rizzoli, Milan, 1982) and has also written articles on Italian culture and politics in the nineteenth and twentieth centuries for the *Journal of Modern History*, the *Journal of Contemporary History* and *The Review of Politics*. He is now writing a history of terrorism in Italy since the French Revolution.

Marie Fleming is Associate Professor of Political Science at the University of Western Ontario and the author of *The Anarchist Way to Socialism: Elisée Reclus and Nineteenth-century European Anarchism* (Croom Helm, London, 1979). She is currently working on a study of the Marxist Neo-Kantian Movement in Imperial Germany.

David Freestone is a lecturer in the Faculty of Law at the University of Hull where he teaches European Community Law and Public International Law. His current work is on the European Parliament, but he contributed an essay on legal responses to terrorism in Juliet Lodge (ed.), *Terrorism: a Challenge to the State* (Martin Robertson, Oxford,

1981) and has written articles and notes for a number of legal journals including the *Modern Law Review* and the *Criminal Law Review*.

Matthew Lippman is a lecturer in Legal Studies at Latrobe University, Melbourne. He has published articles on human rights which have appeared in journals in the United Kingdom, Scandinavia, Australia, the USA and Africa, and currently is working on a text on human rights.

Juliet Lodge is a lecturer in politics at the University of Hull. She was formerly a lecturer in political studies at the University of Auckland, Visiting Fellow in the Centre for International Studies at the London School of Economics and Political Science, and a Leverhulme Research Fellow. She is the author, editor and co-author of several books on international affairs and terrorism and her articles have been published in numerous international journals.

Kenneth Myers is Senior Fellow in European Studies at the Georgetown University Center for Strategic and International Studies. Educated at Colgate University, The Johns Hopkins School of Advanced International Studies and the University of Freiburg, his most recent publications include *North Atlantic Security: the Forgotten Flank* (Sage, The Washington Papers, 1979) and *NATO: the Next Thirty Years* (Croom Helm/Westview Press, 1980).

Yosef Nedava is Professor of Political Science at the University of Haifa, Israel. A jurist and historian, he has published numerous books on Zionism, the Arab-Israeli conflict and Soviet studies.

Dennis Pluchinsky is a member of the Threat Analysis Group at the Office of Security, US Department of State.

Jose A. Trevino is an officer in the United States Air Force with experience in terrorist movements in Latin America, Spain and Italy. He currently is serving as a counter-intelligence officer assigned to the Headquarters of the Air Force Office of Special Investigations, Washington, DC.

INDEX

211